Can I Let You Go?

CATHY GLASS

Can I Let You Go?

A heartbreaking true story of
love, loss and moving on

Certain details in this story, including names, places and dates,
have been changed to protect the children.

HarperElement
An imprint of HarperCollins*Publishers*
1 London Bridge Street
London SE1 9GF

www.harpercollins.co.uk

First published by HarperElement 2016

5 7 9 10 8 6

ISBN 978-0-00-815374-8

Printed and bound in Great Britain by
Clays Ltd, St Ives plc

MIX
Paper from
responsible sources
FSC
www.fsc.org
FSC™ C007454

ACKNOWLEDGEMENTS

A big thank you to my family; my editors, Carolyn and Holly; my literary agent, Andrew; my UK publishers HarperCollins, and my overseas publishers who are now too numerous to list by name. Last, but definitely not least, a big thank you to my readers for your unfailing support and kind words. They are much appreciated.

To Faye.
I'm a better person for knowing you.

CHAPTER ONE

HOPE FOR THE FUTURE?

'Are you sure you are going to be all right alone tonight?' I asked Mum again.

'Yes, love. Don't you worry about me,' she replied, putting on a brave face. 'Phone to let me know you are home safely.'

'I will,' I said. But I didn't move. My children, Adrian, Lucy and Paula, were standing beside me, their expressions sad and serious as they shared my concerns. We were standing in the front porch of Mum's house, trying to say goodbye, but it was very difficult. We were the last to go and would be leaving her alone.

'I could stay with you tonight, Nana,' Paula offered as she had done before, indeed as we all had.

'No, thank you, love,' Mum said. 'That's kind of you, but I'll have to get used to being by myself. I'll see you all again soon. Now off you go home. It's been a long day for us all. I'll watch a bit of television and then after you've phoned I'll have an early night.'

None of us looked convinced, but clearly Mum wasn't going to change her mind about one of us staying, and we had to respect her decision.

'We'll phone as soon as we're home,' I said. I kissed and hugged her again and then stepped out of the porch so that Adrian, Lucy and Paula could hug and kiss her goodbye too.

It was a dark night with no moon, but the porch lamp cast a little oasis of light over our departing group. The air was cool, it was late September, but at least it had stayed dry all day, for certainly heavy rain and dark storm clouds would have added to our gloom and misery. I took the few steps to my car parked on the drive and unlocked the doors, but I didn't get in. I stood beside the car, watching Mum until my children had finished saying their goodbyes and had come over to join me. I still call them children, although they were young adults now: Adrian, twenty-two, Lucy, twenty and Paula, eighteen.

'Don't forget to lock the front door,' I called to Mum. I'd already checked the back doors.

'I won't, dear, don't you worry about me.'

I gave a small nod and the children and I climbed into the car and lowered our windows ready to wave as we departed. I started the engine and then slowly reversed off the drive as Mum stood in the porch waving and we waved back. How many times had we done this? I couldn't begin to guess, for we saw my parents often, usually with the children we fostered. Mum and Dad would stand side by side in the porch, waving and smiling and already looking forward to our next visit, as we did theirs. But now our departure was restrained and a little muted, for it was just Mum seeing us off, bravely. And it would only ever be Mum in the future, for sadly my dear dad had died suddenly three weeks before, and today had been his funeral.

* * *

Once we were out of sight of the house we wound up our windows and I drove steadily and in silence towards our home. The children were silent too. Each of us deep in thought, doubtless thinking of the good, kind man who was no longer with us and the huge gap his passing had left in our lives. Although my father had been in his eighties he'd been in fine health, so it had come as a terrible shock when my brother telephoned my mobile to say he had died. Completely unexpected and a huge loss. The end had been very quick, if that was any consolation. His heart just stopped. He went into his garden to do some weeding and Mum looked through the window and saw him sitting on the damp grass, which she thought odd. She went out and he said her name once and then lay down on his side and closed his eyes, and that was it. She ran indoors, telephoned for an ambulance and then covered him with a blanket to keep him warm. She sat beside him holding his hand and talking to him, while knowing in her heart of hearts that he had probably already passed. When the ambulance arrived there was nothing they could do. He'd died of a massive heart attack.

'I hope he could hear me tell him how much I loved him,' Mum had said to me.

'He knew,' I told her.

'At least he didn't suffer,' Mum said, grasping at this small platitude to try to ease her pain.

'Yes,' I agreed. Although it hadn't helped much in the early days when our grief had been raw.

Dad was well respected in their village, and at his funeral the church had been full of mourners wanting to say their last goodbyes. A loving husband and a devoted father and grandfather, the reverend who'd led the service had said. He'd known Dad personally. My brother and Adrian had read out tributes too, touching and personal.

'Will Nana be all right by herself?' Lucy said from the back seat, breaking into my thoughts.

'Yes, love. I'll phone her as soon as we get home.'

'Why didn't she want us to stay with her tonight?' Paula asked.

'I think she needs time alone to reflect on today,' I said. 'And to start to come to terms with the future.'

'I told her to make a list of anything she needs doing and I'd see to it,' Adrian said quietly from the passenger seat. 'You know, the stuff Grandpa used to do.'

'Thanks, love,' I said, glancing at him. 'That was kind. I'm sure she appreciated that.' I couldn't have wished for more thoughtful children.

I'd stayed with Mum in the week straight after my father's death, when my brother and I had gone through their address book and notified people of Dad's passing and made the funeral arrangements. Then he and I had taken it in turns to stay with Mum, but now I could understand her wish to be alone. The time between a loved one passing and the funeral is a strange and difficult one; normal life is suspended, as you're caught in a limbo of grief and uncertainty. The funeral is supposed to give some closure, and I supposed it had to some degree. But my parents had been married for fifty-eight years and had known each other for longer. They'd been teenage sweethearts and had spent a lifetime together. While Mum was a very positive person, I knew that it would take all her inner strength and resourcefulness to find a way forward in life without Dad. I thought that her insisting on being alone tonight was that first step.

* * *

I was aware that I had voice messages on my mobile; I'd checked my phone briefly at Mum's, and I'd recognized one of the numbers as that of the local authority fostering services that I fostered for. However, I didn't listen to my messages until later that night, after we were home and I had telephoned Mum. We were all upstairs, exhausted, and taking turns in the bathroom to get ready for bed. It was eleven o'clock and as I waited for my turn I perched on my bed and checked the texts and voicemails. Most were from friends saying they were thinking of us on this sad day and wishing me and my family well. The last was from Edith, my support social worker from the fostering services, also known as a supervising social worker or link worker. I'd been going to foster a young boy just before Dad had died, but I'd never met him. This was just after Zeena (whose story I tell in *The Child Bride*) had left us, but I doubted Edith's call was about that boy, as the social services would have found another carer to look after him when I'd become unavailable. I hadn't taken many breaks during the twenty-five years I'd been fostering: when my husband had left us many years before, and now with my father's passing. I'd told the fostering services that I'd be in touch after the funeral when I was ready to start fostering again, but clearly Edith had something urgent to tell me.

'Cathy, I know you're on compassionate leave,' Edith's message began, 'but I've had a referral from a colleague. It's not your normal placement, but I think it would suit you and your family. Adult social services are looking for a short-term home for a young lady who is expecting. She's a lovely person and won't give you any trouble. It would just be for three months until she has her baby. Could you phone me please as soon as you can so we can discuss?'

Whether Edith had remembered that today had been my father's funeral I didn't know – perhaps not, given everything she must have had on her mind. But I was pleased she had telephoned with this referral and my spirits rose a little. I love fostering, it's a huge part of my life, but I doubt I could have coped with a young child with very challenging behaviour at that time. Supporting a mother-to-be until she'd had her baby and then presumably seeing them both settled in their own accommodation could be just what we needed. A new baby, a new life, is uplifting and full of hope, and on a practical level a young woman wouldn't need the constant supervision a young child would. Also, there would be no school run, which would leave me free to go to see Mum without having to put arrangements in place to collect the child from school. It felt right, and when I mentioned it to Adrian, Lucy and Paula before I went to bed they all said they thought it was a good idea too. Fostering is a whole family affair, so everyone's view is important and needs to be taken into consideration.

I slept well – I was shattered – and the following morning, after I'd telephoned Mum to make sure she was all right, I phoned the social services.

'Sorry I couldn't return your call yesterday,' I said to Edith. 'It was my father's funeral.' Mentioning my father's death or funeral was becoming slightly easier and I wasn't tearing up so much.

'How did it go?' she asked.

'Very well, thank you, but we weren't home until late.'

'Good. I'm pleased it went well. So the young lady I referred to, Faye, is a really lovely person. She is twenty-four.'

'Oh, I see,' I said, surprised. 'I'd assumed she was a teenager.'

'No. But because of her condition she functions at a much younger level. She has learning difficulties, and Becky, her social worker, has given me some background details. Faye has been living with her grandparents, but now that she's pregnant they're finding it difficult to manage. They've asked if she can be placed with a foster carer rather than live in supported lodgings, as they don't think she'd cope. We're trying to accommodate their wishes. They have brought her up, but they're in their seventies now and not in the best of health. They are struggling to cope with all Faye's antenatal appointments. Faye's gran has chronic arthritis and her grandpa had a stroke a year ago. They both use walking aids and don't drive, and they rely on the community transport scheme to go out, so it's very difficult. Faye is childlike, apparently. She's a sweet person. It's thought her disabilities are a result of FAS. You're aware of that condition?'

'Yes.' FAS, or Foetal Alcohol Syndrome, refers to a range of physical and mental disabilities that are the result of the mother's alcoholism during pregnancy. The alcohol crosses the placenta and damages the baby.

'Becky would like you to meet Faye and her grandparents as soon as possible,' Edith continued. 'Then arrange a moving date. Faye will still see her grandparents regularly. Her self-care skills are good; she just needs help, support and monitoring, like a child would. She's coping reasonably well with being pregnant and will return to live with her grandparents once the baby is born. They don't know who the father is, and Becky says that the grandmother has taken Faye getting pregnant rather badly. She thinks some of their "not coping" is because of this.'

'I understand,' I said. 'I'm sure her grandmother will feel differently once the baby is born and she sees her great-grand-child. No one can resist a baby.'

There was a short silence on the other end of the phone before Edith said, 'Sorry, Cathy, I should have made it clearer sooner. Faye isn't keeping her baby. You will be supporting her while she is pregnant, but as soon as the baby is born it will be taken into care.'

'Oh,' I said, my heart sinking. 'Why?'

'Faye can't possibly look after a baby. She functions at about the age of an eight-year-old. Realistically her grandparents couldn't look after it either. There is no alternative. Once the baby has been checked over by the doctor, assuming all is well a foster carer will collect the baby from hospital and look after it until adoptive parents are found.'

I was sitting on the sofa in the living room, staring straight ahead. My feelings of hope and optimism at the thought of a new baby were now completely dashed. As a foster carer I'd had to collect a new baby from a hospital without its mother some years previously, and it had been heartbreaking. This would be even worse. Faye would be with me and part of my family for the next three months; we would bond with her and her unborn baby, while knowing all along that she was going to have to give it up as soon as it was born and would never have the chance to be a mother. It would be soul destroying and possibly more than I or my family could reasonably cope with right now. However, foster carers are expected to accept the referrals made to them through their support social worker. It's not a pick-and-choose situation – I'll take this child, but not that one. Carers can be registered to foster a certain age group, but many, like me, foster the whole range, from birth to young adult. Unless there is a very good reason why carers can't accept a specific child, they are expected to take them, for obviously the younger person needs a home. I suppose I could have said that after losing my father we weren't ready to foster again, but that wouldn't have been strictly true.

Edith heard my silence and added: 'You don't have to worry about Faye being very distraught. Becky said she's fine about giving up her baby for adoption.'

'Is she?' I asked, amazed.

'Yes. Becky had a long discussion with her and her grandparents. Faye appreciates she would never be able to look after a baby and her grandparents are in no position to help. They have their own needs. Faye's being very positive. Becky has suggested you all meet at two o'clock on Thursday afternoon. Is that all right with you?'

I was silent again before I said, 'Yes.'

'The meeting is at their flat. I'll ask Becky to contact you with the address and placement details today. Phone her or me if there's anything you're not sure of.'

'All right,' I said. And we said goodbye.

I set down the phone and remained where I was in the living room. Through the patio doors I could see the blue sky beyond. Although it was mid-September it was another fine day, with the sun shining in a cloudless sky. I could hear movement upstairs as Adrian, Paula and Lucy slowly got up. Adrian and Lucy had taken an extra day off work after the funeral. Adrian had finished university and was working temporarily in a supermarket until he decided what he wanted to do (he was thinking of accountancy). Lucy worked at a local nursery and Paula, having passed her A-level exams, was starting at a local college the following week. It was now 10.30 a.m. and the meeting with Faye was the day after tomorrow.

As each of my family came downstairs I told them what Edith had said and asked them for their opinion.

'That's very sad,' Paula said. 'But we can look after Faye.'

'Do you think so?'

'Oh, yes. She sounds nice.'

When Lucy came down her response was, 'Perhaps Faye will change her mind and keep the baby.' So I explained that this wasn't an option because of her learning disabilities.

'Well, someone has got to look after her,' Lucy said pragmatically. 'So it may as well be us.' Lucy had been in and out of foster care before coming to live with me eight years previously and was now my adopted daughter. She had a slightly different view of being in care and I valued her opinion.

'If the baby has to go for adoption,' Adrian said when I told him, 'then I think it's better that it's taken away at birth. I'm sure it would be more upsetting to bond with the baby, love it, and then have to say goodbye.'

'So you think we should look after Faye?' I asked.

'Yes, if you do. But, Mum, I know that whatever happens you'll make sure she is OK.'

'Thanks for your vote of confidence,' I said, although I really didn't see how she could be OK – not a mother having to give up her baby.

CHAPTER TWO

FAYE AND SNUGGLES

At 1.45 p.m. on Thursday I entered the elevator in the high-rise block on the edge of town where Faye lived with her grandparents. The design of the building, once hailed as innovative and the future for city living, with the passing of time now seemed a monstrous piece of architecture, and was the last of four to be left standing. The others had been demolished and the social housing tenants relocated to a new estate. At some point this would be too. The elevator reeked of disinfectant. I pressed the button and began the ride to the eighth floor. I wasn't surprised that Faye's grandparents, exiled up here with their limited mobility, were struggling. What happened when the elevator broke? I wondered. From what Becky, Faye's social worker, had told me, they couldn't manage the eight flights of stairs, and not for the first time in my life I felt very grateful that I had a nice home and my family and I were all in good health.

The elevator ground to a halt and the doors juddered open. I stepped out and over a discarded bag of half-eaten fish and chips that someone hadn't bothered to throw in a bin. I went along the corridor to flat 87 and pressed the bell. The door, like all the others in the corridor, was dark green and in need of a repaint, but that wouldn't happen now the block was due for demolition. Edith, my support social worker, wasn't attending this introductory meeting, and this would be the first time I met Faye's social worker, Becky, although we had spoken on the phone.

A woman answered the door with a cheery, 'Good afternoon, you must be Cathy. I'm Becky. Pleased to meet you.'

'And you.'

We shook hands and I went in and closed the door, then followed Becky down the short hall into the living-cum-dining room. She was a mature social worker with a friendly, relaxed manner that I thought would put anyone at ease.

'This is Cathy, the foster carer I've been telling you about,' Becky said to the three people in the room. 'This is Stan, Faye's grandpa,' she said, introducing me to the portly gentleman sitting in an armchair.

'Hello,' I said.

'Sorry, I can't easily get up,' he said, extending his hand. I went over and we shook hands. In his early seventies, he was wearing a woollen waistcoat over an open-neck shirt and grey flannel trousers; his walking stick was hooked over the chair arm.

'This is Wilma, Faye's gran,' Becky said, referring to one of the two women sitting on the sofa.

'Hello, nice to meet you,' I said.

'And you,' Wilma replied, looking me up and down. She was a similar age and build to her husband and was dressed in navy trousers and a matching jersey. Her walking frame stood within her reach.

My gaze now moved to her granddaughter, who was sitting beside her on the patterned two-seater sofa. 'This is Faye, the young lady I've been telling you about,' Becky said.

'Hello, love.'

Faye threw me a small, anxious smile and immediately looked down.

'Say hello to Cathy,' her gran directed.

'Hello,' Faye said shyly, without looking up. My heart went out to her. Of average height and build, she had straight hair cut rather severely to chin level, emphasizing her plainness. The maroon jersey and trousers she was wearing were very similar to those of her gran; indeed, I thought they could be hers. They were too big, even allowing for her baby bump, and it crossed my mind that one of the first things I should do for Faye when she came to live with us was to take her shopping to buy some pretty maternity clothes.

Becky drew up one of the dining chairs for me and placed it beside hers, so we sat in a small circle. The room was clean and full of the homely clutter of everyday living. I guessed Faye and her grandparents had lived here for a long time. As I sat down I saw Faye snatch another glance at me and I smiled reassuringly. With her small, round face and petite features, she had the classic look of a person with Foetal Alcohol Syndrome. It gave her a childlike appearance. Yet there was also an elderly quality about her, especially in her mannerisms. Her posture and the way her hands were folded in her lap mirrored that of her gran, which was probably a result of Faye's reliance on her and having spent so much time with her.

'Cathy has come here so you can get to know her a little before you go and stay with her,' Becky said positively to Faye. Her tone was gentle and conciliatory as one might use for a child, although it wasn't patronizing. 'I think it would be a good idea if we asked Cathy to tell us a bit about where she lives and her family, don't you?' Faye nodded and stole another shy glance at me. 'Over to you, then,' Becky said, smiling at me.

I was expecting this and had come prepared. 'I've brought some photographs to show you,' I said brightly.

'That's a good idea,' Becky enthused.

Dipping my hand into my bag I took out the small photograph album I'd compiled some years before. I usually took it with me to show the child and their family if the move to me had been planned in advance, but if the child came into care as an emergency I didn't have this opportunity, as they just arrived on my doorstep with their social worker. I opened the album at the first page and passed it to Faye. She immediately passed it to her gran, partly so that all three of them could see, but also, I thought, passing on the responsibility.

'The photograph on the left shows the front of our house,' I began. 'There is a small garden at the front and a much bigger one at the rear.' I knew the sequence of photographs in the album off by heart from having used it many times before. 'The photograph on the right was taken in the hall. You can see our coat stand, where we hang our coats, and our shoes beneath.' I paused while they looked, and then Wilma turned the page. Becky was leaning forward for a look too. 'The picture on the left is the front room and the one on the right is of the back room. That's the one we use most. That's where the television is.' I paused again as they looked at these two photographs and then turned the page. 'There's the kitchen,' I said. 'And then the next photo is outside in the back garden. You can see my family sitting on the patio. Faye, I think they're waving at you, aren't they?' Faye gave a small smile as she studied the photo. This picture was recent and my family were posed, waving and smiling, as though welcoming our new arrival. 'From left to right is my son Adrian, then my daughters Lucy and Paula. Can you see anyone else in the picture?'

Faye nodded and pressed her forefinger on the image. 'A cat,' she said, pleased.

'Yes, that's right. He's called Sammy. We used to have a cat called Toscha, but she grew very old and died. Sammy is only two. We haven't had him long. He's from a rescue centre.'

'That's nice,' Becky said encouragingly. 'You like cats, don't you, Faye?'

Faye gave a small nod and flashed me another cautious smile, then returned her attention to the photographs. The photographic tour continued upstairs with pictures of our bathroom and bedrooms. There were about twenty photographs in all, and every so often Wilma would say something like, 'That's nice,' and Stan would nod, while Faye looked at the pictures very carefully, taking it all in. Doubtless she was overwhelmed by all the changes she was about to face, as most children are before they come into care. These photographs would hopefully help to reassure and prepare her, so that when she arrived my home and family wouldn't be completely strange to her. The last photograph was of what would soon be Faye's bedroom, and she peered at it closely.

'It'll look better once you have your belongings in there,' I said. I'd taken the photograph between one child leaving and the next arriving. It was a comfortable room but plain without personal possessions, and decorated in neutral colours so it would suit a child of any age and of both sexes.

'I like the duvet,' Faye said.

'Good. You can use that one if you wish or choose one from the others I have. Or you may prefer to bring one from home.'

Faye looked at her gran for direction. 'She may as well use yours,' Wilma said. 'No point in moving her stuff if she doesn't need to.'

I hesitated and then Becky said exactly what I was thinking. 'It will be nice for Faye to take some of her possession with her. It'll make her feel more at home and help her settle.'

Wilma gave a small, stiff nod as though acknowledging what Becky had said while not necessarily agreeing with it. I suspected Wilma was used to being agreed with and organizing Stan and Faye.

'I can use my car to move whatever Faye wants to bring,' I offered, wondering if this could be a problem, given the grandparents' limited mobility.

Wilma gave the same small, stiff nod.

'Have a think about what you want to take,' Becky said to Faye.

Having come to the end of the album, Wilma closed it and handed it back to me.

'Thanks for bringing that,' Becky said. 'Perhaps you could say a few words about you and your family, now we know what you all look like.'

This was usual at an introductory meeting and it gave the young person a flavour of what family life with the foster carer would be like. I began by saying a little about what Adrian, Paula and Lucy were doing in terms of work and college, and a description of our weekday routine. 'At weekends we sometimes relax at home,' I continued. 'At other times we go out to places of interest, for a walk, to the cinema or to visit family and friends. It's very flexible. What sort of things do you like to do?' I asked Faye.

She met my gaze and shrugged. 'She's usually with us,' Stan said, joining the conversation. 'We don't get out much.'

'She shouldn't really be going out in her condition,' Wilma added.

I assumed she was referring to Faye's pregnancy. It seemed an odd thing to say, but I didn't comment.

'I'm sure Cathy will think of some nice places to go,' Becky said to Faye, and she smiled shyly. Edith had told me that Faye wouldn't give me any trouble, and I could see what she meant. My first impression was that Faye – compliant, malleable and, it appeared, highly reliant on her gran – could do with being a bit more assertive, as Becky had hinted on the phone. Despite Faye's learning disabilities, she would have opinions and views of her own, but they needed drawing out. Although I still had reservations about how my family and I were going to cope with Faye giving up her baby, I'd obviously do my best for her.

'Faye has a schedule of antenatal appointments,' Becky now said to me, moving on. 'She has a maternity folder containing all the information you need, and notes on her check-ups and antenatal test results. The folder will be passed to you when she moves.'

'And you mentioned a day centre? Will she still be going there?' I asked.

'If Faye wants to,' Becky said. It felt slightly uncomfortable discussing Faye rather than asking her, but to some extent this was unavoidable due to her learning disabilities.

Faye had looked sheepishly at her gran when I'd asked the question about the day centre, as if she'd done something wrong.

'Now she's showing, some of the others who go there talk about her and point,' Wilma said. 'It's not their fault, they don't understand, but it's not nice for Faye.'

'Do you want to go to the day centre?' Becky asked Faye.

She shrugged and looked at her gran again. 'I don't mind.'

'Let's see how you feel after the move,' Becky said, and wrote on her notepad. 'I don't want you to feel uncomfortable going there, but it does give you the opportunity to socialize. Perhaps if I have a word with the care workers?' she suggested.

Faye looked at Wilma, who gave a stilted nod and Faye did likewise. Then Faye suddenly looked up and asked quite forcefully, 'Can I still go to the stables?'

'Not until you've had the baby,' Stan said. 'You know that. We've told you.'

'We've had to suspend her visits to the stables due to health and safety concerns,' Becky explained to me.

'How long?' Faye asked.

'Before you can go to the stables again?' Becky clarified. 'About three and a half months. That's around fourteen weeks.'

'How many sleeps?' Faye asked as a young child might. Clearly she liked going to the stables. She wasn't checking with her gran but talking directly to Becky. I was pleased to see this other side of Faye.

'Ninety-eight sleeps,' Stan said with a small sigh. 'One less than yesterday.' So I guessed this was something he had to explain quite often. 'Once you're home again with us, Sue will start collecting you and taking you to the stables. I promise you, love.'

Faye gave a small, amicable nod, but I wondered if she really did understand the time scale. Time is a difficult concept for young children and adults with learning disabilities, but it was something I'd be able to help her with when she came to me, just as Stan was doing by explaining the number of sleeps.

'How will Faye visit us?' Wilma now asked. 'She can use the bus once she knows the route.'

'I can go with her and show her the route,' I said. 'Or I could bring her in my car. How often will she be visiting you?'

'Every day if she wants,' Wilma said.

'She'll need to spend time with Cathy to settle in, plus she has appointments and check-ups,' Becky said. 'I suggest she visits three times a week, perhaps every other day. Also,' Becky said, now turning to me, 'it's important that Faye is encouraged to be as independent as possible, so once she knows the bus route let her do it by herself. She has a pay-as-you-go phone and knows how to use it. We'll put your number into her contact list so she can phone you if there's a problem.'

'I've got a mobile phone,' Faye said to me, smiling proudly. 'Would you like to see it?'

'Yes, please.'

She tucked her hand into her trouser pocket and carefully drew out her phone. 'I'll tell you all the people in my contact list. They are my friends and I can phone them.'

I smiled and watched as, using all her concentration and a little clumsily, she pressed the icon to display her contacts.

'The first number is my home here,' she said, glancing up at me. 'Then I have Sue's number. She runs the stables and I can talk to her. I have the number of the day centre I go to. My other number is for Emma. She is my friend at the day centre.' Faye looked at me proudly. Bless her. Four contacts, and that was it. The total of her social circle. My heart clenched when I thought of the lists of names most of us have stored in our phones. 'Shall I put your number in now?' she asked me.

'Yes, if you like,' I said.

She passed the phone to her gran to enter the number. 'I don't know how to use these things,' Wilma said and passed it on to Becky.

Becky opened the contacts list and I gave her my landline and mobile numbers to enter. 'If you ever need me, try both numbers,' I said to Faye. 'I'll always answer one.'

'It might be a good idea if you have Faye's number in your phone,' Becky now said to me. 'You have Stan and Wilma's on the placement information forms.'

'Yes,' I said. I took my mobile from my bag and entered Faye's phone number, then Becky returned Faye's phone to her.

'Thank you,' Faye said, her eyes lighting up. 'I've got another contact now!' She looked as though she'd just been given a much-coveted present, which I suppose in a way she had.

'Now, Faye,' Becky said, 'before we arrange a day for you to move to Cathy's, do you have any questions?'

Faye looked sheepishly at her gran and then asked, 'Can I bring Snuggles with me?'

I thought that Snuggles might be a small caged animal, as there was no sign of a dog or cat, but then Becky explained:

'Snuggles is a cuddly toy that goes everywhere with Faye. In fact, where is Snuggles?' She looked around the room.

'I hid him,' Faye said, giving an impish grin. 'Gran said Cathy might think I was a baby if I had him in our meeting. He's here.' With a laugh she turned and, reaching behind the cushion on the sofa, brought out a cute, furry soft toy. It was an animal of indeterminable breed with big doleful eyes and soft silky fur that asked to be petted. Faye held him to her face and rubbed her cheek against him soothingly.

'Hello, Snuggles,' I said. 'Nice to meet you. Yes, of course you must bring him with you.'

Wilma tutted and Stan raised his eyebrows indulgently. 'She's had Snuggles since she was a small child and he goes everywhere with her,' he explained. 'At the day centre and the stables they put him in the office for safe keeping. Heaven forbid if he got lost.'

'I'll keep a close watch on him,' I said.

Faye kept Snuggles pressed to her cheek as Becky asked us, 'Any more questions from anyone?'

Stan shook his head and then Wilma looked at me and said, 'Will Faye be seeing your parents? Becky said you were a close family and Faye gets on very well with older people. Probably because we've brought her up.'

'Yes,' I said. 'We are a close family and she'll see my parents whenever we do, as long as it doesn't clash with when she sees you.' I stopped. A lump had suddenly risen in my throat and I felt my eyes fill. My bottom lip trembled. Don't cry, you silly woman, I told myself. But they'd seen my discomposure and were looking at me. I took a deep breath and swallowed hard. 'I'm sorry,' I said. 'It's just my mother now. We lost my dad recently. It was his funeral last Tuesday.'

21

'Oh, I am sorry,' Becky said, touching my arm kindly. 'We didn't know. The records haven't been updated. I'll tell Edith to change them so this doesn't happen again.'

'Thank you,' I said, fighting to recover my composure. I felt such a fool. I took another deep breath and then said, 'Yes, we are a close family, and Faye will be part of our family while she is with us.' I left it at that, for I knew that to say any more about my parents, or rather Mum, would open the floodgates on my tears.

'Faye,' Becky now said, looking at her. 'It's Thursday today. I suggest we move you to Cathy's at the weekend. Does that suit everyone?' We all nodded. 'Any preference for Saturday or Sunday?' She looked around.

'Sunday,' Wilma said. 'Gives me a chance to sort out what Faye needs to take with her.'

'Sunday is fine with me,' I said.

'Do you want to take Faye in a cab so you can see where she is going to live?' Becky now asked Wilma and Stan.

'There's no need,' Wilma said. 'We've seen the photographs Cathy brought. It would be such a kerfuffle getting us all down and into the cab, and then back again. We're on the council waiting list for a ground-floor flat or bungalow,' she added, glancing at me.

'It must be very difficult for you up here,' I said. 'I can collect Faye. One of my children can come with me and help with her bags so we don't have to make too many trips up and down in the elevator.'

'That sounds good, thank you,' Becky said. 'What time shall we make it on Sunday?'

'I'm easy,' I said.

Stan and Wilma didn't offer any suggestion on time so Becky said, 'Shall we say two o'clock? Then Faye can have some lunch here with you before she leaves.'

'OK,' I said. Stan and Wilma nodded.

'Great,' Becky said and made a note before putting away her pad and pen.

Faye wanted to show me her bedroom before we left, which was a good sign. She was more relaxed with me now. Becky stayed in the living room while I went with Faye. It was a medium-size room, prettily decorated in shades of pink, with shelves of cuddly toys and dolls, much like a young girl's bedroom might be. I admired it and then we returned briefly to the living room, before Faye came with Becky and me to see us out. Stan and Wilma remained seated in the living room and I had the feeling that it was probably such a struggle for them to get around that they only moved when they had to.

At the door Faye threw her arms around Becky. 'She always hugs me goodbye,' Becky explained. Then Faye wanted to hug me, so childlike and innocent in her display of affection and at odds with her obvious pregnancy.

'I like you,' she said after a moment, drawing back.

'Good. I like you too,' I said. 'See you on Sunday. Three more sleeps.'

She smiled and we said goodbye.

'Snuggles says goodbye too,' Faye added.

'Bye,' I said.

Becky and I left and Faye closed the door.

'Well, what do you think?' Becky asked once we were in the elevator. 'She's a nice kid. Her grandparents have done a good job of bringing her up, although they can be overprotective.'

'Yes, she's lovely,' I said. 'But how on earth did she get pregnant when they never let her out of their sight?'

'Exactly what they and I would like to know,' Becky said.

CHAPTER THREE

NOT STUPID

'Wilma is blaming the stables or the day centre,' Becky continued in the elevator. 'But they are adamant it couldn't have happened there. Faye is never left unattended long enough to meet a man.'

'Wilma said that Faye can use the bus once she knows the route,' I said. 'So presumably she's on her own for some periods?'

'Yes, but only for the length of the bus journey. One of the staff at the day centre or the stables sees her onto the bus, and the bus stop here is right outside the flats. If Faye is delayed for any reason or the bus is late one of the staff phones Wilma and Stan. There just isn't a window of opportunity when Faye could have met someone, although clearly she has.'

'And Wilma and Stan have no idea who he might be?' I asked. The elevator stopped, the doors opened and we got out.

'No, or if they do know they're not saying,' Becky continued outside. 'When I tried talking to Faye about it she just looked at me blankly. I'm not sure she even understands how she got pregnant, although I did explain. She'll be spending a lot of time with you after the move, so perhaps she'll open up once she's away from her grandparents.'

I nodded thoughtfully. 'I guess Faye is entitled to a relationship just as anyone is. As long as she gave her consent.'

'Yes. Exactly,' Becky said. We were now standing by her car. 'Adults with learning difficulties are very vulnerable. Statistically they are far more likely to be abused than anyone else in our society. Shocking, isn't it? But I don't know if someone has taken advantage of Faye or if she has been seeing someone. If she'd told me I could have arranged for her to see a nurse for contraception advice. I know some good nurses with experience of adults with learning difficulties. It's something I'll need to consider after the baby is born. I don't want this happening again. So if you can find out if she is likely to see the father again, I'd be very grateful.'

'I'll do my best,' I said. 'But given that Faye only has four contacts in her phone, five now with mine, isn't it unlikely she's in a relationship? How has she been communicating with him?'

Becky shrugged. 'I don't know.'

'And Wilma and Stan never leave her alone in the flat?'

'Not according to Wilma, although she was very quick to blame the stables and the day centre when she first found out. Stan never says much. Anyway, Cathy, hopefully Faye will open up to you. Thanks for taking her. We only have a few foster carers who specialize in adult fostering and they're full. I guess it doesn't appeal as much as looking after children.'

'To be honest, it's not something I'd previously considered,' I admitted. 'But I'm glad Edith thought of me. We'll do our best for Faye.'

'Thank you.' Then, glancing at her watch, she added, 'I need to be going now; I'm in a meeting soon. I'll phone you on Monday after the move. Thanks again.'

We said goodbye. Becky got into her car and I went to mine. Did I feel happier now I'd met Faye? Yes, to some extent I did. Perhaps happy wasn't the right word – she was, after all, still going to give up her baby – but I was slightly more at ease with it, simply because Faye didn't appear upset or distraught about being pregnant or having her baby adopted. Indeed, it had hardly been mentioned. She'd been more concerned about not being able to go to the stables. Becky had said that Wilma had taken the news badly, but she, too, had appeared more relaxed now, perhaps because a fostering placement had been found to help them out.

Yet it was difficult to know, I thought, as I began the drive home, if Faye had really come to terms with what was happening or if she was just ignoring it, or didn't even understand the implications. I'd noticed that she'd seemed oblivious to her baby bump and hadn't rubbed or cupped it with her hand as many expectant mothers do. Was it possible she thought she was just growing fat? Although by now – six months – the baby would be moving inside her. I'd talk to her about it once she was living with me: to prepare her was part of my role.

That evening over dinner I told Adrian, Lucy and Paula about the meeting with Faye, and that I'd be collecting her on Sunday afternoon and was looking for a volunteer to help carry her bags. Adrian said he'd arranged to see Kirsty (his girlfriend) for the day but offered to meet her later so he could help me. There was no need, as both the girls were free and said they would help. After dinner I telephoned my mother as I had been doing every evening since Dad had passed. I always started by asking her how she was and what she'd been doing during the day. Her reply was usually that she'd been tidying up the garden or reading, both of which were solitary pursuits, but perhaps it was still a bit soon to be seeing friends or going on day trips as she and Dad had done. This evening I mentioned that Faye would be coming to live with us for the remainder of her pregnancy. Mum was quite stoical in her response, as Adrian had been. 'I suppose if she has to give up the baby it's best done sooner rather than later,' she said. 'It will have a good home and be very well loved by the adoptive parents. Does she know the sex of the baby?'

'I don't know. It wasn't mentioned,' I said.

We chatted for a while longer and then I said I'd like to come and see her on Saturday and suggested we go out for some lunch. She didn't want to go out, so I said we'd make something there to eat. I didn't think that Mum was depressed, but she did sound sad sometimes, which was hardly surprising given she'd recently lost Dad. It would obviously take time for her to come to terms with a future without him, just as it would for all of us, and I reminded myself of the maxim that time is a great healer.

The following day (Friday) I gave Faye's room a thorough clean and then I did a large supermarket shop, as I would be out all day Saturday. I knew from the placement information forms that Faye had no special dietary requirements, so I stocked up with a range of nutritious foods as well as some treats – biscuits, ice cream, crisps – which I think are fine in moderation. Since I'd learnt that I'd be fostering Faye, I'd been giving some thought to the differences between foster-ing children and teenagers, and an adult with a learning dis-ability. Many aspects seemed similar – for example, the care and support I would give her – but as an adult Faye had a right to make her own decisions as much as possible, which would help maintain and develop her self-confidence and independence. Yet, while I'd had plenty of experience fostering children and teenagers, and the benefit of ongoing training, Faye was my first adult placement. Edith must have been thinking the same, because shortly after I returned home from shopping she telephoned.

'Cathy, I've been looking to see if there is any training that you might find useful, but we don't seem to offer an awful lot specifically for fostering adults. There's a two-day introductory course, but the next session isn't for another eight weeks, which is going to be a bit late to help you. There is some information on the internet, though. I've sent you some links, and if you have any questions or concerns, you can always telephone Becky. She's highly experienced in adult social care.'

'Thank you, I will.'

So that evening I went online and, using Edith's links and a search engine, I learnt quite a bit about foster care provision for adults. At present there are over 10,000 adult fostering placements in England; half of those are living in permanent placements. The ages of the adults fostered ranged from eighteen to over sixty, with three-quarters of the adults having a learning disability, and the others a physical disability or mental health problems. Schemes for fostering adults appeared to vary widely in different parts of the country, with some areas offering far more than others. The big advantage for the care receiver was that they could live with and be part of a family rather than in a care home. I learnt that the process for applying to foster adults was very similar to that of fostering children, with an assessment carried out by a social worker, references, a police check (now known as Disclosure and Barring Service), a health check and introductory training. Once the person was with the foster carer, their social worker visited regularly to monitor and support the placement, which was reassuring. While all this was very interesting, there was virtually no practical advice on fostering adults beyond it requiring patience, understanding and a wish to work with vulnerable adults.

Adrian, Lucy and Paula came with me on Saturday to visit Mum. She lived about an hour's drive away. They were very quiet in the car, gazing out of their side windows rather than listening to music or chatting. I guessed that they, like me, were finding it difficult going to the house again; our first visit after the funeral, the house that for all their lives had been Nana and Papa's home but was now just Nana's. Although we'd already been quite a few times since Dad had passed, it wasn't getting much easier. Arriving and leaving were the worst, with just Mum greeting us at the door and seeing us off, when it had always been the two of them. Once we were inside it became a little easier and today we all found jobs to do. Adrian cut the grass and then washed the car – my brother was selling it for Mum, as she didn't drive – while the girls and I helped Mum prepare lunch and lay the table. It was the first time we'd all sat at the dining table since Dad had died; previously, when we'd been there to organize the funeral, we'd had sandwiches and snacks on our laps. Dad always sat in the same place at the head of the table, and ridiculously I left his place empty, which of course emphasized his absence. As we sat down Mum quietly moved her chair into the space.

'That's better,' she said, and we all relaxed.

After lunch I asked Mum if she would like some help clearing out Dad's clothes, which is a daunting and heartbreaking task. But she said she would do it in her own time and had already made a start. She then produced a gift for each of the children, a memento of their grandpa. His favourite cufflinks for Adrian, an inlaid wooden trinket box for Lucy and his paperweight for Paula, which she'd always admired. Even if they never used the items, they would be treasured as touching personal reminders of Grandpa. I could see the emotion in their faces as they thanked their nana and then kissed and hugged her.

As usual we were reluctant to leave Mum alone and took a long time parting. Eventually Mum said it would be time for her bath soon and shooed us towards the front door. 'Phone me to let me know you're home safely,' she said as she always did. 'I hope tomorrow goes well. I'll look forward to meeting Faye.'

We got into the car and waved goodbye, each of us trying to adjust to seeing one lone figure in the porch.

On our return home Sammy was very pleased to see us and shot in through the cat flap as soon as he heard our voices in the hall. He was a short-haired cat of mixed breed with distinctive black-and-white markings and a haughty air about him, despite his past. He'd been living on the streets, presumably since birth, until someone took him to a cat rescue centre. We'd hesitated about having another cat for many years after Toscha had died, feeling that she was irreplaceable, but we were all pleased we'd gone ahead, as I hoped Sammy was too. He'd been quite feral to begin with and hadn't wanted much to do with us, but now he was gradually accepting our affection, allowing us to stroke him and occasionally sitting on our laps. Although I thought he would always be his own person, and we respected that.

Before I went to bed that night I checked through the placement information forms Becky had sent me to make sure I hadn't missed anything important. As we lived in the same National Health Service area as Faye, after the move she would be able to continue going to the same clinic and hospital she'd already been attending. I made a note to remember to make sure she brought her maternity folder with her, otherwise I'd have to go back for it, as it had to be taken to all her antenatal appointments. I also made a note to remember Snuggles, although I thought Faye wasn't likely to forget him. I knew from what Becky had told me that Faye had lived with her grandparents since the age of two when her mother had died from liver failure, assumed to be a result of alcoholism. The problems that had led to Faye's mother drinking herself to death weren't known, and Faye's father had never been named. Faye had an uncle (Wilma and Stan's son) and two adult cousins, but they seldom saw them. The son had done well for himself and had moved out of the area. Satisfied I knew what I needed to, I closed the folder and went to bed.

The following morning Adrian was up before the rest of us, as he was going out for the day with Kirsty. We had breakfast together and I saw him off at the door in my dressing gown, then the girls and I had a leisurely morning. After lunch, at 1.30, we left in the car to collect Faye. Although Faye knew what my family looked like from the photographs, my family had no idea what she looked like, which is often the case when a move is planned and the child has seen the photograph album. As I drove I tried to describe Faye to Paula and Lucy. 'She's about five feet two inches tall, softly spoken, with a pleasant, round face and straight hair. She looks and acts much younger than her age, but she appears gentle and kind.' They already knew Faye had learning difficulties and lived with her grandparents. 'She might want to hug you,' I said. 'She likes hugging.'

It was just as well I'd said this, for Faye answered the door, took one look at me and threw her arms around me in a big hug. 'I'm coming to stay with you like a holiday,' she said. She appeared excited by the prospect and I was pleased. She could easily have been upset at having to leave her grandparents.

'Yes, you are!' I said, mirroring her excitement. 'We're looking forward to having you stay with us. This is Lucy and Paula, my daughters. You remember you saw their photographs? You'll meet my son Adrian later.'

'Hello,' she said, now a little shy. 'Are you going to be my sisters while I live with you?'

'Yes, we are,' Lucy said.

Faye smiled broadly and then threw her arms around Lucy, hugging her, and then Paula. They looked slightly embarrassed, but I could see they were touched by Faye's easy and open display of affection, and her lack of adult inhibition made their first meeting much easier.

'Are you packed and ready?' I asked as we went in. I closed the door.

'Yes.'

'Bring them in here!' Wilma called from the living room.

'Whoops,' Faye said, smiling as she realized this was what she was supposed to do.

'No worries,' I said.

We followed her into the living room where Wilma was sitting on the sofa exactly as I'd left her three days earlier. Stan was getting to his feet, using his stick for support.

'These are my daughters, Lucy and Paula,' I said to them both.

'Hello,' Wilma said, running her eyes over them. I wondered if she disapproved of what they were wearing. They were dressed fashionably but tastefully, although very differently to the way she dressed Faye.

'Nice to meet you, ladies,' Stan said to the girls, propping himself on his walking stick. They smiled back.

'And you,' Paula said politely.

'Faye is packed, her bags are in her room,' Wilma said matter-of-factly. 'We're seeing her Tuesday? Becky said to check with you first, but she felt Faye should be with you all day tomorrow to settle in.'

'Yes, Tuesday is fine with me,' I said. 'What time?'

'Becky said between eleven o'clock and three. You'll come with Faye on the bus to begin with?'

'Yes, and then I'll return at three o'clock to bring her home. It's only one bus – number forty-seven. She'll soon get used to it.' I smiled at Faye.

'After she's done the journey with you three or four times she should be all right by herself,' Wilma said.

'OK.' Obviously it would have been easier for me to take and collect Faye in my car, but that wouldn't have helped her independence.

'Fetch your things then,' Wilma said to Faye.

'Shall we come and help?' Lucy asked, stepping forward.

'Yes, please,' I said. 'And don't forget Snuggles,' I called after them.

'As if she would!' Stan said indulgently. 'He's been sitting on top of her case all morning.'

I smiled. 'And her maternity folder and mobile phone are packed?' I asked.

'Yes, they're in the case,' Wilma confirmed.

The girls returned almost immediately from Faye's bedroom. Lucy was carrying a suitcase, Paula a shoulder bag and Faye Snuggles.

'Is that everything?' I asked, surprised.

'Yes,' Wilma said. 'She can always collect some more clothes if she needs to when she visits.' Which was true. 'Although she hasn't got that much that fits her now. She's been wearing my clothes, but I need them here.'

I guessed money was tight living on state benefits, and Wilma didn't strike me as the sort of person who would spend money on maternity wear that would only be worn for a few months.

'I was thinking of taking Faye shopping for some maternity clothes, if that's all right with you?' I asked diplomatically. 'As you know, I receive an allowance while Faye is with me.'

Wilma nodded.

'That would be good,' Stan said. 'We've told Faye that staying with you is like going on holiday, so those can be her new holiday clothes.' Which was a quaint way of putting it.

'Good. I'll take her shopping for some new outfits then,' I said. 'See you on Tuesday. Would you like Faye to telephone you this evening?'

'Only if she wants to,' Stan said. 'She sees more than enough of us.'

I smiled. 'But do phone us if you want to chat. You have my phone numbers?'

'Yes, Becky gave them to us,' Wilma confirmed.

We all said goodbye, and Wilma stayed where she was on the sofa while Stan came with us.

'Faye, aren't you going to kiss me goodbye?' Wilma called after her.

Faye stopped in the hall, looked at us and chuckled. 'Oh dear,' she said, clamping her hand over her mouth. 'I nearly forgot!'

The girls and I laughed too, while Stan tutted fondly. Faye clearly had a sense of humour and now that she was more relaxed around us it was starting to come out.

'She'd forget her head if it wasn't screwed on,' Stan said affectionately as Faye returned to the living room to kiss her gran goodbye. 'But she's a good, kind kid. She wouldn't hurt a fly. We're going to miss her.'

'I'm sure you will,' I said. 'But it's not for long and I'll look after her.'

'Thank you,' he said gratefully. I thought that Stan felt a lot more than he showed.

Faye returned from the living room and hugged her grandpa goodbye. 'Look after yourself and enjoy your time at Cathy's,' he said to her.

'I'm going on holiday,' she replied happily. 'Say goodbye to Snuggles, Grandpa.'

'Bye, Snuggles. Behave yourself,' Stan said. It was lovely the way he accepted her for who she was.

Leaning on his stick for support, he opened the front door and then took a couple of steps out of the flat. He stood in the corridor and watched us walk to the elevator, then called goodbye and returned indoors. It was clearly an effort for him to walk and his left side was still weak from the stroke.

'Is your house a long way away?' Faye asked as we waited for the elevator.

'No, not far. About a twenty-minute drive,' I said. I'd mentioned this at my previous visit, but she must have forgotten or not understood.

'I have a watch!' she announced and drew up her left sleeve so we could see her wrist watch.

'Excellent,' I said. 'That's good. I can show you how long it is to my house.' It's so much easier to explain time with the aid of an analogue watch or clock. I always make sure the children I foster have one.

'Which is the minute hand, do you know?' I asked her.

'Yes, the big hand,' she said.

'That's right. It's pointing to five now so in twenty minutes it will be there, on the nine. Do you know what the time will be then?'

She studied her watch for a moment and then said, 'Quarter to three.'

'Well done. So twenty minutes isn't long; it's from there to there,' I said, showing her on the watch.

'It's not long,' she told Lucy and Paula, and they smiled.

The elevator doors opened and we got in. 'The lift smells,' Faye announced, sniffing the air.

'Yes, it's disinfectant,' I said. 'I think it's just been cleaned.'

'Gran says some naughty people use it as a toilet late at night,' Faye said.

'Urgh gross!' Lucy exclaimed, horrified, and peered down at the floor.

Faye looked bemused and a little alarmed at Lucy's outburst. 'What does gross mean?' she asked me.

'Dirty, not nice,' I said.

As the elevator descended I saw Faye eyeing Lucy and Paula curiously and I wondered how much contact she normally had with young people. From what I'd learnt so far she seemed to spend most of her time with her grandparents, apart from two days a week when she went to the stables and the day centre. The elevator stopped, the doors opened and a middle-aged couple who knew Faye were waiting for the elevator. They smiled and said hello to her.

'I'm going away but I'm coming back,' she told them.

'I know,' the woman said kindly. 'Your gran said. See you soon.'

We crossed to the car where Lucy and Paula loaded Faye's suitcase and shoulder bag into the boot. I asked Faye if she would like to sit with me in the front, or in the rear. She wanted to sit in the rear so Paula sat with her, as it was Lucy's turn to sit in the passenger seat. Despite their ages, my children still coveted the front seat, just as they had done when they were younger, and took turns to sit there, unless Adrian was with us, when it was his seat, as he needed the extra leg-room.

'Five minutes has passed,' Faye announced, looking at her watch as I started the engine.

'Twenty minutes was only an estimate,' I said, glancing at her in the rear-view mirror. 'It has taken us five minutes to come down in the elevator and get in the car.'

'Our home is twenty minutes from now,' Paula said. 'So we'll arrive at about ten minutes to three.'

Faye studied her watch and then looked out of her side window. There was a silence for a while and then Lucy asked Faye, 'What sort of things do you like to do in your spare time?'

'Watch television,' Faye said.

'Me too,' Lucy agreed. 'What programmes do you like?'

'I like *Coronation Street*, *EastEnders* and *Emmerdale*, the same as Gran.'

'You're in good company then,' I said. 'Lucy loves the soaps.'

Lucy then talked to Faye about what was happening in these series, and Paula and Faye joined in. Paula watched soaps sometimes, but not as much as Lucy, who updated herself from the internet if she missed an episode. I'm not a great soap fan.

After a while I said, 'Faye likes being at the stables too.'

'I love the horses,' Faye said. 'More than I love Gary in *EastEnders*.' Which made us all laugh.

'So what do you do at the stables?' Paula asked. 'Do you ride the horses?'

'Sometimes, but I also help muck them out.'

'Yuck, what does that mean?' Lucy asked. Considering she worked with children, she was rather delicate in these matters.

'It means we have to shovel up their poo and put it in a wheelbarrow,' Faye said.

'Gross,' Lucy said.

'Gross,' Faye repeated. 'It's very smelly.'

'I don't mind it,' Paula said. 'I go riding sometimes. Do you have a favourite horse?'

I could see that Paula and Lucy, like me, were working out where to pitch the conversation with Faye, and I thought they were doing well.

'Whisper is my favourite,' Faye said. 'She is a Shetland cross and is eleven hands high. You measure horses and ponies in hands. My next favourite is Misty. He is a black gelding and is twelve hands high. I only ride those two because they are very gentle. But I help look after the others and stroke them.'

'That's fantastic,' I said, glancing at her in the interior mirror. 'You know a lot about horses.'

I saw her smile. 'Some of the kids from the flats call me stupid,' she said. 'But Grandpa tells me to ignore them. He says I'm not stupid, I know more than them about horses.'

'That's right,' I said. 'Your grandpa is a very wise man. It's stupid to call people names.'

The thought of anyone calling Faye names or being unkind to her was enough to make me tear up. Gentle, kind Faye. But I could see how vulnerable she was, and I fully understood why her grandparents had become overprotective.

CHAPTER FOUR

IN DENIAL

Although Faye had seen photographs of my house, I still showed her around when we first arrived. As we entered each room she said politely, 'This is a nice room. Thank you for showing me.' This was all rather formal, so I told her to treat the place like home as she would her flat. I introduced her to Sammy who, realizing there was someone new in the house, had shot in through the cat flap to see what was going on. He was usually standoffish when it came to meeting new people and would turn his back and walk away or flee outside, but not with Faye. He came straight up to her, rubbed around her legs, let her stroke him and then rolled over onto his back so she could rub his tummy.

'I think he likes me,' Faye said, pleased, and she knelt to pet him.

'He certainly does,' I said. 'But remember to wash your hands when you've finished stroking him.' It was basic hygiene, but even more important for an expectant mother, as disease could cross the placenta and affect the baby.

When Sammy had had his fill of being petted he went outside again. Faye washed her hands at the kitchen sink and then, examining her watch, said that her gran and grandpa had a cup of tea and a biscuit at home around this time – 3.30 p.m.

'Would you like tea and biscuits now?' I asked, assuming this was part of her routine.

'Yes, please.'

I smiled. 'You must tell me what you have at home so you can have it here. I want you to feel at home.'

'Gran says I mustn't be any trouble.'

'You certainly won't be that,' I said. I filled the kettle. 'But it will help me if you tell me what you want, OK?' Faye was so self-effacing that it concerned me she might not like to say.

She gave a small nod and stayed with me in the kitchen, watching me as I took down the mugs.

'I can make tea,' she said after a moment. 'I make it for Gran and Grandpa.'

'That's good. You can make it here too if you like. But it's nice to have it made for you sometimes, isn't it?'

She nodded accommodatingly. 'Gran and Grandpa can't walk very far so I help them,' she said. 'It was scary when Grandpa had his stroke. We had to call an ambulance. He's slowly getting better. But he says he won't ever be perfect.'

'He's doing very well,' I said. 'Strokes can take a long time to recover from. It's good you can help him.'

'That's what he says. I love my grandpa. I hope he doesn't die.'

'He's getting better,' I reassured her. But I thought it must be a worry for Wilma and Stan, and for any parents with a disabled child, as to who would look after Faye when they did eventually die. I supposed she'd have to go into supported lodgings, as there were no close relatives she could live with.

Once the tea was made we took it into the living room where Lucy and Paula were waiting. I liked them to be sociable when a new child or young person arrived. They hadn't wanted tea but had poured themselves a glass of water each. To start the conversation I said that Faye usually had tea and biscuits around this time at home, and we talked a bit about different families having different routines. Faye talked unselfconsciously, although it was more like an elderly person talking – measured and slow – than a young person in their twenties. How much of this was because of her learning disabilities or from spending so much time with her grandparents I didn't know. But I guessed from what she said that she hadn't spent much time in other people's homes. It appeared that as a child (attending a special school) she hadn't gone to friends' homes to play, nor had she had them home. Now, she only saw her friend Emma at the day centre. She said she went into her neighbour's flat with her grandparents for a cup of tea sometimes, although they were nearer her grandparents' age than hers. But Faye seemed content and accepting of people and situations, which is an admirable quality in anyone.

Once we'd finished our tea I suggested to Faye that we unpack her suitcase. She came with me upstairs while Lucy and Paula went off to do their own thing. Snuggles, who'd been her constant companion, being either held or tucked under her arm, came with us and Faye sat him on the bed. She unzipped her suitcase and on top was the maternity folder, which she passed to me. Together we unpacked her case, folding and hanging the garments into the drawers and wardrobe. As her gran had said, there wasn't an awful lot: two pairs of elasticated-waist trousers in dark green and

43

brown, the same style her gran wore and Faye had on now; two large wash-worn jerseys in grey and beige, which I guessed had also been Wilma's; a dressing gown and duffel coat, which were Faye's but she couldn't possibly do up over her baby bump; a pair of furry slippers; a pair of pyjamas; a vest, bra and pants; a towel and a brand-new wash bag.

'I got that new for coming here,' Faye announced proudly as she took the wash bag from the case.

'It's very pretty,' I said. With a satin finish and a colourful flowery pattern, it was a welcome contrast to the drabness of her clothes.

'I didn't have a wash bag,' Faye said. 'So Grandpa asked our neighbour to buy one for me when she went shopping. He gave her the money. That's was kind of him, wasn't it?'

'Yes, it was. It's beautiful,' I said. 'Lucky girl.'

She beamed and her whole face lit up.

Once the case was empty I stowed it on top of her wardrobe so it was out of the way. Then she took her towel and wash bag to the bathroom and I showed her where to put them: her towel on the rail next to ours and her wash bag on the shelf, ready for later. We returned to her room and unpacked her shoulder bag. It just contained her mobile phone, some well-thumbed women's magazines, which Faye said were her gran's, her hairbrush, some sweets and a small framed photograph of her grandparents which we placed on top of the chest of drawers. This photograph was the only object she'd brought with her that could personalize her room and I suggested that when we went shopping the following day she could choose some posters to put on the walls to make the room look more comfortable. I'd noticed she had some pictures of the Flower Fairies on her bedroom walls at home. Faye liked the idea and, giving me a hug, thanked me. It seemed a big treat for her.

I now suggested we went downstairs and looked through her maternity folder together. I needed to know how Faye was doing with her antenatal care and when her next appointments were, and it would be a reminder for her. I hoped it might also be a starting point for discussion about her baby. So far she hadn't mentioned it and continued to behave as though it wasn't there. She was happy to let me take the folder and we went downstairs where we settled side by side on the sofa with the folder open on my lap. The first few pages contained standard introductory information on the purpose and use of the folder, with emphasis on it needing to be kept with the patient and taken to *all* antenatal appointments. This was followed by the patient's details: Faye's name, address and telephone number (I'd give them mine too at the next appointment), date of birth, age, her doctor's details and the date the baby was expected – 14 December. I'd thought it must be close to Christmas, but seeing it in print gave me a jolt. Faye would be giving birth and then parting with her baby only two weeks before Christmas, possibly closer if she overran her delivery date. The only consolation was that at least she would be home with her grandparents for Christmas.

I continued to the next page, explaining as I went. The results of Faye's two ultrasound scans were included and they were normal. At the time of the second scan the sex of the baby can be ascertained with a reasonable degree of accuracy, and the parent(s) has the right to know if they wish. A note had been made by the nurse that Faye didn't want to know the sex of her baby, which was obviously her decision and perhaps understandable, as she wouldn't be playing any part in its life. While I'd been talking through the notes I'd noticed that Faye had been looking around the room, largely indifferent to the information, much of which was interesting and illustrated with diagrams. I'd been expecting her to ask questions or make comments as she had been doing about other things, for she didn't appear shy any more.

'So you've had two scans and everything is fine,' I said, trying to engage her.

She shrugged, and I wondered if she hadn't understood what a scan was or didn't remember having the scans. 'You know when you went to the hospital and the nurse put cold gel on your tummy, and there was a picture on the screen? It says here Gran was with you.'

Faye gave a half-hearted nod and continued to gaze around the room. I returned to the folder. I read that Faye was going to give birth in the hospital rather than the birthing centre, but there was no mention of a birthing partner.

'Is Gran going to be your birthing partner?' I asked, for clearly she needed someone there.

Faye shrugged again, so I wondered if she hadn't understood. 'A birthing partner is someone close to you, who stays with you while you are in labour. They help and support you. Will Gran be with you when you have your baby?' I tried again, rephrasing it.

For the first time since I'd met Faye her face set. Losing her open, happy disposition, she now looked grumpy. 'Don't say that word,' she said, frowning.

'What? Baby?' I asked, puzzled.

'Yes. We don't talk about that.'

46

I looked at her carefully. 'Faye, love, we are going to have to talk about it. You are having a baby and I need to help you prepare for that.'

'I don't want to talk about it,' she said again. 'Gran knows that. You have to be like Gran.'

This completely threw me. How was I going to help prepare her for what was to come, which was part of my role, if she refused to talk about it? If she wasn't prepared, labour was going to be a very frightening experience for her.

'You can read it,' she said. 'But don't talk to me about it. That's what Gran does.'

'OK.' I'd wait until she'd been with me longer and I'd had a chance to speak to her social worker, Becky, on Monday. I didn't want to upset Faye, but on the other hand she needed to know how her pregnancy was progressing and how the baby would be born. Perhaps she already knew about child-birth, but it was possible she didn't. If not, I had some litera-ture that I used with children that would help explain the process.

I continued going through the folder, looking for the appointment schedule, without making any further comment while Faye gazed around the room. I found a note saying that Faye wouldn't be attending the standard antenatal classes, nor the workshop on breastfeeding, as it wasn't considered appropriate, but she would join the group for a tour of the maternity unit. I didn't know if it wasn't considered appro-priate because of her learning difficulties or because she was giving up the baby. Becky had said that she hoped being away from her grandparents might encourage Faye to start open-ing up and maybe identify the baby's father and the circum-stances in which they'd met, but clearly that wasn't going to happen while she denied the existence of a baby. However, it was still early days.

Once I'd found the list of appointments I closed the folder. 'Good. Everything is going well,' I said with a cheerful smile. 'Do you have any questions?'

'Not about that,' she said, prodding the folder. 'But can I play with Sammy?'

'Yes, of course, if he's in the house.'

'I'll go and look for him,' she said. She stood and with childlike enthusiasm went off in search of Sammy. I heard her go upstairs and then Paula's voice on the landing as they began a conversation. I put away the folder and went into the kitchen to begin the preparations for dinner. Sammy wasn't in the house, but as soon as he heard me in the kitchen he shot in through the cat flap in search of his dinner.

Adrian texted to say he'd be having dinner with Kirsty and would see us later, so the girls and I ate together at around six o'clock. Faye had a good appetite but ate and drank using the same slow, measured movements with which she approached everything. When she'd finished she carefully set her knife and fork in the centre of her clean plate.

'You're a pleasure to cook for,' I said.

'It was nice,' she said. 'Better than we have at home.'

'You shouldn't say that,' Lucy admonished with a laugh.

'But it's true!' Faye protested. With her naïve approach to life and lack of inhibition, she said things as she saw them, unencumbered by tact or diplomacy.

'Do you or your grandparents cook?' I asked lightly, making conversation.

'We all do it,' she said. 'But we have the food in plastic trays that you put in the microwave.'

'Ready meals?' I asked.

'Yes.'

I guessed that cooking, like many domestic tasks, would be difficult for her grandparents with their restricted mobility, so convenience meals were a practical option. 'Would you like me to show you how to cook some easy meals?' I offered. 'The cheese and broccoli bake we just had is very quick and simple.'

'Yes, please,' she said. 'My grandpa will like that too. He doesn't like plastic food. He says you can't tell if you're eating the container or the food.' She chuckled, and I could see where she got her sense of humour.

After dinner everyone helped clear the table and then Faye said she wanted to watch television. Lucy went with her into the living room while Paula went upstairs to wash her hair. I took the opportunity to telephone Mum, using the phone in the hall. I always began by asking her how she was, and as usual she said, 'I'm fine, dear, you mustn't worry about me.' Which didn't really answer my question. Mum was of a generation who rarely shared their problems and just got on with life.

'What have you been doing today?' I asked, as I often did.

'Oh, you know, this and that. Keeping busy. How has your day been? Is your young lady with you?' Which of course directed the conversation away from her to me.

'Yes, Faye's here and settling in,' I said. 'She seems happy enough.'

'Good. I'll look forward to meeting her. I expect you're busy with everyone, so don't worry about me. Thanks for phoning, love.' And so she wound up the conversation and a minute or so later we said goodbye. Mum never wanted to be any trouble, and while she always listened to any problems we might have, I had little idea of hers. I just hoped she was coping without Dad as she led us to believe, but it was difficult to tell.

Faye watched television for the rest of the evening, and I realized she had an even greater capacity for the soaps than Lucy, who was texting as she watched. I joined them for a short while. Paula was in her bedroom listening to music as she dried her hair. At nine o'clock, as the soaps finished, Faye said it was her bedtime. Obviously this was early for a twenty-four-year-old, but being pregnant could have made her tire more easily, and also it wasn't for me to disrupt her usual routine. I asked her if she normally had a hot drink before she went to bed and she said no, just a glass of water. She came with me into the kitchen and I showed her where the glasses were, and then I waited while she filled one from the cold tap. As it was her first night with us I said I'd go with her and make sure she had everything she needed. She said goodnight to Lucy as we passed the living room and then called goodnight to Paula through her bedroom door. 'Goodnight, Faye,' Paula sang out. Adrian wasn't home yet.

Having checked that Faye had everything she needed, I waited on the landing while she was in the bathroom, changing, washing and getting ready for bed. She said she didn't have a bath every night, as she had to take turns with her gran and grandpa, so it was every third night. I assumed that this was because her grandparents, with their disabilities, took a while to bath or shower, so they only had time for one per night. I told her she could have a bath or shower every night while she was staying with me, but she said it was OK, as she'd had a bath the night before. Again, I wasn't about to disrupt her routine, but when she'd been with me longer I'd suggest she showered or bathed every day, as my family and I did.

Faye took a long time washing, changing and brushing her teeth, and when she came out of the bathroom she was in her pyjamas, the buttons on the jacket straining over her bump.

'When we go shopping tomorrow,' I said, 'we can buy you some nice new pyjamas that aren't so tight, or a nightdress. What do you think?'

'Yes, please,' she said, smiling. 'Thank you. I'm looking forward to going shopping for new holiday clothes.' She gave me another big hug. I didn't correct her and say 'maternity clothes'. I didn't want to upset her.

I went with her to her bedroom and checked again that she had everything she needed. I told her there was a night-light on the landing that stayed on, so she would be able to see if she needed to go to the toilet. I reminded her where my bedroom was and that she should come and find me or call me if she needed anything in the night, but not to go wandering downstairs by herself in the dark, just as I did with the children I fostered. She said she understood. I then asked her if she'd like her curtains closed or open (she said closed), the light on or off (she slept with it off, and the door closed). Small details, but they are important in helping a young person to settle in a strange room. Snuggles was already in bed and Faye climbed in and pulled the duvet up to her chin.

'Comfortable?' I asked.

'Yes. Very comfortable,' she said. Just her little face peeped over the duvet. She pressed Snuggles to her cheek and then kissed him. 'Grandpa kisses Snuggles and me goodnight,' she said. 'Gran can't bend down any more.' She smiled.

'Would you like me to kiss you goodnight?' I asked. Some children want a goodnight kiss, others don't, so I always ask, otherwise it's an intrusion.

'Yes.' She held up Snuggles and I kissed his forehead, and then hers. 'Night, love,' I said. 'See you in the morning. Remember to call me if you need me in the night.'

'I will,' she said.

Saying a final goodnight, I came out and closed her door. It felt a bit strange having an adult in the room instead of a child or teenager. Paula was on her way to the bathroom to shower and I said I'd come up later to say goodnight. Downstairs, Lucy was still in the living room with the television on low and texting. I sat beside her on the sofa.

'How are you getting on with Faye?' I asked.

'She's really sweet,' Lucy said. 'And very kind. I like her. I told her about when I was a child – you know, when I didn't have a proper home – and she was really kind and sympathetic. But, Mum, does she know she's pregnant?' Lucy stopped texting and looked at me.

'I'm not sure. Why do you ask?'

'Well, she said how slim I was and I told her she would be slim again once she'd had the baby. She went quiet and then said I mustn't say that, and that she was fat. I tried to tell her it was the baby, but she said no and changed the subject, so I didn't say any more.'

'Thanks for telling me. I'm going to speak to her social worker tomorrow and try to find out how much Faye understands, so we can help her.'

'She's nice, though, really nice. Such a pity she can't keep the baby.'

'Yes, it is,' I agreed thoughtfully.

Adrian arrived home half an hour later, having had a good day out at a leisure park with Kirsty. We chatted for a while and then he went to bed, as he had to be up at six in the morning for an early shift at the supermarket. Lucy went up too and I followed at around 10.30. I never sleep well when there is someone new in the house; I'm half listening out in case they wake. I heard Faye get up at around 2.00 a.m. to go to the toilet and when she'd finished I went round the landing to make sure she was all right. She was, and I didn't hear her again until after 8.00 a.m. when I was up and dressed and Adrian had left for work. He'd meet her that evening.

Faye appeared in the kitchen in her pyjamas and dressing gown and asked if she could make herself a cup of tea. I said of course she could and showed her where the tea, mugs and milk were. She said that at home she always made tea for herself and her grandparents while in her dressing gown, and they drank it in their bedrooms while they dressed. After that they had breakfast together – cereal and toast – at around ten o'clock.

'I help Gran and Grandpa get dressed,' Faye told me. 'Grandpa needs help putting on his vest and doing up the buttons on his shirt. So he sits on the bed and I help him, then I put his socks on for him. Gran needs help with her bra and her socks.'

'That's kind of you, love,' I said. 'Who is helping them while you are not there, do you know?'

'Our neighbour is going in.'

'That's good.'

It was important for Faye to feel at home and to maintain her independence, so I left her to make her tea in her own time. She offered to make me tea too, but I thanked her and said I'd already had a coffee. In keeping with her usual routine, Faye took her mug up to her bedroom and drank it while she dressed. Lucy was up and dressed, and left for work at 8.30, just as Paula was surfacing. She had to enrol at college today but not until eleven o'clock. Unsure of what she wanted to do, she'd opted for a business studies course at a local college, which would give her a good grounding for many careers.

Because Faye didn't have to help her grandparents this morning, she was ready earlier than usual and came downstairs well before ten o'clock. This threw her and she was undecided if she should have breakfast now or wait until ten.

'Are you hungry?' I asked her. She nodded. 'So have your breakfast now then. It's important you eat and drink regularly.' I was going to add 'for you and your baby', but stopped. I'd wait until I'd spoken to Becky before I talked to Faye again about her baby. She poured herself some cereal – cornflakes – while I made some toast. Paula joined us with her breakfast, and at 9.30 I left them at the table while I went into the living room to telephone Becky. I wanted to catch her before we went shopping.

She was at her desk, and when she heard my voice she was immediately concerned. 'Is everything all right?' she asked. A carer phoning the social worker first thing on a Monday morning usually meant they'd had a difficult weekend.

'We're all fine,' I quickly reassured her. 'I collected Faye as arranged yesterday and she is settling in. But I need to ask you something.'

54

'Sure. Go ahead. I'm hoping to visit you both later in the week.'

I could hear Paula and Faye talking at the table. The doors were slightly open, so I kept my voice low.

'You know you said that Faye appears to be coping well with the pregnancy and isn't distressed at the thought of giving up her baby?'

'Well, yes. It's hardly mentioned.'

'Is it possible she doesn't really understand that she is having a baby, or is in denial?'

Becky paused. 'I don't know. It's possible, I suppose, although I spoke to her at length when we first found out she was pregnant. What makes you ask?'

'She completely ignores all aspects of her pregnancy, and yesterday afternoon I went through her maternity folder with her, but she told me not to talk about it. There's no mention of a birthing partner. Will it be Wilma? Then later she told my daughter Lucy that she was getting fat. When Lucy said it was because she was expecting a baby she became withdrawn and changed the subject. We're going shopping today for maternity clothes, but she's calling them holiday clothes.'

'Stan put that idea in her head,' Becky said.

'Yes, I know. But Faye acts as though she isn't pregnant. She hasn't mentioned it and won't talk about it. I think it'll make her upset if I push it.'

There was another silence. 'Let me have a chat with her and we'll take it from there. Are you in on Friday afternoon, around two o'clock?'

'Yes. Faye has an antenatal appointment in the morning, but we'll be here in the afternoon.'

'Good. I'll come to see you both then. We'll have a good chat with her. Apart from that, she's all right?'

'Yes, she's delightful.'

'And, Cathy, on the matter of a birthing partner, Wilma's already said she's not up to it, so I was hoping you'd do it.'

CHAPTER FIVE

BEST OUTCOME

Well, that was a shock. I was going to be Faye's birthing partner. A first for me. Visions of passing Faye the gas and air, holding her hand, dabbing her brow with a cool towel and encouraging her to push when necessary as I'd seen on television ran through my head. Of course I'd do it, if that's what Faye and the adults responsible for her wanted, although I wondered how I would cope when I saw that beautiful baby and then had to stand by helplessly as it was taken away, never to be seen by Faye or me again. Was that how it happened when a newborn went straight into foster care? Or would Faye (and I) have the opportunity to hold her baby? I didn't know and I wasn't sure which was worse. But I would find out so that I could prepare us both. If I was prepared then perhaps there'd be less chance of me breaking down and I'd be better able to support Faye. I'd ask Becky when I saw her on Friday, although there was a great temptation to ignore it all, just as Faye was doing.

After Paula had left to enrol at college, Faye and I left for the shopping mall in town. Snuggles stayed on her bed and Faye told me that her gran didn't allow him to go shopping in case he got lost. I parked in the multi-storey car park and we took the elevator down to the shops. Faye was excited to be going shopping for new clothes, but I wondered what her reaction would be as we entered the store we were heading for. It was huge and sold everything you could possibly want for pregnancy, babies and early years. I wondered if this would be the trigger that allowed Faye to start talking about her pregnancy. If so, I would be considerably relieved.

A very smiley assistant greeted us at the entrance of the store and offered us a basket, which Faye took. Gentle, soothing lullaby music played in the background all around the store, and immediately on our right was the newborn section, with rows and rows of the cutest first-size baby clothes. Faye went straight to them and I followed, feeling that this was a good first step. Although we were here to buy her maternity clothes, if she wanted to buy a first-size outfit for the baby then she could; it would be an acknowledgement that she was pregnant and going to have a baby. Faye picked out the sweetest little pink-and-white dress I've ever seen. 'This would fit Suzie,' she said, holding it up.

'Is that what you're going to call your baby?' I asked, surprised, and feeling we had taken a big leap forward.

'Suzie is my doll at home,' she said, ignoring my reference to the baby.

'These are first-size baby clothes,' I said. 'For newborn babies, not for dolls.'

'It will fit Suzie,' she said.

'It probably will, but we're not here to dress your doll, love. We need to buy you some maternity clothes.'

She was clearly disappointed, which I felt bad about, but she returned the dress to the rail and came with me to the maternity wear section, and we looked around.

'This is a lovely dress,' I said, selecting one. 'I think it would suit you. Would you like to try it on in your size?'

Her face lit up. 'Oh, yes, please.' The doll's clothes were forgotten.

'Excellent. Try on a few different ones.' I helped her select dresses in her size and we put them into the basket for her to try on later. I continued flicking through the rails with Faye close beside me and I showed her some leggings and tops. 'These are good for everyday use,' I said. She nodded enthusiastically. 'Which tops do you like?' She chose a few and put them in the basket. I added black maternity leggings to go with the tops.

'Do you need any help?' another cheery assistant asked.

'I think we're OK, thank you,' I said.

'When's the baby due?' she asked, looking at Faye. I guessed it was part of their sales patter.

Faye smiled but didn't reply.

'December,' I said.

'A Christmas baby, how lovely,' the assistant enthused. 'Please ask me or any of the assistants if you need help or would like to be measured for a maternity bra.' She glanced at Faye.

'Thank you,' I said.

Once she'd gone I asked Faye if she would like to be measured for a bra and I explained what was involved. She pulled a face and said no, so I said I'd guess her size and she could try on some bras in the cubicle, for her present ones must be tight by now. Together we continued round the store and selected some pretty lace-trimmed bras, maternity trousers, a pair of pyjamas, a nightdress, pants and camisole tops, which I explained were like vests. With the basket full we went into the changing rooms, where I hung all the garments on the hooks in a cubicle and then waited just outside while Faye tried them on, ready to help if necessary. Undressing and dressing was a slow process for Faye, but it was important she did it herself. She came out and showed me each outfit once it was on, smiling and twirling in front of the mirror. She was in her element, bless her, but had no idea what fitted or suited her, so I helped her choose. The bras were too small, so I asked one of the assistants to bring in bigger sizes, and eventually Faye had tried on everything. She wanted to wear one of the dresses straight away, so, leaving her in the cubicle, I took the dress to the till, paid for it, and returned it to her. She was delighted.

'I look pretty, don't I?' she said, gazing at her image in the mirror.

'You do, love. Very pretty.' The dress was made from a light grey and pink check material, with long sleeves, and was loosely gathered under the bust to accommodate her growing bump, although I didn't say that to Faye. I just admired it and then, collecting together all the other items we wanted, we went to the till to pay for the rest.

Faye had put on her old duffel coat over the dress. It didn't do up, and I realized we needed to buy her a better-fitting coat or jacket. After trying on a few we chose a three-quarter-length beige quilted jacket, which she would also be able to wear after the birth. I'd spent far more than the clothing allowance I'd receive for fostering Faye – rarely did it cover equipping a child from scratch – but it was completely worth it. Not only was Faye delighted with all her new clothes, I felt proud that she looked smart, as I thought her grandparents would be. Yet Faye had successfully chosen a whole new wardrobe of maternity clothes without so much as acknowledging she was pregnant!

By the time we left the store it was nearly 1.00 p.m. I was hungry and Faye said she was too. I suggested that rather than go straight home we could take the bags to the car and then have lunch in the mall. She loved the idea and wanted to wear her new jacket instead of her old duffel coat, so she changed into it by the car. Faye was like a child in a new dress going to a party as we headed back to the elevator. Her excitement bubbled over and she kept hugging me and thanking me. She didn't look obviously disabled as a person with Down's syndrome or cerebral palsy might, but strangers tended to notice something in her manner and behaviour and so they'd glance at her, smile politely and look away. Which is what the couple in the elevator did as Faye hugged me again and said how much she liked her new clothes and didn't she look pretty.

Many of the restaurants, cafés and bars on the ground floor of the mall were open-plan and as we approached this area we were greeted with an array of delicious aromas from the different cuisines on offer: Chinese, Thai, Malaysian, Mexican, Indian, as well as traditional British food. I asked Faye what she liked but she didn't know. I explained a little about the different foods and Faye stopped at a Malaysian buffet where a large screen on the wall above the counter showed enticing pictures of their range of dishes. She'd never eaten Malaysian food before but wanted to try it, so, aware of her rather conservative tastes in food, I suggested a selection of dishes that weren't too hot and didn't include shellfish, which I knew pregnant women were advised to avoid. I carefully carried the tray with the dishes to one of the bench-style tables and we sat on either side. The food tasted as delicious as it looked in the pictures and Faye enjoyed it. As we ate we talked and I reminded Faye that she was going to see her grandparents the following day. I also asked her if she wanted to go to the day centre on Wednesday; if so, I'd go with her on the bus, but she said she didn't want to.

'I want to go to the stables,' she said.

'I know, love, but do you remember your grandpa and Becky explaining that you couldn't go while you're expecting? Grandpa said you could go again in ninety-eight sleeps. That was when I visited you at your flat. It will be fewer now.'

'How many now?' she asked.

I did a quick calculation. 'Eighty-eight,' I said.

Satisfied, she returned to her food.

A couple with a toddler and a very small baby in a pram were sitting at the table next to us. The little boy was happily trying all the different foods, liking some but not others. When the baby woke the mother picked her up and gave her a bottle. I glanced at Faye to see if there was any reaction, but there wasn't. She just continued eating. I'd noticed in the store earlier, where many of the women had been expecting or had a baby with them, that Faye hadn't given them a second glance, outwardly uninterested, which seemed to confirm that perhaps she didn't fully understand she was pregnant, for I would have expected her to at least look at them, if not comment.

Faye ate well, very well. There wasn't a morsel left on her plate. But as we stood to leave I wondered if she'd overeaten, because she gave a small gasp and, bending forward, momentarily touched her stomach.

'Are you all right?' I asked, concerned.

'No. My tummy feels funny.'

'Do you want to sit down for a while? Perhaps it's indigestion.'

'No, it's gone now,' she said, straightening. 'That food is moving.'

I looked at her carefully. 'It wasn't the food, love. It was the baby.'

'No. It was the food,' she said, ignoring my reference to the baby. 'It has happened before.'

It would, I thought. Many women start to feel their babies move from sixteen weeks, and Faye was twenty-five weeks. 'It will happen again,' I said, and left it at that. I'd explain more once Becky had spoken to her on Friday.

We arrived home just after three o'clock. Paula was already home, having enrolled at college, and she told me about it. The rest of the week for her would be given over to introductory days – fresher's week – then the lectures and work began in earnest the following week. She showed me some literature from college and a reading list. She was looking forward to the course and also being at college rather than school. Adrian arrived home just after four o'clock and met Faye for the first time. While he said an easy, 'Hi, Faye, how are you?' she went shy, threw him a small smile and went to fetch Snuggles, which I noticed she did if she felt insecure.

We all had dinner together, with Snuggles tucked beside Faye on her chair. Adrian, Lucy and Paula did most of the talking, while Faye and I listened. Once we'd finished and cleared the table, Faye wanted to watch television, so I showed her how to work the remote and she settled down for another evening of viewing soaps. Lucy and Paula joined her for a while and then went up to their rooms. Adrian had never been a great television watcher, and certainly not of soaps, preferring his laptop or a book, although he did listen to *The Archers* on the radio sometimes, which the girls were quick to point out was a type of soap. I telephoned Mum as usual. She'd been out with a neighbour to a garden centre for lunch. I was pleased. 'Your dad and I used to go there sometimes,' she said. 'They do a very reasonable two-course lunch at a good price.'

Stan, Faye's grandpa, telephoned and I answered it in the hall. He said he just wanted to check that I'd be bringing Faye on the bus the following day and I confirmed I would be. He said he'd tried to phone Faye's mobile but she hadn't answered. I said she rarely had it with her and often left it in her bedroom.

'That's OK,' he said. 'The phone is really for when she is out alone. What's she doing now? Watching those soaps?'

'Yes, how did you guess?' I laughed. 'Shall I fetch her for you?'

'No, leave her. Just tell her I phoned and we miss her, and we'll see her tomorrow.'

'I will.'

I told Faye straight away, but she was so absorbed in the television she just nodded a response.

At nine o'clock when the soaps had finished Faye switched off the television and went into the kitchen for a glass of water to take to bed, as was her usual routine.

'Would you like a bath before you go to bed tonight?' I asked.

'No, I had one last night,' she said.

'That was the night before,' I said. 'Before you came here.' With a child I would just run the bath each night and insist

64

they had one – nicely so, of course – but it was different with Faye. She was an adult and had her own routine. 'Tomorrow night then.'

'When it's my bath night at home,' Faye said, 'Gran makes me have it before I watch television, otherwise she says I'm too late going to bed.'

'Good idea,' I said. 'We'll do that here then.'

The first week when a new foster child or young person arrives is really taken up with us all getting to know each other. It's a period of adjustment, not only for the young person, who suddenly finds themselves living in a strange house with people they don't know, but also for my family as we adapt to accommodate their wishes and routines. By the end of the week we are usually all jogging along side by side, and even after one day and night together Faye and my family were more relaxed. She called out goodnight as she went up to bed and they sang out, 'Goodnight and see you in the morning.' I waited on the landing until she'd finished in the bathroom. I wouldn't necessarily do this every evening, unless she wanted me to, but it was important while she settled in. She came out of the bathroom looking very smart in her new pyjamas. 'Snuggles likes my pyjamas so much he wants a pair,' she laughed and hugged me. I laughed too. She was such a poppet.

I showed her where the laundry basket was for her washing and then I went with her to her bedroom. I now knew that she liked her curtains closed, the light off and the door shut at night. She placed her glass of water on the bedside cabinet and climbed into bed. I said goodnight and then gave Snuggles and her a kiss, as I had the night before.

'After tonight, how many sleeps before I can see the horses?' she asked, her little face peeping out over the duvet.

'Eighty-seven,' I said.

'That's a long time.' She frowned. 'I wish it was sooner. So does Snuggles.'

I smiled understandingly, stroked a strand of hair away from her cheek, then I had a thought. 'Faye, you can't visit the stables and work with the horses for now, but I could take you to see some horses in a field. Would you like that?'

'Oh, yes please,' she said, her eyes widening with excitement. 'When? Tomorrow?'

'You're seeing your grandparents tomorrow. If you definitely aren't going to the day centre on Wednesday, we could go then.'

'Yes! Thank you,' she cried. 'I'll look forward to it. I'm so happy. So is Snuggles.' Sitting up in bed, she spread her arms for another kiss and hug.

All foster carers in the UK are required to keep a daily record of the child or young person they are looking after, which includes appointments, the child's health and wellbeing and any significant events. When the child or young person leaves the carer this record is placed on file at the social services. In the absence of anyone telling me differently, I was doing the same for Faye. Before I went to bed I wrote up my log notes, and today I included our shopping trip for maternity clothes, that Faye had decided not to go to the day centre on Wednesday, that her grandpa had phoned to confirm arrangements for tomorrow and that Faye was settling in well.

When I'd first been asked to look after Faye I'd had huge concerns that my family and I would find it too upsetting to support Faye through her pregnancy, that we would grow close to her and her unborn baby, and then have to watch as the baby was taken into care. However, the more time I spent with Faye and got to know her, the more I was realizing that she couldn't possibly look after a baby. It took all her skills, time and concentration to look after herself. She was a lovely person, but she functioned like a young child. Her numeracy and literacy skills were such that she wouldn't be able to read and understand instructions on a packet of baby formula, for example, or on how to use a sterilizer or how to take medication (for herself or the baby), or do any of the other many requirements that go into parenting. Faye had little concept of time and lived unhurriedly, largely in her own little world, away from the pressures, demands and commitments that being an adult entails. I had no doubt that if she was immersed in watching a soap on television and the baby began crying for food or needed its nappy changing, Faye would finish watching the television programme first. Not because she was unkind or wilfully neglectful, but simply because she wouldn't comprehend the urgency of her baby's needs and that small babies require feeding and changing regularly. Wilma and Stan weren't in any position to help and support her. They were already finding it too much looking after her and, indeed, needed help themselves. While Faye could still gain much from new experiences, her intellect had probably reached a plateau, which just wasn't sufficient for parenting, sad though this was. I was therefore gradually accepting that finding a loving adoptive family for Faye's baby was the best outcome for all concerned, and hopefully after the birth Faye would be able to resume her old life with her grandparents.

That night I slept easier, although when I heard Faye get up to go to the toilet I went round the landing to check she was all right. She was, and went straight back to bed. Did she know that the reason she was having to wee more often was because she was pregnant? I doubted it, and it was something else I'd explain to her after Becky had talked to her on Friday.

CHAPTER SIX

VULNERABLE

Trying to get Faye ready to leave the house on time the following morning was like trying to get a child to school on time after a great weekend. It wasn't that she didn't want to see her grandparents – far from it, she was looking forward to it – but everything took her so long. She'd start doing one thing and then halfway through she'd wander off and start doing something else. The cat didn't help. Sammy had taken a liking to Faye and kept brushing past her legs, wanting to be stroked, and if he wasn't in the same room as her she'd go off to find him. She was still in her dressing gown at 9.45, and while it hadn't mattered the day before when we'd been going shopping, today we had a bus to catch at 10.20 if we were to reach her grandparents for 11.00. Contact had been arranged for 11.00–3.00, and it was unfair to keep them waiting. My stress levels began to rise as I chivvied her along. Eventually I asked, 'Faye, how do you leave on time when you're at home and go to the day centre and the stables?'

'Gran nags me,' she said with her impish grin. 'She goes on and on. She says I'm too slow to catch a cold. Sometimes I have to miss breakfast, if I'm very slow.'

I could sympathize with her gran, and while nagging Faye or allowing her to miss breakfast wasn't really an option for me, I would have to try to work out a way to help her keep better time. Apart from going to see her grandparents three times a week, she had an antenatal appointment at 9.45 a.m. on Friday. At this rate we'd need to start getting ready the night before!

Faye needed the toilet again just as we put on our coats and were about to leave, but finally we were out of the front door and I set off at a reasonably brisk pace up the road towards the bus stop in the high street.

'I don't like walking fast,' Faye moaned after a moment. 'It makes my feet hurt.' So I slowed the pace.

Somehow we arrived at the bus stop with a minute to spare. 'You want the number forty-seven,' I said, pointing to the number on the front of the bus.

'Forty-seven,' she repeated.

We got on and sat together, then swapped seats, as Faye wanted to sit by the window. As the bus pulled away she turned to me with a frown. 'I've forgotten Snuggles, and my phone.'

I swallowed a sigh of exasperation. She only had two things to remember and she'd forgotten them both. I blamed myself; I should have checked.

'You won't need your phone,' I said. 'You won't be going out alone, will you?'

'No. But Snuggles is in the bathroom and he doesn't like it in there without me. He always sits on my bed when I'm out.'

'Don't worry. As soon as I get home I'll move him into your bedroom.'

'He has to sit on my pillow,' she said.

'Yes, I know. I've seen.'

Reassured, Faye turned her attention to what was going on outside, gazing through the window with the intrigue and wonder of a child. People waiting at the bus stops, a man walking a large dog, cyclists passing on the inside, people getting on and off the bus all held interest for her. She didn't comment, just watched them carefully, looking longer than the cursory glance an adult would normally give. I wondered what she was thinking.

'Penny for your thoughts,' I said after a while, using an expression my father had used.

Faye smiled and looked at me. 'Grandpa says that when I'm staring and don't answer him. But when I'm thinking I don't hear him.'

'It's because you're concentrating,' I said. 'I'm the same.'

Presently we entered the area of town that was familiar to Faye. 'You know where you are?' She nodded. 'Not long now.' I didn't normally use the buses. I either walked or took my car, and the laborious stop-start motion of the bus had lost its novelty for me. 'Only about another ten minutes,' I said, more for my sake than hers.

Faye raised her wrist to look at her watch and then realized she'd forgotten that too. 'Silly me,' she said, tapping her forehead.

'No, you're not. I should have reminded you,' I said. 'All your possessions are in different places at my house. It must be very confusing. We'll remember them tomorrow, don't worry.' I smiled reassuringly.

'Am I seeing my gran and grandpa tomorrow?' she asked.

'No, the day after. It's every other day. It's Wednesday tomorrow. Do you remember we decided that if you're not going to the day centre I'd take you to see some horses?'

'Oh yes, goody. I'm looking forward to that,' she said happily.

We can all forget things and lose track of time, but with someone like Faye, who had learning difficulties and relied heavily on routine and familiarity, it must have been very difficult for her to keep track of what was happening in her life when all that was familiar and regular had vanished. I guessed at home when she took off her watch at night she put it in the same place and then in the morning automatically put it on as part of her routine. We all have similar habits.

It was 10.50 as we stepped off the bus. 'You know that this is the bus stop you get off at, don't you?' I asked her.

'Yes. It's the same place I get off when I've been to the day centre.'

Most of the buses stopped close to the flats – there was a mini-terminus from the days when there'd been four tower blocks here. We walked the short distance to Faye's block of flats and the elevator took us up to the eighth floor. The doors opened and Stan must have been looking out for us as he was waiting in the corridor, leaning on his stick for support.

'Hello, my lovely,' he said, as soon as he saw Faye. 'Don't you look smart!' Faye was wearing one of the new maternity dresses and her new coat.

'I've forgotten Snuggles,' she said, giving her grandpa a big hug.

'Sorry,' I said, feeling responsible.

'She doesn't need him with her the whole time,' Stan said. 'She's a big girl, aren't you, pet?' Faye nodded and gave him another hug. 'Come on in, Gran's waiting to see you.' I guessed they'd been missing her quite a lot.

'I'll just say hello to Wilma and then I'll be on my way,' I said.

'Won't you stay for a cuppa?' he asked.

'That's kind of you, but I've got a few things to do. I'll be back later, though.'

I followed them into the flat and to their living room where Wilma was sitting in her usual place on the sofa. We said hello as Faye went over and hugged her.

'Where's your duffel coat?' she asked Faye.

'At Cathy's. I've got new clothes now,' Faye added, proudly pointing to her coat and dress.

'Don't forget to bring your other clothes home with you,' Wilma said. 'They'll fit you later.'

'She won't,' I said. 'I've put them all in her suitcase. None will go missing.'

Wilma nodded, but that was all she said about Faye's new clothes. She didn't compliment her and I hoped she approved of what I'd bought. 'What have you been up to then?' she asked Faye.

Faye looked to me for an answer.

'On Sunday we unpacked, then after dinner Faye watched some television,' I said. 'And yesterday we went shopping.'

'They've got a cat,' Faye said.

'Yes, we saw him in the photograph,' Wilma said. 'Are you managing to sleep there?'

Faye nodded.

'She's doing very well,' I said. 'Becky is coming to see us on Friday.'

'Yes, she phoned here this morning.'

There was a small silence and then I said I'd better be going. I confirmed I'd be back around three o'clock and, having said goodbye, I saw myself out.

I had to wait ten minutes for the bus, so by the time I arrived home it was twelve o'clock. I'd have to leave again shortly after two o'clock to collect Faye, so the days she saw her grandparents were going to be very short for me, until she felt confident using the bus alone.

Upstairs I found Snuggles sitting on the edge of the bath and I took him to Faye's room where I positioned him as she liked him on the pillow. Her bed was unmade, her pyjamas were on the floor and the curtains were only partially open from where she'd left in a hurry. Her phone was also on her bedside cabinet. I had a quick tidy up and then went downstairs to make the most of the time I had left.

It was while I was vacuuming, with one eye on the clock, that I had the idea of making a time chart for Faye, also known as a routine chart. It had helped children I'd looked after in the past and I thought it might help Faye too. Leaving the rest of the housework, I went to our toy cupboard. I found white card, felt tips and a ruler and settled at the dining table.

A time or routine chart shows a child or young person what they need to be doing at any particular time of day. It's a timetable, really, and is used by parents, teachers and childcare workers to help a child establish a routine. It is especially useful for morning and evening routines and can include homework and out-of-school activities. Faye's bedtime routine wasn't an issue, apart from having a regular bath or shower; it was the morning when she needed constant reminders, and I hoped this would help. It also encourages self-reliance. Adults automatically create time charts in their minds so that, for example, if a person needs to leave the house at 8.30 to get to work by 9.00, and they know it takes them an hour to get ready, then they set their alarm clock for

7.30, aware they have to be showered and dressed by 7.50 and having breakfast at 8.00 to leave by 8.30 without chronic indigestion. Young children and those with learning difficulties can't conceptualize this, so writing it down can help.

Using the ruler, I divided up the page into grids, then wrote the time on the left and what Faye needed to be doing on the right; for example, 8.45–9.00. *Get dressed*. She could read the time and there was a clock on the wall in her bedroom, so all she had to do was check the time with the chart, which I would pin beneath the clock. Friday would be slightly different, as we had the antenatal appointment, so she would have to be ready earlier. I made a second chart just for Friday morning. I would explain to Faye how they worked when she got home.

Before I left to collect Faye that afternoon I texted Paula to say where I was going, as she might be in before me and wonder where I was. We usually let each other know our plans. I caught the 2.20 bus, this time taking a book with me to read to stave off the monotony of the journey. When I arrived at the flat I was slightly surprised to find Faye sitting in the living room with her coat on. I was five minutes early.

'Everything all right?' I asked, glancing at the three of them.

Wilma gave a stiff nod.

'She wouldn't take her coat off,' Stan said. 'She loves it so much. Thanks for getting it. It's good quality.'

'You're welcome,' I said. 'I'm glad she likes it, but sorry it caused a problem. Faye,' I said, now looking at her, 'the coat is for outdoors, not in. You'll be too hot.' Indeed, her cheeks were flushed.

'We told her,' Wilma said. 'But when our Faye puts her mind to something she won't be told.' I hadn't seen this side of Faye, but clearly it had caused some friction. 'She tells me you're taking her to see horses tomorrow?' Wilma added.

'Yes, just to see them in a field. I'm aware of the health and safety concerns. She won't be riding them.'

Wilma nodded, and again I thought I detected slight hostility.

'Enjoy yourself,' Stan said to Faye as she stood, ready to leave. Despite their disagreement, Faye hugged her gran goodbye and then Stan came with us to the elevator.

'Don't you fret over what your gran says,' he said once outside. 'She's a bit out of sorts today. Her arthritis is playing up.'

'I know,' Faye said with a sigh. 'But she does go on.'

'It must be very frustrating not being able to do the things she wants and being in constant pain,' I said.

'It is,' Stan said. 'But her bark is worse than her bite.' Which was another expression my father had used.

The elevator arrived and Faye gave her grandpa a big hug as we said goodbye.

'See you Thursday,' he said as the doors closed. 'Look after yourself.'

'Is everything all right?' I asked Faye as we descended.

She nodded. 'I love Gran, but she does get on my nerves some-times. Grandpa tells her to be quiet and press the off switch.'

I smiled. 'No family ever gets along all the time. But it was OK?'

'Yes. Did you put Snuggles on my bed?'

'I did. I've also made a time chart for you and pinned it to your bedroom wall. I'll explain about it when we get home.'

Outside I asked Faye if she remembered which bus to catch and she didn't.

'Number forty-seven,' I said.

'Can you write it down for me? That's what Grandpa does. He says I'd forget my head if it wasn't glued on.' She chuckled.

I laughed too. 'I like your grandpa. He reminds me of my own dad. I'll write down the number of the bus and also put it in your phone. But Faye, you won't be travelling on the bus by yourself until you're sure of the journey, so don't worry.'

When the bus arrived I pointed out the number on the front.

'Number forty-seven,' Faye repeated loudly as we got on, and then made a dash for a window seat. I saw a couple glance at her.

After a few moments Faye started asking questions about the time chart and I explained as best I could without having it with me to show her.

'We have a chart like that on the wall at the stables,' she said. 'It's got the names of the people and which horses they have to muck out and feed.'

'Yes. That's similar,' I said. 'It's a rota. Your chart just has your name on it and the times you need to be doing things.'

'If it works, you can give it to my gran when I go home. Stop her nagging me,' Faye said.

'Yes, I could. Although she probably has her own techniques for helping you.'

'It's called nagging!' Faye said after a moment, and we both laughed.

Halfway through the journey the schools finished for the day. The bus quickly filled with secondary school children and the noise level rose. Two lads sitting directly behind us were particularly loud, guffawing and whooping at whatever it was they were sharing on their mobile phones. I heard Faye sigh a couple of times, and then she suddenly turned in her seat and said very forcefully, 'Keep the noise down, won't you!' Much as her gran would probably have done, I thought.

'Sorry,' one of the lads said, and they lowered their voices. But I was concerned.

'Faye,' I said quietly. 'You shouldn't really talk to strangers like that. Not all strangers are nice.'

'But they needed to be told,' she said. 'My gran yells at the lads on our estate from the kitchen window if they make a lot of noise.'

'But that's different,' I said. 'She's safe in the flat. It's not a good idea to talk to strangers for any reason, especially if you're alone.'

It was at times like this that Faye's vulnerability was high-lighted. She couldn't see danger as someone else might. I was with her now and she'd chosen two decent lads who'd simply looked a bit surprised and had apologized. But if she'd been alone on the bus and had decided to reprimand a thug, the outcome could have been very different, for I doubted many thugs would excuse her on the grounds of her disability. I thought it must be a constant worry for parents and carers looking after young people with learning disabilities to allow them the independence they needed while keeping them safe.

'Have your grandparents talked to you about strangers?' I asked.

'Yes, lots of times,' Faye said a little testily. 'I know I shouldn't talk to them, but those boys were making a noise.' So I left it at that.

As the bus neared the stop where we had to get off, I began pointing out landmarks so that Faye would know when to press the bell to tell the driver she wanted the bus to stop.

'The church is on the right,' I said, pointing. 'Then that row of shops is on your left.' I pointed again. 'Once the bus has passed the last shop you press the bell and then stand.' The traffic in the high street usually meant that the bus was moving quite slowly at this point, so she should have plenty of time to see the landmarks.

I let Faye press the bell and we stood as the bus stopped. Two other passengers got off with us. 'Now we go to the crossing,' I said. 'It's the only safe place to cross the road here.' She nodded.

We waited at the edge of the crossing for the cars to stop. 'You know you never step onto the crossing until the cars have stopped in both directions,' I said.

'I know.'

We crossed and then walked along the pavement until we came to the end of my street. Faye recognized it.

'Excellent,' I said. 'Do you know our address?'

'No. Should I?' she asked.

'I'll write that down and put it in your phone. You've already got my telephone number stored there.' I always made sure the young people I fostered either knew our home address when they started using the buses alone or had it written down. Obvious, but it was something that could easily be overlooked.

We were the first ones home and Faye was eager to see the time chart, so we went up to her room. She kissed and hugged Snuggles and then stood next to me as I explained the chart. I hadn't pinned up Friday's chart yet, as that could be confusing for her – I'd do so on Thursday evening. Faye seemed to grasp the concept of the time chart.

'So what are you doing between six and six-thirty in the evening?' I asked.

'Having my dinner,' she answered correctly with a smile. Then, looking at the clock on the wall, 'That's in two hours.'

'Yes, it is. Well done.'

I'd added a bath into the evening schedule, hoping it could become part of her routine, but if having one every day became an issue she could revert to every third night as she did at home. As long as her hygiene was good, it wasn't for me to change what was a well-established and working routine, as she'd be home again in three months.

All my family were in for dinner and as usual we chatted as we ate, mainly about what we'd been doing during the day. My children made a point of including Faye by asking her about her day with her grandparents, and she also told them a few times that she was going to see horses tomorrow. Faye ate well, helped to clear away the dishes and then settled in front of the television. Lucy was with her for a while and then left to chat to a friend on her phone. Paula was on the computer and Adrian went out to check something that wasn't working correctly on his car. It was his first car, which he'd saved up for, but it was starting to give him some problems.

At 7.30 p.m., after Faye had been watching television for an hour, I told her it was time for her bath.

'But I'll miss my programme,' she said.

'If you have your bath now you'll have time to watch more television afterwards, just as you do at home with your gran. That's what the chart shows.' She didn't move. 'Faye,' I said, non-confrontationally but picking up the remote, 'I'll fill your bath while you fetch your pyjamas from your bedroom. That will speed it up.'

'Nag, nag, nag,' she said good-humouredly. 'You're just like my gran.' But she stood and came with me upstairs.

In the time it took her to fetch her pyjamas I had run her bath. I checked she had everything she needed and then I left her to wash. As it was the first time she'd used this bath I waited on the landing in case she needed anything. I could hear water splashing as she washed herself, and she also hummed a tune. Then it went quiet. 'Is everything all right, Faye?' I called from outside the door.

'Yes. Can I get out now?'

'Have you finished washing?'

'Yes.'

'OK. Do you need any help?'

'No. You mustn't come in. I haven't got any clothes on.'

'I won't,' I replied quickly. Faye needed her privacy as much as anyone.

I heard the water drain, but it was another quarter of an hour before she came out in her pyjamas and dressing gown, and her hair was wet. She said she always washed it in the bath and I asked if she wanted a hair dryer, but she said she dried it on the towel. Not wanting to miss any more television, she took the towel downstairs with her and continued drying her hair as she watched her programme. If I thought she watched too much television when she could be doing something more stimulating, it wasn't for me to say. She enjoyed watching television and these programmes had been part of her life with her gran at home.

As with the previous evenings, Faye watched television until nine o'clock and then, when the last soap finished, she stood, poured herself a glass of water and went up to bed. I kissed her and Snuggles goodnight and came out of her room. I heard her get up to use the toilet once in the night, but now I was more confident she was all right alone I didn't get up. Once I heard her bedroom door close I turned over to go back to sleep. It was only then that I realized I hadn't telephoned Mum. I was annoyed with myself. I'd telephoned her every evening since Dad had passed, but it was too late now. I'd phone first thing in the morning.

CHAPTER SEVEN

COMPROMISE

'You don't have to telephone me every evening,' Mum said as I apologized again for not phoning the day before. 'You're worrying too much about me. I'm doing all right, really I am.'

'Are you?' I asked. It was 7.30 a.m. and I knew Mum would be up. She and Dad had always been early risers. I, too, was showered and dressed, and sitting on the edge of my bed.

'Yes, I'm all right,' Mum said. Then there was a small silence before she added, 'You know, love, it's different when you're young, when you have your whole life ahead of you. You don't think about death. But as you get older you know that if you are a couple then eventually one of you is likely to pass before the other. Your dad and I talked about this not that long ago and we both agreed it was important that whoever was left behind made the most of the time they had left, until we could be together again.' She paused. 'Of course I miss your dad dreadfully – he was my best friend as well as my darling husband – but he wouldn't want me sitting here night after night, depressed and in tears. He wouldn't want you fretting and worrying about me being alone either. I don't really feel alone. I have a wealth of happy memories that brings your dad closer to me. I am sure he's watching over me. Yesterday I tried to hang a picture …'

'We could have done that for you,' I said, swallowing the lump that had risen in my throat.

'I know, love, but I wanted to have a go at it myself. I found his tool kit in the garage, but when I hammered the nail into the wall it was wonky. I had to laugh, and I could hear him laughing too. We shared the joke. "Well, at least you had a go," I heard him say, which of course is what he would have said in life.'

'Yes, it is,' I said quietly. 'Dad always encouraged us to try new things, even if they were difficult and we might not succeed.'

'That's right, he did. I expect you feel his presence some-times, just as I do. We were a close family, we still are. Because we can no longer see him doesn't mean he isn't with us. He's with us constantly in our thoughts. So promise you'll stop worrying about me. I'll ask you if I need help.'

'All right,' I said, and wiped the tear from my eye.

'Good. So how's your young lady settling in? Faye?'

'Yes. She's doing well. I thought I might bring her over to meet you at the weekend. I'm not sure which day yet. It will depend on when she is seeing her grandparents.'

'I'll look forward to meeting her. Life goes on.'

'Yes. But you don't mind me phoning you each evening if I want to?' I asked.

'No, of course not, love. Just don't feel you *have* to.'

'OK.'

After we'd said goodbye I remained sitting on the edge of the bed. Yes, I did feel Dad was with me, watching over me, just as Mum did, but it didn't stop me from missing him. My parents had always been the backbone of the family, and after my husband, John, had left when the children were little, Dad had fulfilled not only the role of grandpa, but father too. But for now, at least, my chat with Mum had reassured me, and it was the start of a new day.

The time chart, combined with the promise of seeing horses, resulted in Faye being ready at 9.30 a.m., an hour earlier than I'd planned to leave. She wanted the television on to fill the gap (*The Jeremy Kyle Show*), but instead I took some books from the shelf about animals and horses and suggested she might like to have a look at those while I saw to the laundry. The books were aimed at junior-school-aged children, but the beautiful coloured plates of different breeds of horses and ponies soon had Faye captivated. She sat engrossed for the full hour. She could read some of the sentences and came to me with any words she didn't know. Then in the car I explained again to Faye about the place we were going to: that it was a ten-minute drive away and the field held about twenty horses and ponies, and one donkey.

I'd never known whom the animals belonged to, but they'd been there for as long as I could remember. I used to take my children when they were little, and more recently the children I fostered. Up until about three years ago you could feed the horses, but then a notice had appeared on the gate asking people not to feed them as it upset their stomachs. However, they still liked to be stroked and petted and they galloped over as soon as anyone approached the gate. It was a popular spot in the school holidays, but now there was just Faye and me; she'd left Snuggles in the car.

Faye stood beside me at the gate, smiling broadly and in her element as she gently stroked one of the horses.

'I'm sorry we haven't got anything for you to eat,' she said as she patted his neck. He nuzzled her shoulder and she laughed. The larger horses, the stallions, had arrived first and were at the front, with the ponies behind them, almost waiting for their turn in a hierarchy of size and dominance. The donkey was alone and standing some way off.

Some of the horses at the front were leaning over the gate and the fences either side of it, trying to reach fresh grass. 'It's all right to feed them grass,' Faye said, bending down and tearing off a handful. I assumed it was, as they were grazing in a grassy field.

I fed the horses too and then took the packet of antibacterial wipes I kept in my bag and wiped the slobber from my hands. I'd make sure Faye wiped her hands well when she'd finished and then wash them once we were home.

'You've had some,' Faye said, lightly admonishing one of the horses that had already taken grass from her hand. He seemed to understand and moved aside to let another horse take his place.

I took some photographs on my phone, which I would have printed for Faye and her grandparents, and I breathed in the fresh September air. The day was warm but without the muggy heat of August. Birds fluttered in and out of the hedgerow and occasionally rabbits could be seen hopping along the far side of the field. I watched Faye tearing off the grass and feeding the horses, and I was very pleased that I'd suggested we come. Although it wasn't the stables, it was a good second best for Faye. She clearly had a rapport with the horses, and I could see why she loved going to the stables. As she stroked them her touch was light and rhythmic, which must have felt good, for they stood very still as she petted them and partially closed their eyes, almost swooning. Once the horses at the front had had their fill of grass and petting, Faye sent them off to make room for the smaller ponies. They galloped away across the field, their tails held high and manes flying out behind them. Eventually most of the horses and ponies had taken a turn to be fed and there was just the donkey left. He stretched up his neck so that his chin was just able to rest on the top rung of the gate and looked at Faye with large doleful eyes. Then he suddenly gave a very loud hee-haw, which made us both start. Faye quickly tore up another handful of grass and fed him. He was one of the oldest animals in the field and his coat was patchy and dusty. It always had been. My father had once remarked that he looked as though he'd 'spent a night on the town', meaning he was looking rough after an evening out celebrating, which rather summed him up.

'What's your name, lovely?' Faye asked him.

He let out another hee-haw in response. Faye laughed and patted his neck, and dust motes flew.

'I don't think these horses have names,' I said. 'If they do, we've never known them.'

'All the horses in the stables have names,' Faye said. 'I'm going to call him Dancer, like Santa's reindeer. I'm sure he could dance if he wanted to.' Dancer appeared to nod his head.

Faye gave him some more grass and then gently tried to untangle the hair of his mane. 'I really need the mane and tail brush we use at the stables,' she said.

'Sorry, I haven't got one of those with me,' I said with a smile.

'I'll bring my hairbrush next time,' she said seriously.

She petted and talked to Dancer for some time. He was in no hurry to leave. Then one of the stallions returned, his hooves thundering across the field, and Dancer, clearly aware of his place in the pecking order, ran off.

'That was rude,' Faye said, mildly chastising the stallion. 'I know you're bigger than Dancer, but you shouldn't throw your weight around. I'm going to call you Boxer, because you're like the fighting men Grandpa watches on television.'

Boxer was soon joined by a couple of other horses and Faye continued petting and naming them. Eventually, all twenty or so of the horses in the field had a name. I couldn't tell some of them apart, but she seemed to be able to, perhaps from working with horses. We were there for over an hour, and the only reason we left was because Faye needed to use a toilet and she didn't fancy squatting behind a hedge.

'Can we come here again tomorrow?' she asked as I passed her the antibacterial wipes for her hands.

'You're seeing your gran and grandpa tomorrow,' I reminded her. 'Then on Friday we have your antenatal appointment in the morning and Becky is coming in the afternoon. But we could come again next week.'

'Yes. I want to come here every week,' she said, pleased.

Once her hands were reasonably clean she called goodbye to the horses, said she'd see them again soon, and we returned to the car. On the way home Faye told Snuggles all about the horses and the names she'd given them, remembering most of them. Once home, after she'd been to the bathroom, she wanted to watch television. Faye told me that the television was on for most of the day at her home. I didn't usually have the television on all day, so I suggested she might like to draw some pictures of the horses we'd seen instead, and show them to her grandparents. She liked the idea, so I took paper, crayons and a pencil from the cupboard and set them on the table. I sat with her for a while as she drew and then left her colouring in while I saw to some housework. Every so often Faye came to find me to show me the pictures and I admired the work in progress. Her drawings were at a very basic level, the artwork of the average seven- to nine-year-old. Three brown horses with legs in straight lines stood in the bright green field, below a solid blue sky with a huge round yellow sun. She drew two pictures, very similar, one for her gran and one for her grandpa. 'So there won't be any arguments,' she explained in a tone similar to one her gran might have used.

When Paula arrived home Faye proudly showed her the finished drawings, childlike in her enthusiasm. Paula praised them and then Faye tried to remember the names of the horses. Not for the first time since I'd met Faye, I saw the disparity between the innocent child, the little girl who loved ponies and was proud of her drawings, and the pregnant woman – a fact she was still ignoring. My family might have seen the discrepancy too, but they didn't say. I wondered how Faye was going to cope on Friday at the antenatal appointment when she was refusing to acknowledge her pregnancy. Wilma had taken Faye to the previous antenatal appointments and I thought it would be a good idea if I had a chat with her so that I was better prepared. This would be awkward with Faye present, so after dinner, while Faye was watching television, I took the phone into the front room and telephoned her grandparents. Stan answered. I could hear the television in the background.

'It's Cathy, Faye's carer,' I said. 'Sorry to disturb you. Everything is all right, but I wanted to check a couple of things with you.'

'Sure. Fire away,' he said jovially.

'Which day were you thinking of seeing Faye this weekend? I'll work my plans around it.'

'Saturday. If that's all right with you.'

'Yes. That's fine. I'll see my mother on Sunday. And the other thing –' I hesitated. 'Is it possible to have a quick chat with Wilma? I wanted to ask about the antenatal appointments she took Faye to.'

'Sure, women's stuff. Hang on a moment and I'll take the phone to her.' The sound went from the television and then I heard him say, 'It's Cathy. She wants to talk to you about Faye.'

There was a small silence and then Wilma said a tentative 'Hello.'

'Hi, Wilma. How are you?'

'Not so bad. Legs playing up as usual, but I mustn't complain. What did you want to talk to me about?'

'You know Faye has her twenty-five-week antenatal appointment on Friday?'

'Yes.'

'You went with her to the previous ones and I was wondering how you got on.'

'It was a struggle. First getting in and out of the lift here, then the taxi, and those stairs in the doctor's are a killer. Stan came with us and stayed in the waiting room. I've taken her to four appointments, including the two scans, but I can't do any more. It nearly did me in.'

'Yes, it must have been very difficult,' I sympathized. 'But I was wondering how Faye got on in the actual consultation, when she saw the midwife. She would have measured her stomach, taken her blood pressure, checked her urine and generally talked to her about how the pregnancy was progressing. How did Faye cope with all of that?'

'I see. Well, she completely ignored the midwife and left me to do all the talking. I think the midwife put it down to Faye being disabled, but it wasn't. Faye's got her problems, but she can talk. When we got out of the surgery I told her off for sitting there like she was dumb, but Stan said to leave the girl alone. So that's what we've done since. We don't mention it unless we have to. It's easier for us all.'

'I see,' I said. 'I can appreciate that. And the ultrasound scans? Did the radiographer give Faye a print-out of the baby? It's usual now.'

'She offered, but Faye didn't want it. She wouldn't talk to the radiographer or look at the monitor, which I can understand. It's lovely if you're keeping the baby, but do you really want to see an image of it if you know you're never going to be its mother and look after it? I didn't want a picture and neither did Faye.'

'No,' I agreed. 'I understand. Thank you. It's helpful to know. I feel a little more prepared now.'

'Faye might be different with you and talk,' Wilma added.

'I'm not so sure. She's not saying anything to me about the pregnancy – she doesn't want it mentioned – which is making it difficult for me to help prepare her. Becky is coming to talk to her on Friday.'

'Yes, I know. When she phoned here she asked me how much I thought Faye understood about being pregnant. I said a lot more than she's letting on. Faye has always been good at ignoring what she finds difficult, but she can't ignore this for much longer.'

'No, indeed,' I agreed.

'To be honest, Stan and I are counting off the days until all this is over and Faye can come home. Then we can get back to normal. We try not to show it in front of Faye, but the strain this is putting on us is enormous. First our daughter goes off the rails and kills herself with alcohol, and now this. It's our great-grandchild, after all, although Stan and I try not to think of it that way.'

At a loss to know what comfort I could offer, I sympathized, thanked Wilma again for taking the time to talk to me and then we said goodbye.

Faye didn't have a bath that evening. I'd been on the telephone at the time she was supposed to have it, and she didn't want it later, as she'd miss 'the best bit of the programme' she was watching. I find that parenting is full of compromises, where you have to balance what should happen with what the young person wants. Faye had had a bath the previous evening and could have one the following, so I let it go. She stayed in front of the television until nine o'clock when she stood, poured herself a glass of water and, calling goodnight, went up to bed.

Thursday followed a similar pattern to Tuesday. I took Faye on the number forty-seven bus to her grandparents' to familiarize her with the route. Stan was waiting in the corridor outside the elevator to greet us, and he hugged Faye affectionately. When I went into the flat to say hello to Wilma I sensed that her attitude towards me had softened, perhaps because of our chat on the telephone the evening before. She smiled at me, used my name and thanked me for bringing

Faye and for all I was doing for her. Then, later, when I collected Faye that afternoon, Wilma said to me, 'Good luck for tomorrow. I'll be thinking of you,' referring to the antenatal appointment.

'Thank you,' I said.

That evening after dinner I showed Faye the time chart I'd made for the following morning and explained to her that we had to leave the house at 9.20 to be at the doctor's surgery for her antenatal appointment at 9.45.

'So you can still have your cup of tea in your dressing gown at eight o'clock as you usually do,' I said, pointing to the relevant box on the chart. 'Then you get dressed between eight and eight-thirty. There,' I said, pointing to the next box. 'Breakfast between eight-thirty and nine o'clock. There. Then you brush your teeth – five minutes for that – then you come downstairs straight away, and we put on our coats and shoes ready to leave.' I finished by pointing to the last box, which showed a big 9.20 – the time we had to leave. 'I know it's different from the other mornings, but it will work fine, and will save me from having to nag you,' I added with a smile. 'I'll pin it to your bedroom wall.'

'Can I watch television now?' she asked.

'Yes. But remember you're having a bath tonight.'

'I know. It's on my chart.'

The time chart seemed to be working, although I had to remind Faye when it was time for her bath. However, she left the television without protest, had her bath and then watched some more television in her dressing gown. At nine o'clock, as the last soap finished, she stood, went into the kitchen and poured herself a glass of water as usual, which she took up to bed. When I went into her bedroom to say goodnight I asked her if she had any questions or worries about the antenatal appointment the following morning.

'Yes,' she said, 'I have a question.' And for a moment I thought we had a breakthrough and she wanted to talk about her pregnancy. But then she said, 'Can I take Snuggles with me?'

'Yes, if you want to.'

'Gran makes me leave him at home sometimes. She says I'm too old to be carrying around a cuddly toy. But he's not just any cuddly toy. He's Snuggles.'

'I know, love. If it helps you, then take him with us. I don't mind, and I'm sure your gran doesn't either. She only wants what's best for you.'

'Snuggles is best for me,' Faye said and, giving him a big kiss, she lay her head on the pillow, ready for sleep.

CHAPTER EIGHT

DON'T WANT TO HURT THEM

The doctor's surgery Faye attended was situated in a bungalow-style building that housed a number of different health clinics, including speech and language therapy, podiatry, diabetes, ophthalmology, as well as a maternity unit. Built around the same time as the tower blocks, it now also served the needs of those living in the streets of modern terraced housing that were gradually replacing the flats. The last block of flats still standing, where Faye lived with her grandparents, towered over the new-builds and could be seen from outside the clinic.

'Shall I wave to Gran and Grandpa?' Faye asked as we got out of the car, glancing up at the flats.

'They won't see you from here, love,' I said. 'It's too far away. We can see the flats because they're tall, but if they were looking out, we'd just be small dots to them.'

'Like ants, Grandpa said.'

'Yes.' So I guessed he'd already explained this to her before.

Faye was holding Snuggles loosely by her side and I was carrying her maternity folder. We'd left the house on time and had arrived a couple of minutes early. Faye appeared unfazed by the prospect of the antenatal appointment, possibly, I thought, because she was still in denial or didn't fully appreciate her condition. A situation I hoped would change when Becky spoke to her that afternoon. I assumed Faye was likely to remain silent during the consultation with the midwife, as she had done at the previous appointments when her gran had accompanied her, although at present she was chatting quite amicably. We entered the health centre and approached reception.

'Hello, Faye,' the receptionist said, looking up and smiling warmly. 'How are you?' Because this had been Faye's family's doctor for many years, some of the staff knew her.

'I'm very well, thank you,' Faye said politely.

'Good.' The receptionist smiled at me and then checked us in. 'Take a seat through there until you are called,' she said, pointing to the waiting area.

'Thank you,' I said. I saw no need to explain to her who I was. Faye wasn't a child, and possibly her grandparents or Becky had informed the doctor's surgery that Faye was living with me until the baby was born.

Like most National Health Service waiting rooms it was adequately but not lavishly furnished: vinyl chairs arranged in rows, a small corner table containing some old magazines and a few children's toys, but no potted plants, pictures on the walls or similar accessories, as one might expect in a private healthcare waiting room. There were a dozen or so adults waiting to be seen and two children, as various clinics ran at the same time, as well as general doctors' appointments. One small boy, who was sitting on his mother's lap, looked very pale. A toddler I guessed to be about eighteen months old was running around chuckling and generally entertaining those waiting. Patients were called to their appointments via a digital monitor suspended in one corner of the room, which announced their name, the person they were seeing and the number of the consultation room.

Faye settled into the chair beside me with Snuggles on her lap. I checked in my bag that my mobile phone was on silent. Faye had left her phone in her bedroom as usual. The only time she'd need it would be when she started going alone on the bus to see her grandparents; then I would make sure it was fully charged and in credit. Faye vaguely watched the toddler running around, as most of us were doing, but there was nothing to be read in her expression other than slight intrigue. Then she turned her attention to the others waiting and studied them closely, as she tended to do with strangers. The antenatal appointment before ours overran by ten minutes and then Faye's name, the name of the midwife and the room number flashed up on the monitor, while a digital voice simultaneously announced the same information. Faye seemed to know where the room was; she immediately stood, and with Snuggles dangling at her side she led the way out of the waiting area, down a corridor and to a room on the right. I knocked and opened the door. The midwife sat at the desk writing.

'Take a seat, I won't be a minute,' she said, glancing up.

Faye and I sat in the two chairs that were positioned at right angles to the midwife's desk and waited until she'd finished. I passed her the maternity folder. 'Thank you,' she said, smiling at us both. Then glancing at the name on the front of the folder she said to Faye, 'I remember, I saw you before with your grandmother.' Unlike the receptionist and other permanent staff here, the midwife would serve a number of practices and would only have met Faye at her first antenatal appointment.

I thought it was appropriate to introduce myself. 'I'm Cathy Glass, a foster carer. Faye is staying with me until after the baby is born.'

The midwife nodded and began looking through the folder, familiarizing herself with how Faye's pregnancy was progressing. She would see many women each week, all at different stages in their pregnancies. Faye sat beside me in silence, head down and fiddling with Snuggles in her lap. After a few minutes the midwife stopped reading and looked at Faye. 'So how is the pregnancy going, Faye? How are you feeling?'

Faye gave a small shrug and didn't look up.

'No problems?' the midwife asked.

Faye shook her head.

'And you can feel the baby moving?'

Faye kept her head down and said nothing.

'Let's bring your details up on screen.' She swivelled her chair slightly to face the desktop computer, which would give her access to Faye's medical records; the maternity folder just monitored her pregnancy.

Faye and I sat quietly again while the midwife read. I couldn't see the screen; it was angled away from us. After a couple of minutes she turned to us again. 'So, Faye, we're going to check your blood pressure today, weigh you and I'll measure your stomach. We'll also listen to the baby's heartbeat, and I'll need to check your urine. Have you brought a specimen with you?'

Eyes down, Faye shook her head.

'I'm sorry,' I said. 'I should have realized it would be needed.'

'No problem. She can do it once we've finished here. Ask at reception for a sample pot and then return it there. The toilets are at the far end of the waiting room. Collect an extra sample pot for next time.'

'Thank you,' I said.

Clearly it was now time for the midwife to examine Faye. A couch was against one wall with a retractable screen. The midwife stood and, picking up the blood pressure monitor, turned to Faye. She didn't move or look up – I was starting to see some of the stubbornness Wilma had mentioned.

'I see you've already bought the baby a first toy,' the midwife said, trying to engage Faye and referring to Snuggles. But of course it was totally the wrong thing to say.

'Snuggles is actually Faye's,' I said. 'They're inseparable. You know the baby will be going for adoption?'

The midwife grimaced, realizing her faux pas. 'Sorry,' she mouthed to me, so I didn't know if she knew or not. Faye sat stubbornly in her seat.

'Come on, love,' I said, turning to her. 'The nurse needs to take your blood pressure.'

'I can do it with her sitting there,' the midwife said, and took the couple of steps to her side.

'Role up your sleeve,' I said to Faye. 'Do you want me to help you?'

'No, I can do it,' she said moodily.

'Excellent,' I said.

Faye pulled up her sleeve and the midwife wrapped the cuff of the blood pressure monitor around her upper arm. 'That's a pretty top you're wearing,' she said to Faye, again trying to engage her in conversation.

Faye remained perversely silent.

The monitor did its job. The midwife said the reading was normal and marked the result on the appropriate graph in the maternity folder. 'I'd like to weigh you now,' she said to Faye. 'Can you stand on those scales for me?'

Without lifting her gaze, Faye stood and with Snuggles at her side went over and stepped onto the scales. Although she wasn't responding she was at least cooperating.

'That's good,' the midwife said, reading out her weight.

Faye stepped off the scales and waited by them as the midwife noted the reading in the folder.

'Now, we need to measure your tummy to make sure baby is growing as it should be. Can you lie on the couch for me?'

Faye did as she was asked, lying flat on her back with Snuggles at her side. The midwife lifted Faye's top a little so she could slide the tape measure underneath her back and then round the front and over her bump to get an accurate measurement.

'Good,' she said, and made a note of the figure. 'Now we'll have a listen to baby's heartbeat.' She squeezed a little gel from a tube onto Faye's stomach and smeared it over her skin. Then she picked up the foetal Doppler and ran it over her bump until the baby's heartbeat could be heard loud and clear. 'There it is,' she said, pleased. 'Your baby's heart beating healthily.'

Emotion welled up in me, for here was the irrefutable proof of the life living within Faye. The tiny baby perfectly formed but only the size of a small bag of sugar. A baby's heartbeat is twice as fast as an adult's; it sounded like the clip-clop of a galloping horse or a high-speed train running over the tracks. It's the sound expectant parents cherish – confirmation that their baby is healthy – and it's a connection before the baby is born and they hear its first cry. But Faye remained staring at the ceiling, her face expressionless, as the sound echoed in an otherwise silent room.

'That's all fine then,' the midwife said after a moment, switching off the Doppler and returning it to the table. The air was suddenly unnaturally quiet without the heartbeat. She pulled a paper towel from the dispenser and wiped the gel from Faye's stomach. Faye tugged her top down into place and climbed off the couch.

'Can we go now?' she asked me.

I looked at the midwife.

'Everything is fine. The baby is the right size. Do you have any concerns?'

'No.' I didn't in respect of Faye's physical health. It was her non-acceptance of being pregnant that worried me. 'She's eating and sleeping well,' I added.

'Good. Before you leave, make an appointment at reception for her next check-up in three weeks. And don't forget the urine sample. I'll test it after you've gone. If you don't hear from me, assume it's normal.'

'Thank you,' I said.

'Can we go now?' Faye asked again.

'Yes,' the midwife said with a smile.

I wasn't so pleased. I thanked the midwife again and we left. In the corridor outside I said to Faye, 'That was rude.'

'I don't like her,' Faye said sulkily.

'Why not? She seemed pleasant enough to me.'

'I don't like what she says.'

'What? About Snuggles?'

'No. About babies.'

'But that's her job. She's a midwife, a nurse with extra training. Her job is to help and monitor women who are expecting.'

'Snuggles doesn't like her either,' Faye said, holding him up and ignoring my last comment.

At reception I asked for two urine sample pots and gave one to Faye. 'Do you know what to do?' I asked her.

'Gran showed me,' she said, still a little moody.

'Do you need help?'

'No. I've got Snuggles.'

The receptionist must have heard and flashed me an indulgent smile. 'I'll wait for you here then,' I said to Faye.

Faye went through the waiting area to the Ladies at the far end, while I turned to the receptionist and booked Faye's next appointment.

'She's a sweet kid,' the receptionist said. 'It must be difficult for her.' The phone rang before I needed to reply, and from then on she was busy answering the phone and attending to people at the counter.

Ten minutes passed and Faye still hadn't appeared, so I went through the waiting area and knocked on the door of the Ladies. It wasn't the most private place to site a bathroom, and a few of those in the waiting area looked over. 'Faye?' I knocked again. 'Are you all right?'

'Yes,' came her small voice from the other side of the door.

I waited by the door and five minutes later she came out and handed me the sample pot. 'Well done. I know it's awkward,' I said quietly to her. 'It'll be easier next time. You can do it at home before we come.'

We returned through the waiting room and I handed the sample pot to the receptionist and we said goodbye. Faye was still looking disgruntled and once outside I said again that the midwife was just doing her job.

'Snuggles says can we go and see the horses?' she asked.

'Not today, love. There isn't time. Becky is coming to see us at two o'clock. We'll go next week.'

I wondered if I should say anything further about the midwife's role, but I decided to leave it until we'd seen Becky. I was pinning a lot on Becky's visit – she was a highly experienced social worker and used to working with adults with learning disabilities. Faye's grumpiness vanished in the car and once home she asked if she could watch television, but I produced some jigsaw puzzles from the cupboard instead.

Her face lit up. 'My grandpa does jigsaws,' she said.

I smiled. 'So did my father.'

The two puzzles Faye did first had about forty reasonably large pieces and were aimed at six- to eight-year-olds. But she quickly completed these and progressed to a more difficult puzzle with sixty slightly smaller pieces. When she'd finished that one we had lunch and then Faye took another jigsaw puzzle from the cupboard. This one was far more complex than the previous, with 150 small pieces forming an intricate, colourful geometric design. Adrian had bought it with his pocket money when he'd been into doing jigsaw puzzles as a child. We took it into the living room and set it on the coffee table where it could remain undisturbed until it was completed. Faye was still working on the puzzle twenty minutes later when Becky arrived and I showed her into the living room.

'Wow! I am impressed,' Becky said, going over for a closer look. Faye smiled, pleased.

I offered Becky a coffee and left her sitting on the sofa beside Faye while I went to make it. Sammy was in the kitchen trying to decide if he should go into the living room and introduce himself to our guest, but decided otherwise and went out through the cat flap. I returned to the living room with Becky's coffee and set the cup and saucer on the small occasional table within her reach.

'Thanks, Cathy,' she said, taking a sip. She was watching Faye as she carefully selected another piece of the puzzle and tried to fit it in. 'You're doing well,' she said to her.

I agreed and sat in one of the easy chairs with my fostering folder and diary at my side.

'So how did your antenatal appointment go this morning?' Becky asked Faye, taking another sip of coffee.

Faye didn't reply, although she had clearly heard Becky. She kept her concentration on the puzzle.

'Everything was fine,' I said. 'Blood pressure and weight, and the midwife measured her stomach. It was all normal. We also heard the baby's heart beating.'

'Excellent,' Becky said. Setting down her coffee she took a notepad from her bag and made a few notes. Faye was still looking at the puzzle, pretending she hadn't heard. Becky saw this.

'Could you leave that for a moment,' she said, lightly touching Faye's arm. 'I'd like to talk to you for a few minutes. It won't take long.'

'What do you want to talk about?' Faye asked, without looking up.

'I'd like to talk about how you're feeling, and about the baby you're carrying.'

'I don't want to talk about that,' Faye said firmly.

'Why not? Can you tell me?' Becky asked kindly.

'Because it makes Gran and Grandpa sad.'

'I see. Does talking about it make you sad?' Becky asked.

Faye shrugged. She put down the piece of puzzle she'd been holding and, picking up Snuggles, held him to her. 'I want all of us to be happy again,' she said quietly. 'Grandpa,

104

Gran, me and Snuggles. I want to go home and it to be like it was before.'

'I understand that,' Becky said. 'And you will be going home as soon as you've had your baby. Do you understand about the baby in your tummy and why you are staying with Cathy for now?'

'Yes.'

'Why do you think that is?'

'Because Gran can't cope with all the appointments and stuff.'

'Yes, that's more or less it.' Becky paused to collect her thoughts. 'Faye, Cathy and I are a little concerned that you're not talking about how you feel about being pregnant and the baby. There must be a lot going on in your mind, but you don't say what it is. You don't like the baby being mentioned, so it's difficult for us to know how you're feeling. We want to make sure you're all right and to help you through this.'

'I know,' Faye said, her face setting. 'But I already told you, I don't want to talk about it because it makes Gran and Grandpa sad.'

'Is that the only reason?' Becky asked. Faye nodded. 'You understand why your tummy is growing bigger? We talked about it a few weeks ago. It's because there is a baby inside that will be born in three months' time.'

'I know,' Faye said.

Becky paused and studied Faye. 'All right, but I want you to remember that Cathy is good at listening and answering questions. So if you don't want to talk to your gran and grandpa, perhaps you could talk to Cathy. You can phone me, but Cathy is here with you all the time.'

'I'd like it if you could talk to me,' I added.

'All right,' Faye said, finally looking up. 'I'll talk to you, but not to Gran and Grandpa. I don't want to hurt them any more. I just want things to be how they were.'

CHAPTER NINE

INNOCENT REMARKS

One of the issues a parent or carer may encounter when looking after a child or adult with a learning disability is with communication and language difficulties: understanding their wishes and needs. Faye had adequate language skills to see her through everyday situations, but she wouldn't necessarily be able to define, identify or verbalize complex emotions, as the average adult would. In children I'd seen this come out in angry, frustrated outbursts, but in Faye's case it appeared she'd been internalizing her feelings to protect her grandparents. Although Becky hadn't said an awful lot, it was enough to persuade Faye that it was all right for her to start talking to me about being pregnant and the baby. After Becky left, Faye continued doing the jigsaw puzzle and then asked if she could help me cook dinner tonight. I said of course she could and that I was planning on making a casserole, which I needed to prepare now, as it required a long, slow cook.

In the kitchen Faye helped me to collect together the ingredients we needed from the fridge and cupboards, and to wash them. I then gave her a knife and, following my example, she stood beside me at the worktop, peeling, chopping and slicing the ingredients and placing them into the casserole dish. Snuggles sat propped up at the end of the counter, watching us.

'Have you ever had a baby in your tummy?' Faye suddenly asked as we worked, which took me by surprise.

'Yes. Twice. First with Adrian and then Paula. It seems incredible now that they were that small once,' I added reflectively.

'What about Lucy?' Faye asked.

'She wasn't in my tummy. She was in another woman's tummy, her birth mother's. She is my adopted daughter.' I glanced at Faye. 'Like your baby is going to be adopted, but you will always be her birth mother.'

'Becky said she is going to find a really nice mummy and daddy for my baby,' Faye said.

'Yes, I'm sure she will.' I didn't know what stage the process of identifying adoptive parents for Faye's baby had reached, but I guessed the search for a suitable match had already begun, and it wouldn't take long. There are thousands of childless couples wanting to adopt a baby, although the baby would be placed with a foster carer to begin with until the legal process was complete. It hadn't really been appropriate to ask Becky how soon after the birth the baby would be taken from Faye as I'd intended to, but Faye now said, 'Becky told me I could have a photograph of me holding my baby, if I wanted to. I've told her no. Gran and Grandpa said it would be too upsetting.'

'I can understand that,' I said. 'Some find it helpful.'

'Gran says that once I've had the baby and go home we need to try to forget it, and carry on with our lives.'

I nodded noncommittally but thought that might be easier said than done.

'Does Lucy's birth mother have a photograph of her?' Faye asked, placing another slice of carrot into the casserole dish.

'Yes. She still sees her sometimes.' I stopped, wondering if this was the wisest conversation to be having and if it might confuse Faye. 'It was different with Lucy,' I said. 'She was much older when she came to me – eleven, not a baby.'

'Why?' Faye asked.

'Lucy had a very unsettled and unhappy childhood. She had to live in a number of different homes before she came to me. That won't happen to your baby. It will have a lovely mummy and daddy right from being a baby, which will be much better.'

Faye nodded. We'd finished chopping the carrots and I now passed her a celery stick to chop, while I took an onion. 'Same chopping motion,' I said. 'And be careful of your fingers. We don't want finger in the casserole.'

Faye laughed while I mused, feeling relieved, that not only was Faye now talking about her baby, but also adoption. All it had taken was a few appropriate words of encouragement from her social worker.

'Is Lucy's mummy …' Faye began.

'Birth mother,' I corrected.

'Is Lucy's birth mother happy that Lucy is living with you?'

'Yes, I think she is. She struggled for a long time to try to look after Lucy, so she's pleased she's settled now.' I felt tears spring to the backs of my eyes, as they always did when I thought of Lucy's early life and her suffering. I tell Lucy's story in my book *Will You Love Me?*

'I won't struggle, will I?' Faye asked.

'No, you won't. You will have your gran and grandpa to look after you. And when you think of your baby, which you

will do sometimes, you'll know it is loved and well cared for.'
I reached for a tissue to wipe my eyes. 'It must be those
onions,' I said.

When I served the casserole that evening I told Paula, Lucy
and Adrian that Faye had helped me make it and they were
very complimentary. Far more complimentary than when I
alone made dinner. Their praise and kind comments pleased
Faye, and she said she wanted to help me again another time.
As it was Friday – the end of the working week – Adrian
and Lucy went out in the evening and Paula had a friend
over. I asked Faye if she would like to invite Emma, her
friend from the day centre, here one time. I explained I could
speak to her parents and collect and return her in the car if
necessary.

'No,' Faye said, pulling a face. 'I don't want her here.'

'Why?'

'She doesn't like watching the television programmes I do.'

I kept my smile to myself. Faye was serious. 'I see. How do
you know that?'

'We talk about what we do in the evenings at the day
centre. That's how I know.'

'Well, if she came here you wouldn't need to watch television. You could do something else, like puzzles, board games,
play cards, or we could do some cooking – maybe make a
pizza? Or you could sit and chat and listen to music, like
Lucy and Paula do.' I tried to make it sound exciting and
enticing. I thought it would do Faye good to see her friend, as
she wasn't going to the day centre. I appreciated how difficult
it was for her grandparents with their limited mobility to
organize a visit.

'Nah,' Faye said, sounding like a teenager. 'I'll see her when I go to the day centre again. I'd rather watch television.'

'OK. Tell me if you change your mind.'

On Saturday I took Faye on the bus to see her grandparents, and once I was home again I had a small window of opportunity to spend time with Lucy, Adrian and Paula before I had to leave again to collect Faye. Lucy asked why I didn't collect Faye in the car and I explained that I had to familiarize her with the route so she could visit her grandparents alone, but that we hadn't reached that point yet. Going was fine; the correct bus stop in the high street was easy to identify, as was the stop at the other end, because it was in the area Faye knew well. But on the return journey Faye wasn't recognizing the landmarks in the high street in time to push the bell to signal to the driver she wanted the bus to stop.

Stan and Wilma greeted me warmly when I arrived at three o'clock to collect Faye, and Wilma asked after my family. Then, as I waited for Faye to put on her coat and shoes, Wilma asked how the visit from the social worker had gone the day before.

'Very well,' I said. 'Didn't Faye say?'

'No,' Stan said. 'We couldn't get a word out of her about it.' I could understand why. It would be uncomfortable for Faye to tell her grandparents that she'd agreed to talk about her pregnancy to me but not to them, so it was easier to say nothing, which was what she tended to do when faced with awkward situations.

'The antenatal appointment yesterday morning went well too,' I said. 'Although Faye didn't say much. Health-wise, everything is as it should be.'

They nodded, and I knew this was probably as much information as they wanted about the antenatal check-up, preferring to ignore the pregnancy as Faye had been doing, and was still doing with them.

Before we left to catch the bus back I confirmed that Faye would be visiting them again on Monday – she was seeing them every other day when possible. Stan came with us to the elevator to say goodbye, and then as we descended I asked Faye if she'd had a nice day, as I usually did. She said she had and that their neighbours had 'popped in for a cup of tea and a chat' and had spent the afternoon with them. The couple were a similar age to her grandparents and Faye had clearly enjoyed their company.

As the bus approached our stop I reminded Faye of the landmarks she had to look out for, and with my prompts she pressed the bell in plenty of time. Once home she completed the jigsaw puzzle she'd been doing and we all admired it before packing it away. After dinner she watched television. Paula joined her and presently I heard them chatting. Later, when Faye went for her bath, Paula said to me, 'Did you know Faye is talking about the baby?'

'Yes. Her social worker explained to her that it's better to talk about worries than to keep them bottled up when they can upset you.'

'She wasn't worried or upset,' Paula said. 'There was an advert for baby things on the television and it showed a pregnant woman. Faye said, "She's like me," and rubbed her stomach.'

'Good. That sounds positive,' I said.

But while Faye wasn't worried or upset by talking about her baby now, I soon learnt that I'd unintentionally upset

Lucy. She came to me with a type of frown I hadn't seen in a long while. 'Why have you been talking about me to Faye?' she asked, slightly confrontationally.

'What do you mean?' I asked. 'I often mention you and your brother and sister to others, because I'm so proud of you all.'

'Not like that,' she said a little moodily. 'You've been talking to Faye about me being adopted.'

'Oh, I see,' I said, immediately realizing my error. 'I'm sorry. I was just trying to make her feel better about her baby being adopted. I didn't say much, but I should have realized. I won't say any more.' Like many children who'd been in and out of care for much of their childhood, Lucy had craved a normal family life, which of course she had now with us. That she was adopted was rarely mentioned, and she was as much a part of my family as if she'd been born to me. I couldn't have loved her any more. But she remained sensitive to some issues from her past, and I needed to remember that.

'I'm sorry,' I said again. 'It was thoughtless of me. It won't happen again.'

'OK,' Lucy said, recovering. 'You're forgiven. Big hugs.' She spread her arms wide.

I hugged her and held her close. 'I love you so much. You know that, don't you?'

'Yes. I love you too.'

'But, Lucy, you need to be prepared for the possibility that Faye might mention adoption again or want to talk about birth mothers. She doesn't understand what is appropriate, and I can't tell her not to talk about these things when Becky and I have been encouraging her to talk.'

'I know,' Lucy said easily. 'It's fine, really. It was just a shock when she suddenly said, "My baby is being adopted like you are."'

'I can see that, but be prepared for the fact that she may say something similar. She won't know it could upset you.'

'I understand,' Lucy said.

Paula, Lucy, Adrian and Faye all came with me to visit my mother on Sunday, so there was a car full. Adrian sat in the front passenger seat for the extra leg-room and the three girls were in the back. The radio was on, but Lucy and Paula were plugged into their phones, either listening to music, texting or making and taking calls. I'd asked Faye if she wanted to bring her phone, but it didn't hold the same appeal to her as it did for many young people who like to be in regular contact with their peers through social media. However, she did have Snuggles on her lap. Faye was looking forward to meeting my mother, and I'd telephoned Mum the evening before to check it was still all right for us all to descend on her, and if she wanted us to bring anything.

'Just bring yourselves,' she'd said, as she often did. Although of course we were taking her flowers and chocolates.

'Do you have a grandpa?' Faye asked as I drove. I'd told her that my father had died, but she must have forgotten. Thankfully Lucy and Paula hadn't heard, as they had earphones in, but Adrian looked at me a little disconcerted.

'No, love,' I said to Faye. 'Grandpa died recently.' I glanced at her in the rear-view mirror.

'That's sad,' she said, her face dropping. 'I hope my grandpa and gran don't die.'

'I'm afraid we all have to die some time,' I said. 'But I'm sure it won't be for a long time yet.' I hoped Faye didn't talk like that at Mum's, as it could be upsetting for everyone. But as with Lucy's adoption, I couldn't give Faye a list of taboo subjects that she wasn't to talk about. Much of the time she saw life through the eyes of a child and had their same lack of inhibitions. She said things as they were, and if her innocent remarks touched a nerve with us then it fell upon us to make allowances and accommodate them. It wasn't Faye's fault she could be tactless sometimes; it was part of her learning disability.

I sensed the atmosphere in the car shift as I drew onto the drive at Mum's house and cut the engine. It was still difficult arriving, aware that just Mum would be answering the door. Lucy and Paula took out their earphones and there was a sharp silence for a second when no one moved or spoke, before Faye said brightly, 'Is this where your gran lives?'

'Yes,' I said.

'Doesn't she live in a flat?'

'No, in this house.'

'It's a nice house,' she said. Then she told Snuggles the house was nice and that Paula, Lucy and Adrian's gran lived here, which lightened the atmosphere.

Mum appeared at the front door – I guessed she'd been looking out for us – and we smiled and called hi as we got out of the car. As soon as Faye was out she ran to Mum. I looked over anxiously, concerned as to what she was going to do, but she just wanted to hug her, greeting her as she did her own grandparents. Mum looked a bit surprised. 'Well, that's a lovely hello,' she said, returning the hug. 'You must be Faye.'

Faye beamed and stepped back. 'Yes, I am Faye, and this is Snuggles.'

I'd already told Mum about Snuggles.

Faye went indoors as Mum hugged and kissed each of us in turn. As I gave Mum the flowers and chocolates I remembered how Dad used to joke to Mum, 'The flowers are all yours and the chocolates are all mine.' I smiled at the recollection.

Indoors, I went with Mum into the kitchen to help her make hot drinks and put the flowers in water, while Lucy, Adrian and Paula showed Faye into the living room. The house was as it had always been. Mum hadn't made any changes, other than removing Dad's personal possessions from downstairs. His spare glasses, crossword book (he always had a crossword on the go), coat and umbrella were no longer in their usual places.

We arranged a plate of biscuits and the drinks on a tray and I carried it into the living room, where I handed out the drinks while Mum offered the biscuits. Adrian was sitting in what had been Dad's armchair and I was pleased; it seemed to be another little step towards coming to terms with Dad's passing and making it a little easier for us all. We settled with our drinks and biscuits and Mum talked to Paula about college, to Adrian and Lucy about their jobs and to Faye about horses. I'd mentioned to Mum that Faye liked horses and Mum always made sure she included any child we were fostering in the conversations (as Dad had also done). 'Cathy tells me you like to go horse riding,' she said to Faye.

'Yes,' Faye said. 'But I can't go now, so Cathy takes me to see horses in a field.'

'That's nice,' Mum said. 'I think we might have been there.'

'Yes, we have,' I agreed.

'I feed the horses grass,' Faye said. 'And I've given them all names.' She told us some of the names she could remember.

Once Adrian had finished his drink he said he'd go out and cut the grass. Mum began to protest, saying he hadn't come here to work, but I said that Adrian liked to help and preferred to be doing something rather than sitting and chatting. Dad had been the same. Presently we saw Adrian through the patio windows, pushing the electric lawnmower up and down the grass. Lucy and Paula then went with Mum into the kitchen to help her prepare lunch. They often did. They loved spending time with their gran without me there and I respected that. I think grandchildren can have a special relationship with their grandparents, sharing and confiding in a way they wouldn't necessarily do with their parents. The difference in age seems to close the generational gap, rather than widening it, and of course grandparents are generally relieved of any disciplining role, so they can more easily be the young person's friend and confidant.

I stayed with Faye in the living room while Lucy, Paula and Adrian were occupied, and I asked her if she'd like some books to look at, but she asked if Gran had any games like I had. I pulled over the upholstered footstool that doubled as a toy box and lifted the lid. Faye knelt beside me and began searching through it. She took out the box of dominoes, which she said she sometimes played at the day centre. She and I played a couple of games and then we helped lay the table for lunch, although it was more like dinner with a main course of chops and roasted vegetables, followed by blackberry and apple pie and custard. The pudding had been one of Dad's favourites as well as ours. 'It's nice to have the opportunity to make it again,' Mum said. 'It's not worth making for one – I'd be eating it all week.'

After we'd finished lunch and had helped clear away, Adrian found some more jobs to do, including fixing the bolt on the side gate, which had broken when the gate had slammed in the wind, and oiling its hinges. The girls and I helped Mum wash up and put away the dishes, so it was soon done. Faye said she often did the dishes at home, as her gran and grandpa couldn't stand at the sink for long. We then sat in the living room and chatted for a while, and then at Faye's request we played some card games she knew from the day centre. Despite my initial reservations that Faye might say something to upset Mum, the day had gone well. Faye was relaxed around Mum, and while she often mentioned her own grandparents and that she liked to help them, as their legs were bad, she didn't make any untoward remarks about my father that could have been upsetting. Neither did she mention being pregnant or the baby. In the car going home I found out why. 'I made sure I talked about things that wouldn't upset your gran,' she said. 'Like I have to with my gran and grandpa. I don't like seeing them upset, so we had a nice day and were all happy.'

I smiled. 'Yes, indeed.'

CHAPTER TEN

CHANGE OF HEART

On Monday I took Faye on the bus again to visit her grandparents, and then on Tuesday we went to see the horses in the field. Faye was delighted when she called their names and they cantered over, although I think they would have come anyway with the promise of handfuls of fresh grass and being stroked. I'd found an old hairbrush at home and had given it to Faye so that she could brush their manes. A few of the horses stood still to let her brush, but the others shied away, probably not used to having their hair done, for I doubted many visitors arrived with a hairbrush! 'We could bring some mascara next time,' I joked.

'Yes, like Lucy,' Faye said. 'She wears mascara. I've seen her putting it on.'

'Would you like some?' I asked, wondering if this was a hint.

'No. My gran wouldn't like it, and I try to please Gran and keep her happy.' Said without any hint of dissent or regret. Faye was a truly selfless person.

'I know you do, love.'

The hairbrush was filthy by the time Faye had finished brushing the horses' manes, so I put it into a carrier bag to wash on our return home, and gave Faye plenty of antibacterial wipes for her hands.

On Wednesday I took Faye to see her grandparents again, and on the return journey she finally remembered, without prompting, when to press the bell button to stop the bus. 'Well done,' I said. I decided that if she did it correctly on two more journeys then she could travel to see her grandparents by herself, as Becky wanted her to. Faye didn't seem too bothered if she made the journey alone or not. True to her character, she tended to go along with everyone else's wishes.

Edith, my support social worker, telephoned on Thursday afternoon for an update and to see how Faye had settled in. When I was fostering a child she would visit every month to check I was caring for them to the required standard, assess my ongoing training needs, give support and advice where necessary and sign off my log notes. As Faye had been referred from adult services it was felt that Becky could support and supervise me, although I could phone Edith if I needed to and I still sent her my monthly reports.

Now Faye knew that Becky and I wanted her to talk to me about her feelings and her pregnancy, she continued to do so in a relaxed and spontaneous manner. The number of comments and questions steadily increased, and they weren't just to me but to Lucy, Paula and Adrian as well – as and when the moment arose, although Adrian usually told Faye to ask me if she wanted to know something about pregnancy or childbirth. I always answered her questions honestly, in detail, and using language appropriate for her level of understanding, rephrasing and repeating if she didn't grasp it the first time. I found some books that I'd used with my own children and children

I'd fostered, which explained how babies were conceived, grew inside the mother's womb and were born. One of the books had large colourful illustrations and told the story of a new life as if it was an incredible adventure. Faye loved the story with the passion a child shows for a fairy tale, which in a way it was. She wanted me to read it over and over again. The wonder of creation never ceases to amaze me: a microscopic sperm joining with a single-cell egg and growing into a baby. It's pretty awe-inspiring, even for adults, and it was true magic for Faye. However, in all our readings and discussions about babies I was no nearer to finding out who the father of Faye's baby was, although we got close a few times.

'You understand that it takes a man and a woman to make a baby?' I asked Faye one time.

'Of course I know,' she said a little indignantly.

'Good. So you know that every baby must have a daddy, even though he might not see the mother. He gave the mummy the sperm to make the baby.'

'Yes, I know. There's a picture here,' she said, flipping back through the book.

'So your baby has a daddy, although you may not see him now.'

'I know,' she said matter-of-factly.

'Do you want to tell me about him?' I asked.

'No. Gran wouldn't like it.'

'But you know you can talk to me or Becky about him?'

'Yes, but I don't want to. It's our secret.'

'Did he tell you that?'

'Yes. And I agree with him,' she said emphatically.

I could have continued my questioning, but I felt to do so would have been unreasonably intrusive and would possibly have forced her into saying something she'd later regret or even to make up something. Becky had asked me to try to find out who the father was, as she had concerns that Faye might have been forced into having intercourse, but from Faye's manner when I'd mentioned the father I didn't think so. She wasn't distraught or tearful as surely she would have been had she been raped. It was still possible she'd been persuaded or coerced into having sex, and, if so, the circumstances in which that had happened would need to be looked into if they ever became known. But, then again, Faye had sexual feelings as much as anyone, so she might have entered into the relationship of her own free will, although where and with whom would remain a mystery for now.

Faye began making the journey alone to her grandparents' flat the following week. Each morning before she left I checked she had her phone and bus ticket with her, but I was on tenterhooks until Stan phoned to say she'd arrived. On the return journey I telephoned her grandparents to say she was back. I didn't think we were being overprotective, for although Faye had used the buses to go to and from the day centre for many years, the route to my house was very different and in the opposite direction, so checking she'd arrived seemed a sensible precaution. The first three trips went without incident, but then on Saturday, at the time Faye should have been leaving to catch the bus to me, Stan telephoned and asked if I could collect her in the car. He said that while she'd been waiting at the bus stop outside the flats some boys who lived locally had begun taunting her and calling her names. She had tried to ignore them for a while, but then she'd felt threatened and had fled back to the flat. I was horrified, angry and upset that anyone could be so cruel as to pick on someone with a learning disability – as, I expected, her grandparents were. But when I arrived Stan was philosophical.

'It's not the first time it's happened and I doubt it will be the last,' he said. 'Faye does her best to ignore them, but today it got personal. It was worse when she was at school. They'd surround her and take her snack money. Bullying was one of the reasons we moved her to a special school.'

It was pitiful and I felt my eyes well. Poor, gentle Faye, who'd never hurt anyone, having to put up with that. Yet while I was incensed, Faye and her grandparents seemed to accept bullying was part of her life. Wilma said that these lads were part of the group who'd picked on her at school.

'They want reporting to the police,' I said.

'We have done in the past,' Stan said. 'But by the time the police arrive they're long gone. The sooner we move away from here the better.'

'Is there any news on that?' I asked.

'No,' Wilma said with a sigh. 'I phoned housing again on Monday. We're gradually moving up the waiting list for either a bungalow or a ground-floor flat, but there are others ahead of us.'

'I'd have thought you would be a priority.'

'We are, but because of the ageing population there are many others like us who need ground-floor housing too.'

'Can't Becky put a word in for you?' I asked. I knew that social workers could write to the housing department if there were special circumstances.

'She has,' Wilma said. 'And our doctor has sent a letter. We'll just have to be patient and wait now.'

Faye kissed her gran goodbye and then Stan came into the corridor as usual to see us to the elevator. Outside the block of flats there was no sign of the bullies, but I saw Faye glance around. I wouldn't bring up the subject unless Faye did. There wasn't much I could say. She'd probably had far more personal experience of dealing with bullies than I had, and there wasn't any advice I could give her beyond what she was already doing – ignore them. However, once in the car Faye confided that this time they'd been calling her names because she was pregnant.

'They asked me if Snuggles was the baby's father,' she said.

'That was stupid of them.'

'I didn't tell Gran, it would have upset her.'

'Yes.' I paused. 'Faye, I'm wondering if perhaps it would be wiser if I started giving you a lift in the car when you visit your grandparents. Not just because of what happened today, but as you're getting bigger now you don't want to be standing around waiting for buses.'

'Yes. I like going in your car,' Faye said easily.

That evening I telephoned Faye's grandparents and suggested that in future I brought and collected Faye in my car. I didn't tell them the nature of the boys' bullying, but I said, as I had to Faye, that I thought it would be more comfortable for her. They agreed.

'Faye's proved she can do the bus journey alone,' Stan said. 'She doesn't have to prove it any more.' Which I thought was a sensible view. I'd mention our decision to Becky next time I spoke to her. From then on I took and collected Faye in the car. It saved a lot of time and worry.

* * *

The days passed and Faye continued to talk openly about her pregnancy and what she now referred to as 'my baby'. My family and I were happy for her; her openness seemed preferable to ignoring her condition, as long as you didn't think about the end result: that it would never be *her* baby. But with all the talk and openness, something else was starting to happen: I was bonding with her baby, as I was sure Faye was, and possibly my children too. When Faye had refused to acknowledge her pregnancy the baby had remained a vague and indistinct entity – something apart from our lives. But now she was sharing her pregnancy openly, by telling us when the baby moved and what it felt like, and that it was uncomfortable at night, for example, and she was now sitting with her hands resting over her bump, it had gone from being an 'it' to a real living person. As we didn't know the sex of the child we couldn't refer to it as 'he' or 'she', so we used the term 'baby'. We always asked Faye how baby was today and she'd reply with, 'My baby is very well, thank you,' or something similar. So in a few weeks we'd effectively gone from fostering Faye who was pregnant to fostering Faye and her unborn baby, which felt very different. And perhaps part of me saw what was coming next, for I wasn't as surprised as I might have been.

In complete contrast to Faye's previous antenatal check-ups, she was very enthusiastic about the next one, at twenty-eight weeks gestation, and was looking forward to learning how her baby was doing and hearing its heartbeat. As we entered the consultation room she smiled at the midwife and said a bright hello, then answered her questions and generally engaged with her, interested in all aspects of her developing baby. We'd brought the urine sample with us from home and the midwife dipstick-tested it in the surgery and said everything was normal. Faye was pleased and thanked her. She then took her blood pressure and that was normal too, as was her weight gain.

'You're doing very well,' the midwife said.

Faye smiled, thanked her again and then, looking down at her stomach, said, 'Did you hear that, baby? You're doing very well.'

The midwife was looking slightly bemused and I felt I had to say something.

'We've had a change of heart and we're more accepting,' I said.

'So she's going to keep the baby?'

'Oh no. I didn't mean that. But Faye has accepted it is better to talk about the pregnancy.'

'Good. That makes life easier for us all.'

Faye was ready and lying on the couch to have her bump measured even before the midwife asked her to.

'Am I fat enough?' she asked as the midwife read out the measurement.

'Yes. That's perfect,' she said.

'Are you going to put that jelly on my tummy now?'

The midwife smiled. 'The ultrasound gel? Yes, here it is.'

She put on the gel and then ran the Doppler over Faye's stomach until the steady clip-clop of the baby's heartbeat could be heard. Beaming, Faye clasped her hands together in delight. 'That's my baby's heart.' Then she asked the midwife: 'Can I hear the rest of my baby?'

'There isn't any more to hear,' the midwife said kindly. 'But you would have seen your baby on the monitor when you had your scan.'

Faye didn't say anything, but I knew from Wilma that she hadn't seen the baby on the monitor at either of the previous scans, because she'd refused to look. There were no more scans scheduled, so I hoped she didn't regret not looking and not having a print-out of her baby's image to keep.

Thankfully, Faye either didn't understand or remember this and was still smiling as she climbed from the couch with Snuggles in her hand. We waited while the midwife wrote in the maternity folder, then she handed it to me, reminding us to book the next appointment for three weeks' time on the way out, and also to collect another urine sample pot.

'But I've already done one,' Faye protested.

'For your next appointment,' I said.

We said goodbye and left the midwife updating her computer. I wondered if she was adding anything about Faye's change in attitude.

'I heard my baby,' Faye told the receptionist. The couple waiting at the desk glanced at her.

'It's a lovely sound, isn't it?' the receptionist said kindly.

'It is,' Faye agreed. 'When can I hear it again?'

'At the next appointment,' I said. 'In three weeks.'

Outside, Faye asked again when the next appointment was. 'In three weeks,' I said. 'Then it's every two weeks until you have your baby. Don't worry, I've written it all down.'

'How many sleeps until I have my baby?'

'Oh gosh. I think it must be about seventy-five,' I said. 'I'd have to look on the calendar and work it out.' I was now expecting Faye to say that this was when she would be able to go to the stables again, which was the context in which sleeps had been mentioned before. But she didn't.

'So about seventy-five sleeps and then I have my baby?' she asked.

'Yes, about that,' I said.

'Seventy-five sleeps. I'm looking forward to seeing my baby.'

'That's good,' I said, my voice slightly flat. Any mention of the birth was bittersweet – the joy of a new baby undermined by the sadness of losing it.

We climbed into the car. I put the key into the ignition and then waited while Faye fixed her seatbelt around her bump. 'Cathy,' she said, turning to me, 'I can't talk to Gran about my baby, so can I tell you?'

'Yes, of course, love. Anything. What is it?'

'I think I'm going to keep my baby. Will you tell Gran?'

I took my hand from the ignition key and looked at her. 'Faye, love, that isn't possible, is it?'

'Why not? It's my baby. I can keep it if I want. Snuggles says I can.'

I instinctively glanced at Snuggles sitting in her lap and then looked at her. 'Is it because of what the midwife said after I'd said you'd had a change of heart?' I wondered if her words about Faye keeping her baby had given her the idea.

'No. I've thought about it before and I want my baby.'

How to explain? Where to begin? I thought. I didn't want to hurt Faye's feelings, but she needed to understand. 'Faye, love, babies need a lot of looking after. They can't do anything for themselves for a very long time. They're not like Snuggles. You can't pick them up and put them down when you want to. A baby is with you all the time and needs feeding and changing all day and all night.'

'I can feed and change my baby if you show me,' Faye said. 'You showed me how to cut those carrots. You can show me how to feed and change my baby.'

My heart went out to her. If only it were that simple, I thought. 'It's a lot more difficult than cutting up carrots,' I said, touching her arm reassuringly. 'There is so much to learn.'

'I can learn things. I know it takes me longer, but I can learn. I want to learn. I'm happy about my baby and I want to learn so I can keep it.' A lump rose in my throat.

'Faye, do you remember Becky talked to you when you were first pregnant?' She nodded. 'You agreed then that it would be better if she found a lovely mummy and daddy for your baby who will look after it very well.'

'I know,' Faye said, her face setting slightly. 'But I don't want them to have my baby. I've changed my mind. I'm not going to give them my baby and they can't make me.'

The truth was that the social services could 'make her' give up her baby if there was sufficient reason, which there was. They could apply to the court for an order to remove the baby at birth, but I didn't say that. It would have been too cruel. I then realized that in all the talk about pregnancy and giving birth I'd never mentioned the reality of parenting a baby. It hadn't seemed appropriate or relevant, as Faye wouldn't be keeping her baby. She hadn't gone to the antenatal parenting classes for the same reason. As a result she'd built up a completely unrealistic, probably romantic, view of what it was like to look after a baby.

'Faye, once we get home I'll explain to you what looking after a baby is really like. Then I think you'll understand why you and Becky made the right decision when you agreed it would be better if she found a mummy and daddy for your baby. OK?'

Faye nodded. I desperately wished the outcome could have been different, but it was impossible. Faye could never parent a baby without twenty-four-hour support, and her grandparents weren't in any position to give her that. There really was no alternative. Hopefully, once I'd had a good chat with her, she'd be able to see that.

Faye's thoughts tended to hop from one idea to another and by the time we were home she appeared to have forgotten about wanting to keep her baby. She hadn't mentioned it again in the car but had talked happily about other things: when we could see the horses again, that it was her gran's birthday soon and she wanted to buy her a present, and finally that she desperately needed a wee. Once indoors Faye went to the bathroom while I put the maternity folder away and then made us a hot drink and a snack. Faye asked if we could go shopping for her gran's present and card that afternoon, and I agreed, as I had a few things I needed to buy from the shopping centre too.

In the mall I was careful to keep away from the store we'd been to previously that sold maternity wear, baby equipment and clothes. But Faye didn't mention her baby; she was too engrossed in choosing a present, card and wrapping paper for her gran. I decided that if she brought up the matter of keeping her baby again, I'd explain the complex and all-consuming needs of a baby so she'd see the impossibility of keeping it. I could have done with one of those baby simulators – the life-size dolls that cry out for care day and night. Faye would soon tire of its relentless demands, for she loved watching television, playing and her sleep.

We had lunch out, then returned home and Faye helped me to make a cottage pie for dinner. We all ate together, chatting as usual about what we'd done that day. College lectures had begun for Paula and she said she had a lot of research to do that evening for an essay. After dinner Faye settled in front of the television for an evening of soap viewing, only interrupted by her bath. Lucy joined her for a while. Adrian was mainly in his room on his laptop. Although Faye hadn't mentioned keeping her baby again, it soon became clear that she hadn't forgotten it. When I went to say goodnight to her (and Snuggles) she said, 'Cathy, I really do want to keep my baby. Will you tell Gran and Becky?'

I sat on the edge of the bed and, taking her hand in mine, I explained in laborious detail all the negative things I could think of about looking after a baby: the constant crying, the smelly, pooey nappies, the non-stop demands of feeding and changing, the exhaustion, and the fact that there was no time to do anything you enjoyed, like watching television or playing games, as a baby required all your time. My *pièce de résistance* was that she wouldn't be able to go to the day centre or the stables again. Her face fell and I felt guilty, but I had to make her see that keeping her baby wasn't an option.

'But I like going to the stables,' she protested. 'I want to see the horses again.'

'I know you do, love. Have a think about what I've said and we can talk about it again tomorrow. If you have any questions, I'll answer them.'

'OK.'

Then she brightened, asked when we could see the horses again in the field and hugged me goodnight. I hoped that when she'd reflected on what I'd said she'd understand and that would be the end of the matter. My hope was soon dashed.

CHAPTER ELEVEN

ANNIVERSARY

The following day I took Faye in the car to see her grand-parents, and when I collected her she said they'd had a really nice time and had gone into their neighbours' flat for a cup of tea. The couple had their niece and nephew visiting and Faye knew them well. Our afternoon and evening continued with dinner and then Faye watched her usual television programmes. When she went up for her bath she saw Paula on the landing and I heard them chatting for a while. But when Faye was in the bathroom Paula came down to find me, and she was looking worried.

'Mum, I think you should know that Faye's just told me she wants to keep her baby, but you won't let her.'

My heart sank. 'That isn't what I said, and it's not my decision. Thanks for telling me, love. I'll talk to her.'

'She can't keep it, can she?'

'No, but she needs to hear it from her social worker. Don't you worry, I'll sort it out.'

When Faye finished her bath she came downstairs in her nightdress and dressing gown as she usually did, towel-drying her hair. I had switched off the television.

'Where's my programme?' she asked, put out.

'You can have it on in a moment. I need to talk to you first. Sit down, please, love.'

She sat in the chair she used for watching television and looked at me questioningly.

'Faye, it's not my decision whether you keep your baby. You, Becky and your grandparents decided together some weeks ago that adoption was best. Do you remember?'

'Yes, but I've changed my mind.'

'I understand, but it's not that simple. Tomorrow I'll telephone Becky and tell her what you've said. I expect she'll want to talk to you.'

'Will she be cross?'

'No, not cross. But she'll be able to advise you on what's best for you and the baby.'

'Will she tell Gran?' Faye asked, now looking concerned.

'I don't know. Why?'

'I hope she doesn't. Gran will be cross and Grandpa will be unhappy.'

Faye's simplistic, childlike view of the world meant that she saw things in absolutes. People were either cross or happy, good or bad, right or wrong, on your side or against you. There was no in-between middle ground, where most adults live their lives. I hoped that Becky could make Faye see that this was far more complex than upsetting her grandparents.

'Can I have the television on now?' she asked.

It was on the tip of my tongue to say, *And supposing your baby is crying when you want the television on, what then? Or you've just stepped into your bath and the baby starts crying. Would you immediately get out, dripping wet, to answer its cries? And how would you know what the baby wanted? Feeding, changing, winding or soothing? Parenting is a sharp learning curve. How would you cope?* But I'd explained this to Faye already and it wasn't her fault that she hadn't grasped it.

'Yes, you can have the television on,' I said. I passed her the remote and then went into the hall to telephone Mum.

I was still phoning Mum most evenings for a quick chat, but tonight as we talked I thought she sounded a bit down.

'Are you sure you're all right?' I asked for a second time.

'Yes. How's Paula doing at college?' she asked, changing the subject.

'Very well. There's a lot of work, but she's enjoying it.'

'Good, and Adrian, Lucy and Faye are all right?'

'Yes, they're fine. What have you been doing today?' I asked, bringing the conversation back to her.

'Sweeping up leaves in the garden,' she said slightly despondently. 'Autumn's here.'

'Yes. Indeed. I'll have to do ours.'

'I'm going to the cemetery tomorrow,' Mum added.

'Oh, yes?' I said, a little surprised. As far as I knew Mum hadn't visited Dad's grave since the funeral. It was a bus journey away, so I'd assumed either my brother or I would take her in the car on a weekend.

'I'll come with you,' I said. 'We can go in the car.'

'There's no need for you to come rushing over,' Mum said, as usual not wanting to be any bother.

'I'd like to. I'll have Faye with me, but she can wait in the car while we're at the grave.' I thought that Mum might not want to share such a private moment. 'She's no trouble.'

'I know she's not. But are you sure? You do so much rushing around.'

'Yes. I'd like to come, if you'd like some company.'

She immediately brightened. 'Yes, I would.'

'Good. We'll be with you around eleven o'clock and perhaps we can get some lunch out after.'

'Yes, that would be nice. I was feeling a bit gloomy. Tomorrow is the anniversary of the first time I went out with your father, our first date. I felt I wanted to go to the cemetery.'

'Oh, I see. I didn't know.' I obviously knew the date of my parents' wedding anniversary but not the date of their meeting. I doubted my brother knew it either.

'I've bought a red rose to place on his grave,' Mum said. 'Your father gave me a red rose on our first date, all those years ago.'

My eyes immediately filled as I pictured my darling mum going into the florist to buy a single red rose to put on my father's grave in memory of when they'd first met. He'd always given Mum a single red rose on their wedding anniversary, as well as other gifts, but I'd never appreciated the significance of it until now.

'That's lovely,' I said. 'Dad would appreciate that. We'll see you tomorrow then.'

'Yes, looking forward to it. Thanks, love.'

When I told Lucy, Paula and Adrian where I was going the following day and about the red rose they were as moved as I was.

'How wonderfully romantic,' Paula said. 'Grandpa loved Nana so very much.'

'He still does,' Lucy said. 'Death doesn't stop that kind of love.' Which made me tear up all the more.

Then Adrian shared something I hadn't previously known. 'Kirsty and I celebrated the anniversary of our first date. I took her out for a meal. I booked the table in secret and gave her some flowers. She said it was very thoughtful and the best surprise ever.'

'That's lovely,' I said, touched and proud of my son.

Anniversaries and other family celebrations are often diffi-cult in the years immediately after a loved one has passed, when their absence is even more obvious. I wrote the date my parents had first met in my diary, as I thought Mum would probably want to mark the day in future by taking a red rose to his grave. Now I knew I would always go with her if she wanted me to.

The following morning Adrian, Paula and Lucy left the house first, calling their goodbyes as they went, and then while Faye was getting ready I telephoned Becky. The call went through to her voicemail, so I left a message asking her to phone me when she was free. I said I needed to talk to her about Faye but that it wasn't an emergency. I then waited for Faye to finish getting ready. The time chart was still in place, although Faye seemed to be slowing down the bigger she got, so I had to make allowances and lightly chivvy her along. I'd already explained to Faye we were going to take my mother to visit my father's grave, and once in the car I told her that I'd left a message for Becky to phone me.

'And you'll tell her I'm keeping my baby.'

'I'll tell her what you've said, yes.'

'Good.'

Faye sat in the passenger seat with Snuggles on her lap without a care in the world, totally oblivious to the enormity of what she was now proposing and the worry her change of mind would cause to all involved. I'd had a restless night worrying, but Faye had slept like a log. As far as she was concerned, she wanted to keep her baby and that was that. If only it were that simple, which of course for Faye it was.

My mobile began to ring just as I pulled into Mum's driveway – it was Becky. 'Thanks for returning my call,' I said. Mum was at the front door and, seeing me with the phone to my ear, beckoned to Faye to go in. 'Just a second, Becky,' I said. Then to Faye, 'You go in with my mother and I'll be with you soon.'

'Tell Becky I want to keep my baby,' Faye said.

'What was that?' Becky asked.

'Here, you can tell her,' I said to Faye, and passed her the phone.

I gestured to Mum to go indoors and we'd be in when we'd finished on the phone. She disappeared inside and closed the door.

'I want to keep my baby,' Faye said to Becky. But that was all she said before handing the phone back to me. 'You tell her the rest,' she said, and jumped out of the car.

I put the phone to my ear again as Faye went up to the front door and pressed the bell.

'What's this about?' Becky asked. Mum opened the door and Faye went in.

'Faye says she has changed her mind about giving up her baby for adoption and now wants to keep it.'

'When did this happen?'

'The day before yesterday, after we'd been to the antenatal appointment. Although Faye said she'd been thinking about it for a while. I think that as we've been talking much more about her pregnancy, she's grown closer to the baby. It's all become more real to her, so she may have suddenly grasped the enormity of what she's giving up.'

'And she didn't before?' Becky asked. 'I discussed it with her.'

'I don't know. I've emphasized how difficult it is to look after a baby, but Faye now thinks I'm trying to stop her from keeping her baby. I've told her it's not my decision.'

'Has she told her grandparents she's changed her mind?'

'No. She's worried how they'll react. She doesn't want to upset them.'

'I need to talk to Faye,' Becky said. 'I'm up your way tomorrow afternoon. Could you be in around four o'clock?'

'Yes. Faye's seeing her grandparents in the day, but we'll be back then.'

'Thank you. Tell her I'll talk to her tomorrow, although I really don't know what else I can offer. Obviously Faye has the same rights as anyone else, but I don't see how she could parent a child without full-time help. Her grandparents can't offer that level of support, even if they were all moved to a bigger flat. There's nothing in the public sector. There just isn't the funding for the type of placement Faye would require, much as I wish there was. I'll talk to her tomorrow.'

'OK. I'll tell her you're coming.'

Becky hesitated before ending the call. 'Cathy, you've got to know Faye. I am right, aren't I? She couldn't manage the baby.'

'No. Faye is a lovely person, but she would need constant support. She does now, really.'

'Yes.'

We said goodbye and I returned my phone to my bag and let myself into Mum's house. I could hear Faye and Mum talking, and as I went into the living room I found them side by side on the sofa with a cup of tea and a biscuit, smiling and chatting like old friends.

'Is everything all right?' Mum asked.

'Yes. It was Faye's social worker.' Then to Faye I said, 'Becky is coming to see you tomorrow.' Faye didn't say anything.

'Shall I make you a coffee?' Mum asked, going to stand.

'No, I'll do it. You stay put.'

I went into the kitchen as Mum and Faye resumed chatting, now talking about the leaves that were blowing past the window. I wondered if Faye would tell Mum the reason for Becky's visit, but she didn't. When I returned with my coffee she was telling Mum about brushing the horses' manes and how the horses at the stables would be missing her. Perhaps she realized that the matter of her wanting to keep her baby might be upsetting for my mother, as it would be for her own grandparents. I helped myself to a biscuit and settled in a chair. Faye was very relaxed and comfortable chatting to someone my mother's age, even more so than talking to Adrian, Lucy and Paula, who were more her age and with whom she got on reasonably well. She asked Mum how her legs were, which made Mum and me smile. Mum said her legs were fine, thank you, and Faye said that was good, as her gran and grandpa suffered with their legs. Once we'd finished our drinks Mum suggested we went to the cemetery, as rain was forecast later. She fetched her coat and also the red rose, which she'd kept in the fridge so it would stay fresh. It was neatly wrapped in a cone of cellophane and tied with a small red-ribbon bow, similar to the one Dad would have given Mum on their first date and those he always gave her on their wedding anniversary. I was touched by its simple beauty and the love enshrined in that one small bloom. A first date, a romance, and a lifetime of happiness. It moved me deeply.

'That's a nice flower,' Faye said as she put on her coat.

'Thank you,' Mum said. 'My late husband gave me a rose like this on our first date, and for all our wedding anniversaries.'

'That was kind of him,' Faye said.

'Yes, love. He was a kind man,' Mum said.

'I used to put flowers on my mummy's grave,' Faye said. 'But we haven't been for a long time because of Gran's legs and Grandpa's stroke.'

I looked at her. 'I didn't know that. If you'd like to go, I can take you.'

'Yes, I'd like that. Can you ask Gran how we get there?'

'I will.'

The cemetery where Dad lay was about a fifteen-minute drive from Mum's house. Situated in a beautiful spot in the heart of the countryside, it was accessed through large patterned wrought-iron gates that were locked at night, and then down a long winding drive. There'd been a cemetery on this site for centuries and the inscriptions on the tombstones in the oldest part dated back to the 1700s. I parked the car in the area close to Dad's grave and cut the engine.

'Snuggles and I can wait in the car,' Faye said.

'Thank you. You'll be able to see us through the window.'

Mum and I got out. I linked arms with her and we began walking along the path towards the area that had been most recently dug. One of the groundsmen working in the immaculate gardens paused to say a polite good morning and then continued tending the flowerbeds of winter pansies. A chilly wind ran through the trees, sending a flurry of leaves to the ground. Despite the cold, an elderly gentleman sat on one of the benches, taking in the peace and tranquillity. He smiled and nodded as we passed.

Dad had been joined by others since his funeral; four fresh graves now lay in a line to the right of his. We hadn't decided on the finish of the grave yet, whether to plant bulbs and flowers, to have a vase for cut flowers or to cover the top with decorative stone chippings, as some had done. Mum was thinking about what she wanted to do, and then my brother and I would arrange it.

Mum stood at the edge of the grave and spoke to Dad just as if he was there. 'Hello, love. It's our anniversary. My turn to buy you a rose after all those years of you buying one for me.' My eyes filled.

She bent down and carefully laid the rose on the grave near the headstone, then, brushing away a couple of leaves, she straightened. We stood side by side in silence for some moments, our eyes down and concentrating on the grave as we thought of Dad. 'Much-loved and greatly missed husband and father', the engraving on the marble headstone read. The marble, as yet unweathered, shone brightly, as did the other stones around him that were recent.

'He was always there for us,' I said after a few moments.

'Yes. He was a good man. The best,' Mum said, her voice catching.

Another leaf blew onto the grave and I removed it. The grave didn't need tending in any other way, as it was too new for the surrounding grass to have encroached. I glanced over to the car to check on Faye and could just make her out, sitting as we'd left her in the back of the car and looking through the window.

Mum and I stood silently for a few moments longer, taking in the chance to be alone with our thoughts and close to Dad. Then the first drop of rain fell.

'It rained on our first date,' Mum said. 'Your dad had just given me the rose and the first drops fell. He'd brought an umbrella with him and we huddled together under it. He said later he was pleased it had rained, as it gave him an excuse to get close to me.' She smiled.

'It's a pity I didn't think to bring an umbrella with us,' I said as more drops fell.

'Best return to the car,' Mum said. Then, looking at the grave one last time, she added, 'Bye, love. Happy Anniversary.'

I took her arm and we walked at a slightly quicker pace back along the path. As we went Mum told me more about their first date, details I'd never known. 'Your dad wore his best suit,' she said with a smile. 'He did look smart. It was navy and he'd had it pressed especially. Dating was different then, more formal. We were both nervous and shy. We didn't even hold hands until the second date, and it was weeks before he kissed me.'

I smiled. 'Very different from now then.'

'Oh yes.'

As we climbed into the car Faye asked Mum if she'd had a nice time, which was obviously inappropriate, but Mum understood and said, 'Yes, thank you, dear. Have you been all right?'

'Yes. Snuggles and I could see you.'

We went to a country pub for lunch where I'd been before with my parents. You could sit outside to eat in the summer and there was a children's play area, but it was too chilly to eat out today. Mum and I helped Faye choose from the menu and then while we waited for our food we sipped our drinks and talked. Presently Mum nudged my arm and said quietly to me, 'Those two women over there are really staring.'

I looked over and saw immediately whom she meant. It was Faye they were staring at, and it was clear they were talking about her. As I met their gaze they quickly looked away. 'Just ignore it,' I said to Mum.

I'd noticed recently that now Faye was obviously pregnant she was attracting more stares, and some of them appeared judgemental, almost condemnatory, suggesting a comment along the lines of: *What's someone like her doing being pregnant?* When the two women looked again I was ready with my questioning raised eyebrow and they quickly looked away. I was used to fending off critical and intrusive looks when out with some of the children I'd fostered, especially if their behaviour was bizarre or they had a meltdown or tantrum in public. As a foster carer I'd learnt that there was no room for self-consciousness and I fended off unwanted stares and comments and protected the children, just as I did my own.

When we'd finished eating (Faye had a pudding while Mum and I had coffee) I took Mum home. The rain had stopped and the watery autumnal sun made a brave appearance. We stayed at Mum's for about an hour and then, mindful that Paula would be home soon, we said goodbye. It was still very difficult leaving Mum alone, although she assured me she was fine and would telephone either my brother or me if she needed help. As I reversed off the drive and Mum stood in the porch waving, I felt that same stab of sadness that Dad was no longer by her side.

'Your mum is nice,' Faye said, waving.

'Yes, she is,' I agreed. I pulled away.

'I think your dad was nice too.'

'Yes. Definitely.'

'My mum was nice. I wished I'd known my mum. It's sad when people die, isn't it?'

'Yes, it is. Very sad.' I blinked to clear my eyes and concentrated on the drive home.

CHAPTER TWELVE

'GOOD ENOUGH' PARENTING

Faye often expressed her thoughts as they occurred to her, just like a child would. There was no internal filter, which most adults acquire in order to screen a comment for its appropriateness of content or timing. The following morning I took Faye to her grandparents' for the day, and as soon as we walked into their living room, even before she had taken off her coat, she said, 'Cathy's going to take me to see Mummy. Can you tell her where she is?'

Little wonder Stan and Wilma looked surprised. 'What are you talking about, love?' Wilma asked, not unkindly. 'You know your mum's been dead for years.'

'Yes, but I want to see her like we used to.'

'You want to visit her grave?' Stan asked. Faye nodded. 'What's brought that on?' he said.

Faye looked to me to explain. 'Faye came with me yesterday when I took my mother to visit my father's grave,' I said. 'Faye said she used to visit her mother's grave but that you hadn't been for a while. I offered to take her, if that's all right with you.'

'I see,' Stan said thoughtfully. 'Yes, we did used to go regularly. Then all the buses became a bit much. I hadn't realized she wanted to go.'

'Perhaps you and Wilma would like to go too,' I suggested. 'I could fit you all in my car.'

'You don't want to be bothering with us,' Stan said. 'We're not the easiest bodies to move around, me relying on a stick and Wilma her walking frame.'

But then Wilma said, 'Cathy, if it's not too much trouble, I'd like to go, thank you.'

'Good.' I looked at Stan.

'Well, yes, if it's not too much trouble.'

'It's not,' I said. 'How about the day after tomorrow? I could bring Faye here at the usual time and we could go from then. I'll bring you back, of course.'

'Thank you,' Wilma said.

'If you're not in any rush afterwards, I could treat us all to a cake and a drink in the café,' Stan offered. 'It's not far from the entrance to the cemetery. We always used to go in there after we'd visited Mary's grave and before we caught the bus back.'

It was the first time I'd heard Faye's mother's name and suddenly she became that more real, a person.

'Stan, I've always got time for a cake and a coffee,' I said to him with a smile. 'That would be lovely. Thank you.'

'Good,' Wilma said. She was smiling broadly, clearly appreciating the outing. She didn't often smile and yet all it had taken was the thought of a visit to her daughter's grave and a drink and a cake in the café afterwards. I was very moved. This clearly meant a lot to her and Stan, who was now reminiscing about the delicious hot chocolate and home-made cakes they served in the café.

I said goodbye to Wilma and Faye, and Stan saw me to the front door. As he opened it he lightly touched my shoulder.

'Thanks, love,' he said quietly. 'You're a good person. Not many would go that extra mile. We greatly appreciate your kindness.' Embarrassingly, I teared up.

'You're very welcome,' I said.

The rest of the day vanished in a trip to the supermarket and a quick tidy of the house in preparation for Becky's visit later that afternoon. When I returned to collect Faye at three o'clock she was sitting in the living room with her coat and shoes on. 'She said Becky was coming to see her, so I thought best have her ready so you're not late,' Wilma said. 'What's she coming for?'

Faye looked at me a little guiltily. Clearly she hadn't told her grandparents the reason for Becky's visit, only that she was coming to see us.

'To talk about what happens after the birth,' I said, which wasn't a lie.

Wilma and Stan nodded. It was all they wanted to hear, and if Faye hadn't told them the reason – that she'd changed her mind and now wanted to keep the baby – it wasn't for me to tell them.

Confirming that I'd see them the day after tomorrow for our trip to the cemetery, I said goodbye and Faye kissed her gran. Stan came out with us to say goodbye and then waited in the corridor outside the flat until the elevator arrived, when he called another goodbye before returning inside. Once the elevator doors had closed Faye said, 'I'm glad you didn't tell them. Becky can tell them, then they won't be cross with me.'

'They'll have to know some time,' I said. This was typical of Faye. In her simplistic world, Becky would tell her grandparents that she was keeping her baby and magically

148

everything would be fine. Only of course it wouldn't, and if Becky couldn't persuade Faye to change her mind back again then her grandparents would have to be told. I could imagine how upset they'd be. They weren't in good health and they'd had a lot to cope with in the last few months: learning that Faye was pregnant and having to accept that adoption was the only practical solution. To then hear that Faye wanted to keep her baby (which would likely result in a court case) would cause them even more anguish and heartache. They seemed vulnerable and not at all robust, and I didn't doubt that the resulting stress would impact on their health.

Paula was home when Faye and I arrived. She'd had a tutorial that afternoon followed by private study. I asked her how it had gone and she said well, then I reminded her that Faye's social worker would be coming at four o'clock. Like any family that fosters, we were used to visits from social workers and meetings taking place in our home. The children knew that they weren't to disturb the social worker while she was with the child. Paula and Faye chatted for a while and then Paula went up to her room. Faye went into the living room where she sat on the sofa beside Sammy with Snuggles in her lap. She began petting the cat with her right hand while holding up her left so she could see her wristwatch, and she started counting off the minutes. She wasn't nervous, but sometimes she liked to show how well she could tell the time by counting down to an appointment. Four o'clock came and went and then at five minutes past four the doorbell rang. I showed Becky into the living room.

'You're five minutes late,' Faye declared, holding up her watch for Becky to see.

'Oh dear, that's not good,' Becky said indulgently, and went over for a closer look. 'You're right. I'll have to do better next time.'

Faye smiled, satisfied she'd been right.

I offered Becky a drink, but she didn't want one. 'Shall I leave you to talk to Faye alone?' I asked.

When I fostered children it was usual to give the social worker time alone with the child or young person so that they had the opportunity to discuss any issues they might not feel comfortable sharing in front of their foster carer. It's a slightly unsettling feeling to be shut out of a meeting in your own home, aware that they may be talking about you, but it's something foster carers have to get used to. However, in this instance Becky said, 'If Faye is happy, it would be easier if you stayed. You need to know the options.'

Faye nodded and I sat in one of the easy chairs as Becky took a notepad and pen from her bag, and then carefully looked at Faye, who kept her gaze down and concentrated on stroking Sammy.

'Faye,' Becky began, 'I need you to tell me what you've told Cathy, about what you would like to happen once your baby is born.'

'I want to keep it,' Faye said, pausing from stroking Sammy. 'I'm not going to give my baby to someone else.'

'Can you tell me why?' Becky asked, leaning forward slightly and trying to make eye contact. 'When we talked about this before we all agreed it would be best for you and your baby if I found a mummy and daddy to adopt it.'

'But I'm not giving them my baby now,' Faye said, her face setting. 'I've changed my mind.'

'What's changed your mind?' Becky asked.

Faye shrugged and then, taking her hand from the cat, said, 'It's my baby and I can keep it if I want to.'

'Faye, I know it's your baby,' Becky said patiently. 'But babies and young children need a lot of looking after. How would you look after the baby? Do you know?'

Faye was silent for a moment and then, looking at Becky for the first time, said, 'Cathy can teach me. I can learn. I learnt to tell the time and cook.'

'Yes, you did,' Becky said. 'And that's good. But looking after a small baby is very different. It's far more complicated and you can't afford to make mistakes or forget things.'

Faye was quiet again.

'Where would you live?' Becky continued patiently, trying to make Faye see the impossibility of the situation.

'I could stay here with Cathy,' Faye said.

'Permanently?' Becky asked. 'What about your gran and grandpa?'

'I could visit them, like I do now,' Faye replied, clearly having considered it. 'Cathy can take me in her car or I could go on the bus. I know which bus to catch now. I've learnt that.'

'Have you told your grandparents of your plans?' Becky asked gently.

Faye shook her head. 'You can tell them. They won't be annoyed with you.' My heart went out to her. She was so sincere, but unrealistic in her expectations.

Becky gave a small, sad smile. 'I'm afraid it's not possible for you to stay here with Cathy permanently,' she said. 'But you'll be here until you go into hospital to have the baby.' She paused and took a breath, as though gathering her thoughts. 'Faye, I've been talking to my manager and I'll be speaking to her again after I've seen you. We both feel that adoption is best for your baby, but if you're sure you want to try and look after it then it's possible I could arrange for you to stay in a specialist mother-and-baby unit. It's a special type of home and there will be other mothers staying there with their babies or young children. You each have your own room. There are staff there who are trained and on hand to help and advise you. They will also watch how you look after your baby, assess your parenting skills and then write a report. I will visit you as well, and then we will decide what is best for your baby.'

I was looking at Faye. Did she have any idea what Becky was talking about? That she was being given a chance to parent her baby and prove she was capable. I should have felt elated, but I didn't. No more elated than Becky, who'd just delivered this in a flat monotone voice, aware, as I was, that all this was going to do was delay the inevitable: that Faye would fail the parenting assessment and still have to part with her baby at the end of it.

'What do you think?' Becky asked. 'You'll have your baby with you and you'll look after it in the home for about six months.'

'I want to stay here,' Faye said. 'Cathy can help me.'

'It's not just about helping you,' Becky said gently. 'The staff at the home will assess you too. To see if you can meet the needs of the baby.'

'Cathy can assess me,' Faye said.

Foster carers do sometimes play a role in assessing a child, young person or even a mother with a baby or child. I'd had to do this with Jade (whose story I tell in *Please Don't Take My Baby*), but that was very different. Jade didn't have learning difficulties and had stood a reasonable chance of being able to keep her baby if she changed her lifestyle and acquired the right parenting skills. But even then I'd felt uncomfortable assessing her and had helped her too much, so in the end she'd gone to a mother-and-baby unit, although not the same one that Becky had in mind for Faye.

I was relieved, therefore, when Becky said, 'Faye, you can stay here with Cathy until you go into hospital to have your baby, and then you will need to go to the mother-and-baby unit. While you are here, Cathy will continue to help prepare you for the birth and she can also teach you some parenting skills, but after the birth you will have to go to the mother-and-baby unit. Places are limited, so you will need to tell me if this is what you want. Then I'll discuss it further with my manager and apply for a place for you. There's only a little over seven weeks before your due date.'

'Will you tell my gran?' Faye asked, still more worried about what her gran would say than the enormity of the decision before her.

'Yes. I can tell your grandparents if you decide you want to go to the mother-and-baby unit,' Becky said.

'I do,' Faye said.

Becky looked at her carefully. 'Faye, you understand the choices here, don't you? You could give up your baby for adoption after you've had it at the hospital, and then return to your gran and grandpa to live. Or you can go to the mother-and-baby unit?'

'Then can I come back here with my baby?' Faye asked, confused.

'No, love,' Becky said. 'At the end of the six months we will make a decision on what is best for the baby long term. It's possible we will decide it would be better for it to be adopted.'

Faye fell silent, her face unreadable. Who knew what she was thinking? Becky had explained the options and she now gave her a few moments to consider what she'd said, before she asked, 'What do you think, Faye? You have the right to decide what you want to do. We've found a lovely couple to adopt your baby, or do you want to go to the mother-and-baby unit?'

'Baby unit,' Faye said.

Becky nodded and, opening her notepad, began writing. 'OK. I'll speak to my manager, then I'll phone you later in the week.'

'Will you tell Gran and Grandpa?' Faye asked again.

'Yes. Once I've spoken to my manager,' Becky said. 'Is there anything else you want to ask me?'

Faye shook her head.

'If Faye goes to the mother-and-baby unit, will I be able to visit her?' I asked.

'Yes, if Faye wants you to, which I assume she will do.' She glanced at Faye, but she was deep in thought. 'It's about a forty-five-minute drive from here. I'm not sure how practical it will be for Stan and Wilma to get there,' she added.

'Possibly I could give them a lift in my car,' I suggested. 'I'm taking them to the cemetery the day after tomorrow.' I then explained to Becky that Faye had wanted to visit her mother's grave and that I'd offered to take her grandparents too. I also mentioned that I'd begun giving Faye a lift in my car when she visited her grandparents, rather than her using the bus, and why.

'That seems sensible,' Becky said. 'Thank you.' Then, looking at Faye, she asked, 'Is there anything else you want to ask me?' Faye shook her head. 'Well, if you think of anything, you can telephone me or ask Cathy.' She put away her note-pad and pen. 'I'll be in touch later in the week. Goodbye then, Faye. Take care.'

'Goodbye,' Faye said.

As I saw Becky to the front door she said, 'I have to give her the chance, as she's asked, but Stan and Wilma are going to be upset. So will the adoptive parents. They were expecting this baby as much as Faye, and this is the second time they've been let down at the last moment. They're a lovely couple in their mid-thirties who can't have children. They're going to be devastated.'

I nodded. This was a side of adoption that is little considered: the childless couple who will have gone through years of fertility testing and treatment to finally be told they will never conceive a child. Then comes the painful acceptance, the soul-searching decision to apply for adoption, the long and gruelling assessment to be considered as adoptive parents and, at last, the heart-stopping elation of being approved. Then another long wait until an infant is matched with them and the jubilation of that call – their prayers have finally been answered and they will soon be parents. Followed by the devastating news that it's off, the baby is no longer theirs – not once, but twice.

'The nursery is ready,' Becky added as she opened the front door. 'It's beautiful. The baby would be so loved and wanted. Now someone has to tell them it's not going to happen. And sadly I fear Faye's parenting assessment will only tell us what we already know, although I'd like nothing more than to be proven wrong.'

* * *

Foster carers worry about the children and young people they look after just as most parents worry about their children. Sometimes we worry more about them than we would our own. As a parent you know you've given your child the best start in life and have equipped them with the skills to make appropriate decisions and to meet challenges. But Faye, because of her learning disability and despite her grandparents' best efforts, remained ill equipped for life's challenges and certainly not for parenting. She was naïve, vulnerable and relied heavily on others. I could see she was going to be badly hurt and I worried about her on and off for the rest of the evening and most of the night. Tossing and turning through to the early hours, I heard her get up to use the toilet twice and then return to bed. Would it be possible for her to learn the skills necessary to parent a baby? I doubted it as much as Becky did, and she'd had plenty of experience of working with adults with learning disabilities. If Faye went to the specialist mother-and-baby unit, how would she feel at the end of the six-month assessment? Would she realize and accept that she couldn't parent her child and therefore feel adoption was the best outcome? Or, having bonded with her baby, would she be even more upset and unwilling to part with it? I'd been slightly surprised that Becky had made the offer of the specialist mother-and-baby unit. Social services' budgets are tight and to fund this type of placement would be expensive. Hardly money well spent if the prognosis for Faye being able to keep her baby at the end of it was so very poor.

But was it feasible to change that prognosis? I wondered as the hours towards morning passed. Faye would receive help and support from the staff at the unit, but would it be enough to change the outcome? She also had seven weeks left with me. What could I teach her in that time? Enough to give her a chance of keeping her baby? I doubted it, but I had to try. Assuming that when Becky phoned she would confirm that Faye was to be given the chance to go to the unit, I would do everything in my power to teach Faye how to look after a baby. If Faye wanted to keep it enough then perhaps this would accelerate her learning and she could understand and retain what was needed to pass the parenting assessment. But what *was* needed? What were the criteria for assessing a parent? What goal posts were we aiming for?

It was not yet 6.00 a.m. but while the rest of the house slept I slipped on my dressing gown and went downstairs and switched on the laptop. I left it in the living room to boot up while I made a large mug of coffee and gave Sammy an early breakfast. He meowed a thank-you. I took the mug of coffee into the living room, set it on the corner table within my reach and brought up the search engine on the computer. I typed in *social services parenting assessment criteria* and up came a page of links to articles and to some of the specialist family centres. I began reading and five minutes later I'd found exactly what I wanted: the criteria used by social workers when assessing what I now learnt was known as 'good enough' parenting. 'Good enough'. I liked the term and felt a surge of optimism. Not perfect – no parenting is perfect, regardless of how hard we try – but 'good enough', adequate. I felt we were in with a chance and I read on.

'Good enough' parenting essentially requires meeting the child's health and developmental needs, putting the child's needs first, and providing routine and care. As well as giving basic care, it includes keeping the child safe, providing emotional warmth, stimulation, guidance, boundaries and stability. The assessment took into account the parent's ability to ask for support where necessary, and wider factors such as family circumstances, income, education, housing, employment and own upbringing. Then I found a few paragraphs specifically on assessing parents with learning difficulties, and it said that when a parent with a learning disability neglected their baby or child it was usually as a result of them forgetting to do something, rather than intentionally harming the child, which made sense and resonated with me in respect of Faye. It warned professionals against presuming incompetence (that is, assuming the parent wouldn't be able to adequately parent purely because they had a learning difficulty), which could result in their strengths being overlooked. It said that the parent's disability should be identified within the assessment but must not be the overriding factor. Other factors that should be noted were the parent's early childhood experiences (which could affect their own parenting); the parent's ability to learn and retain new information; to be able to assess and respond to changes; to prioritize the needs of others and themselves, and to be able to communicate adequately. It said that it was unlawful for a social worker to remove a child from a parent purely on the grounds of the parent's learning disability. The decision had to be based on whether the parent could meet the needs of the child and provide 'good enough' parenting.

There was a lot to take in. Faye could communicate to a reasonable level and I felt sure it would be adequate, but whether she could process and retain information to the required standard to parent a child I wasn't sure. But I was now completely committed to doing all I could to help her. Lowering the lid on the laptop, I drained the last of my now-cold coffee and, deep in thought, went upstairs to shower and dress. I wouldn't say anything about what I'd learnt to Faye until we'd heard from Becky that she would definitely be going to the specialist unit. I knew from experience that decisions can and do change in social work. This wouldn't just be Becky's decision but that of the adult social services team responsible for Faye.

CHAPTER THIRTEEN

A SENSE OF OCCASION

It was pouring with rain the following morning, so Faye and I didn't go to see the horses as we'd planned but stayed indoors. After breakfast and once she was dressed I took the opportunity to explain more to her about her developing baby and reinforce what I'd already told her. I used the children's book I'd used before and also the internet, although much of the writing on the webpages required a level of reading far in advance of Faye's. I'd tried to find a website especially for parents who had leaning difficulties, but there was nothing. Some websites made reference to the problems that adults with learning difficulties faced when trying to parent, but none actually addressed the issues. However, the diagrams and pictures on the general parenting websites were useful and some showed what the developing baby looked like in the womb. I read out that at thirty-one weeks gestation, which was the stage Faye was at, the baby weighed approximately 1.5kg and measured about 40cm from the top of its head to its toe. I showed her on my arm roughly how long this was – from my elbow to the tip of my finger. We could see from the pictures that the baby's arms, legs and body had filled out and were now in proportion to its head, so it no longer looked like a foetus but a newborn baby. We learnt that it wouldn't be moving around so much now, but that if Faye ever noticed it had stopped moving then she needed to tell me straight away so we could see the doctor for a check-up. Faye pulled a face when I read out that the baby was now passing small drops of urine, practising for when it was born.

The weather was still poor in the afternoon and Faye asked if we could go to the cinema. Adrian had mentioned at the weekend that he'd been to see the new James Bond film and Faye said she wanted to see it, as she liked James Bond films. She told me she had been to the cinema before, but not for a long time, because her gran and grandpa found the seats too uncomfortable and had difficulty getting in and out, and up and down the steps. She brought her purse with her, as she wanted to buy herself some popcorn, which she remembered doing before at the cinema. The little bright-red zip purse she clutched contained her pocket money, which her gran topped up as and when necessary from the state allowance she received.

I paid for us to go in and Faye bought her popcorn. I helped her count out the money from the coins she had in her purse; it took a while. The cashier was patient, appreciating that Faye was struggling, but it made me realize how difficult it would be for Faye if she ever had to cope alone. She had no experience of managing money beyond a bit of pocket money. Would she ever cope with a household budget? I doubted it. So what would happen if she passed the parenting assessment? How would she manage living independently, just her and the baby? Unless she returned to live with her grandparents, but was that feasible? Then I caught myself worrying about the what-ifs of her as-yet-undecided future and drew back. One stage at a time. Faye had yet to have her baby and go to the specialist unit and attempt to pass the parenting assessment.

Faye loved the film – the noise, music and action – nearly as much as she loved the popcorn. She ate slowly and consistently throughout the film, taking one piece of popcorn out of the box at a time. Having eaten the last husk from the box, she wanted to buy some more, but I said it would spoil her appetite for dinner. I also wondered about the effect all that popcorn was having on her baby, as everything a mother eats or drinks passes through the umbilical cord to her baby. I explained this to Faye and she accepted that she'd had enough for one day. As we were leaving the cinema a well-meaning woman glanced at Faye's bump and said to her, 'It won't be long, love, before you're bringing your little one to see the films.'

Faye paused and then replied, 'If my social worker lets me keep it.' While the woman looked uncomfortable, I was relieved that Faye had understood at least some of what Becky had told her and that keeping her baby wasn't definite.

That evening just the girls and I were in for dinner, as Adrian was working a late shift. Faye told them she'd been to the cinema and what a nice time she'd had.

'All right for some,' Lucy replied a little tartly. 'Some of us have to go to work.' They were short-staffed at the nursery where Lucy worked and she hadn't had a lunch break so wasn't in the best of moods.

Faye went quiet for a moment and I hoped she hadn't taken Lucy's comment personally. Faye never made sarcastic retorts like that to anyone, it wasn't in her nature. After a moment, looking at Lucy, she said, 'You are so lucky being able to go to work. I wish I could, but no one wants someone like me.' It was so sincere and heartfelt, I knew Lucy felt her words as much as I did.

The following day I was pleased that the rain had stopped for our visit to the cemetery where Faye's mother rested. I dressed casually but smartly in light-grey trousers and jumper and a navy coat. Faye was dressed smartly, too, in black leggings and a royal-blue maternity top we'd bought her, and carried her coat to the car. On the way she wanted to stop to buy some flowers to place on her mother's grave. She said there was a man selling flowers at the gate of the cemetery but her gran never bought them from him as they were too expensive. I stopped at a petrol station and helped her choose a bunch of flowers. I hadn't heard any more from Becky, so I didn't know what, if anything, the grandparents had been told about the possibility of Faye going to the mother-and-baby unit. However, when we arrived at their flat they greeted us warmly and unreservedly, so I assumed they hadn't yet been told. They were ready and dressed in their Sunday best. Stan was wearing a suit and tie and Wilma a floral-pattern winter dress under a black coat. Stan had his walking stick at his side and Wilma her walking frame.

'You do look smart,' I said.

'Well, it's not every day I get the chance to take three young ladies out to lunch,' Stan said. Wilma smiled and touched her hair into place. I could see just how much this outing meant to them. It wasn't just going to visit their daughter's grave; it had become an occasion, they so rarely went out. But it soon became evident just what an effort it was for them to leave the flat.

Using his walking stick, Stan went out of the living room first, followed by Wilma with her walking frame. She had a carrier bag containing a bunch of flowers looped over one of the handles of the frame and her handbag over the other. As she went through the doorframe one of the flowers caught against the wood and a bloom fell off. She tutted. I offered to carry the bag, as did Stan, but, independent, she brushed off our help and transferred the bag to her hand. Then she struggled to manoeuvre the walking frame out through the front door and eventually, with a sigh of frustration, she passed the carrier bag to Faye and we all left.

I closed the door behind us and Wilma wanted to deadlock it. She slipped her handbag from her walking frame and took a moment to open the clasp, her arthritic hands clumsy and not doing what she wanted them to. I could see her frustration. Having opened her handbag, she spent more time grappling with the contents before she found the key and then locked the door. It would have been easier if one of us had done it, but it was clear that Wilma needed this independence and considered it her responsibility. Stan, clearly aware of this, was waiting patiently by the elevator and didn't press the button for it to come until we approached. Wilma walked slowly, evidently in pain, and I could see why she moved around the flat as little as possible. I knew she was waiting for an operation to replace one knee and hip joint, but I had no idea to what extent that would help her general mobility. Her whole body seemed very stiff.

The elevator arrived and Stan kept his hand on the open door to stop it from closing while we all got in. Wilma first, then Faye and me, and lastly Stan.

'We're on our way,' he said brightly to Wilma with a wink as the doors closed behind us.

'We certainly are,' she said, smiling, despite the pain she was in.

'I've bought flowers for Mummy,' Faye said. 'They're in the car.'

'Good girl,' Stan said.

'Our neighbour got ours,' Wilma said to me. 'She's good like that. She's always popping in to see if we need anything before she goes shopping.'

The elevator stopped at the third floor, but the two teenage girls who were waiting there decided they'd let it go rather than try to squash in with us. At the ground floor Stan again kept his hand on the door while we all got out. 'Are you fit, love?' he asked Wilma, meaning was she managing all right.

'I am, love,' she said happily. It was lovely to see them out together and enjoying themselves.

I'd parked as close as I could to the flats, but even then it was a difficult walk for Wilma. Stan seemed to manage better with his stick, although it was obvious his left side was still weak from the stroke. I unlocked the car doors and it was decided that Wilma would sit in the front. Using her frame for support, she slowly eased herself down into the passenger seat and then lifted in her legs. I took the walking frame and the carrier bag and stowed them in the boot. The frame just fitted in. Wilma said that as well as the flowers the bag contained a gardening trowel, cloth and a pair of scissors to tend the grave.

I helped Stan into a back seat and he kept his stick with him. Faye sat beside him, her flowers on her lap. She'd left Snuggles on her bed at home. Stan then gave me instructions on the most direct route to the cemetery – a different cemetery to the one where my father lay. In between giving me instructions he made light conversation.

'It's a while since we've been this far,' he said to Wilma.

'Yes, must be two years. Quite an expedition for us.' She chuckled.

'I wonder what state we'll find her memorial stone in. It'll need a clean.'

'It will. Although the council will have mown the grass.'

Faye listened and then joined in, very comfortable with their familiar and easy everyday conversation.

As I drove in through the main gates of the cemetery I saw the flower seller Faye had mentioned, and Stan gave me instructions on where to park – the parking bays closest to Mary's grave. As it was a weekday there were plenty of spaces. I took the walking frame from the boot and then opened the passenger door and stood it ready for Wilma. It was even more of a struggle for her (and Stan) to get out of the car than it had been to get in, as they had to heave themselves into a standing position. I helped Wilma as Faye helped her grandpa, and they accomplished it in stages: swivelling their legs round and out, and then straightening up using their walking aids. Once standing, it took Wilma a few moments to get her balance, then I passed her handbag and carrier bag to her, which she hooked over the handlebars of the walking frame, and we all began along the path in the direction Stan pointed. The day was bright but the wind cold, and Wilma paused to do up her coat. 'Don't want to be catching a chill,' she said. Stan agreed, and then helped her fasten the buttons that her arthritic fingers couldn't manage. It was touching to see, and the type of thoughtful act my father would have done for my mother.

It was only about fifty metres to Mary's grave, but it took us some time and I recognized this was probably as far as Wilma could walk; any further and she would have needed a wheelchair. Mary had been cremated, so there was no grave as such but a marble memorial stone over the spot where her ashes were buried. As Wilma had predicted the main grass had been cut, but the memorial stone needed wiping clean and the edges of the grass trimming; this and the empty vase at one corner of the stone made the grave look slightly unkempt.

'We used to bring fresh flowers every week,' Wilma said a little sadly, and Stan and Faye agreed.

It was obvious that neither Stan nor Wilma could kneel or bend to tend the grave, so I said that if they told me what they'd like to do, I'd see to it.

'Thank you,' Wilma said. 'Could you rinse the vase out and fill it with fresh water? The tap is over there.' She pointed. 'And if you wet this cloth, we can use it to wipe the stone.' She took the cloth from her carrier bag.

Faye came with me to the tap and together we washed and filled the vase and then wrung out the cloth. Returning to the grave, I wiped the marble clean as Stan held the vase and Wilma and Faye arranged their flowers in it. Now the stone was clear, the inscription became visible:

No pain, no grief, no anxious fear
can reach our loved one sleeping here.
Mary, darling daughter of Stan and Wilma
and beloved mother of Faye.

Beneath the inscription were the dates of her birth and death. I was deeply moved. Mary had only been twenty-five when she'd died, a year older than Faye was now. I felt the words – no pain, grief or fear – probably referred to her illness and the years of suffering when she'd battled with alcoholism. How very sad. What a dreadful waste of a life and what a huge strain it must have put on Stan and Wilma. Who knew what Mary might have achieved without the ravages of alcohol addiction, the legacy of which – foetal alcohol syndrome – would remain with Faye forever.

I used the scissors Wilma passed to me to trim the edges of the grass and then, following her instructions, I used the trowel to dig back the edges of the turf so that a little soil frame was created around the stone, which Wilma said would slow the grass growing over. This was how she'd tended the grave when they'd come to the cemetery regularly. It looked so much better already. Then, under Wilma's guidance, Faye carefully set the vase full of flowers into its holder. They looked lovely.

'Job well done,' Stan said, stepping back to admire the finished effect.

We all stood for a moment, looking down at the stone in respectful silence. Then Wilma said, a little embarrassed, 'Cathy, I hope you don't mind but I usually say a short prayer before we leave.'

'Of course not,' I said. I lowered my gaze.

Wilma, Stan and Faye closed their eyes and stood with heads bowed and hands folded loosely before them, as Wilma said: 'Mary, until we meet again, may God hold you in the palm of his hand and keep you safe. God bless you, love. You are in our hearts forever.'

Simple words yet touching, and I felt drawn into their loss and sorrow.

'Amen,' I joined in with them at the end. We stood for a moment in quiet contemplation and then raised our heads.

'God bless,' Stan said before turning. We began slowly back to the car.

Once in the car Stan gave me instructions to the café, which I thought I'd spotted on the way in: out of the cemetery, turn right and about 200 yards on the left. Fortunately there was room in the small car park or I would have had to drop them off and park elsewhere. I took the walking frame from the boot and once again Faye and I helped them out of the car. I had never been in this café before, although I'd passed it a number of times. It was a typical English tea room, selling light lunches and afternoon teas that included a selection of sandwiches, homemade cakes and scones.

Once settled at a table, Stan gave the menu only a cursory glance, then looked at his watch and declared, 'Lunchtime. I'm having the all-day breakfast.'

'Me too,' Wilma said. So I guessed this was what they used to have when they visited the cemetery regularly.

Faye spent some time studying the menu and then asked her gran if they still did the jacket potato with beans and cheese. Wilma said they did and pointed it out on the menu. I ordered a toasted cheese sandwich, despite Stan protesting that I should have something 'more filling'. As we waited for the food to arrive we made light conversation and Stan and Wilma asked me about my family and how my mother was. They said Faye often mentioned her. They were also keen to know about fostering, as many people are. Although I'd seen Wilma and Stan regularly when I'd taken Faye to their flat and collected her, we'd never really had a proper chat. Some parents of the children and young people I fostered I got to know well, others not so, and a few I never met for my own security and protection. Yet despite our conversation, which continued as we ate, the one subject that didn't come up was Faye's pregnancy, although it was now very obvious. She had to sit a little back from the table to accommodate her bump and often rested her hands on it or rubbed it if the baby moved or she felt uncomfortable. I saw Wilma glance at it, but she didn't comment. I knew that their way of coping was to ignore the pregnancy as they had been doing. And of course at present, as far as they were concerned, the care plan was still for Faye to return home to them once she had given birth and for the baby to be adopted. They needed to be told of the new developments soon.

The food was delicious and the portions very generous. Once we'd finished, Stan asked if anyone wanted a pudding or cake, but none of us could manage one. When the bill arrived I offered to pay my share, but Stan wouldn't hear of it. I thanked them both and said how much I'd enjoyed it, and that I appreciated being treated, for as a single parent it usually fell to me to organize and treat my family, so this made a very pleasant change. Stan smiled and seemed to grow with my thanks. I could see how much my gratitude meant to him; he was such a dear, kind man.

We returned to the car and I drove to their block of flats. Stan and Wilma said that I needn't go up in the lift with them but to drop them off in the car park, which was where the community transport collected and dropped them when they had a hospital appointment. As it was two o'clock, they said Faye should come back with me rather than go in just for an hour, and they'd see her again the day after tomorrow. Faye and I helped them out of the car and then watched as they made their way along the path to the entrance of the flats. Before they went in they turned and waved. Faye and I waved back.

'We've all had a nice day,' Faye said as we returned to the car. 'I like it when my gran and grandpa are happy.'

'Yes, it all worked out very well,' I said.

Faye was silent for a moment and then, as I started the car's engine, she said, 'When will Becky tell them I've changed my mind about the baby?' So I guessed she'd been thinking about that too.

'As soon as she knows for sure that you will be going to the mother-and-baby unit,' I said. 'It shouldn't be long.'

Indeed, it wasn't long, for half an hour after we returned home Becky telephoned.

CHAPTER FOURTEEN

UNETHICAL

Becky said straight away that it had been decided that Faye and her baby could go to the specialist mother-and-baby home, and I could tell her. She said she would telephone Wilma and Stan, and then arrange a short meeting – a review – probably at their flat, as the care plan had changed. She'd advise me of the date. Becky finished by asking how Faye was and I told her briefly of our day out. We said goodbye and I replaced the handset, my thoughts buzzing, partly from joy that Faye was being given the chance to keep her baby, but also at the prospect of how much Faye had to learn in a relatively short time. A list immediately formed in my head, like revision topics for an examination: feeding baby – bottles/breast; keeping baby clean – bathing/changing nappies; how to hold a baby – supporting its head; answering its cries; interacting with and stimulating the baby, and so on and so forth, all of which were crucial for parenting and would be observed and assessed at the mother-and-baby unit.

Faye was in the living room – we were the only ones home – and I went in. She was sitting comfortably on the sofa, stroking Sammy who was curled on her lap and enjoying the attention. Sammy had really taken to Faye and now spent more time on her lap or rubbing against her legs than anyone else's. They both looked very content, and perversely it crossed my mind that when Faye had her baby and it began to cry, would she put the cat aside and answer her baby's cries or would she continue stroking the cat? I honestly didn't know.

'Faye, that was Becky on the telephone,' I said as I sat beside her on the sofa. 'She said to tell you that you can go to the mother-and-baby home if that is what you'd like.'

'And I can keep my baby?' she asked, without looking up from Sammy.

'Yes. While you are at the home.' I couldn't promise her any more than that.

'That's good,' she said with a small smile and continued to stroke the cat. 'But I don't want to go there now.'

'No. You go after you've had your baby. In about seven weeks.' I often had to repeat and clarify points. It was part of Faye's learning difficulties that she couldn't process and retain information as other adults could. I watched her stroking Sammy, relaxed and without a care in the world.

'Faye, we've got a lot to learn about how to look after a baby. I'm going to teach you as much as possible so that you stand the best chance of being able to keep your baby long term, all right?'

'Yes.' Sammy opened one eye and gazed at her before closing it again.

'We could start now,' I said. 'Before I make dinner.'

'Yes. After dinner I watch television.'

Not once you've had the baby, I thought, but didn't say. 'So, let's start by you telling me what you know. What do you think are the most important things about looking after a baby?' I wasn't trying to catch her out; I just wanted to see how much she knew.

'Giving it food,' she said, glancing at me.

'Good. What sort of food. Do you know?'

She shrugged.

'Babies have milk, don't they?'

'Oh yes. Do they have it on cornflakes?' She was serious. Faye liked cornflakes and had lots of milk and sugar on them for breakfast, so I could see why she'd made this connection.

'No. To begin with all babies have is milk. They don't have teeth to chew with, and their stomachs can't digest anything other than milk for at least four months. So all they have is milk, but it's not the same milk that we have. Do you know where their milk comes from?'

'A bottle,' Faye said. 'I've seen babies with bottles.'

'Yes, babies can have milk from a bottle, that's right. The milk in it is called formula and you buy it from a chemist or supermarket. But babies can be breastfed too.' Her eyes rounded in astonishment. I didn't lose heart. This was new to her. She'd grasped a fair bit of what I'd told her about her baby's development and birth, but I hadn't gone beyond that because she hadn't been going to keep her baby.

I reached for the laptop and googled breastfeeding. Up came pages of information and a short video clip. I pressed play to start the video clip, which showed a mother breast-feeding her baby with a background commentary about the benefits of breastfeeding. Faye couldn't have understood much of the commentary, as it was spoken too quickly and the terms used were too complex, but she could see the baby suckling at the mother's breast.

'Oh, I remember,' she said. 'I saw a woman doing that on television and she got told off.' Then she explained that a character in one of the soaps she watched regularly had been told off for breastfeeding in a bar.

'You don't have to worry about breastfeeding in a bar,' I said. 'You won't be doing that. But a mother's milk is very good for her baby, and the midwife at the hospital will teach you how to breastfeed.' For as any mother knows, establishing breastfeeding is not as simple as it first appears, and a patient midwife is invaluable at the start. 'Some mothers find they can't breastfeed,' I said. 'So they use bottles. Some do both, breast and bottle. We will need to buy a set of bottles for your baby, formula and a sterilizer,' I said, thinking aloud. 'You'll also need nappies, creams, lotions, a thermometer, first-size baby clothes, vests, a shawl, a warm suit for outdoors. You won't need a crib as the mother-and-baby home will have one, but you may need a stroller. I'll have to ask Becky what you need.'

I reached for the notepad and pen I kept by the phone and jotted down these items while I thought of them, and also a note to remind me to ask Becky what we needed to buy. Faye had stopped stroking Sammy and was now looking at me a little concerned. 'Don't worry,' I said. 'We've got plenty of time to buy what we need. It'll be fun going shopping again.' She smiled. But I knew I mustn't overload her with too much information and also that I needed to make learning fun, for her ability to grasp the basics of parenting was as important, if not more so, than choosing the right clothes for her baby. It was then I thought of using a doll and the toy feeding bottle I kept in the games cupboard. I had stored games and toys for all ages of children, and the bottle I had in mind was a favourite.

* * *

Five minutes later, instead of having Sammy on her lap, Faye had the baby doll cradled in her arm. It had a soft, floppy body so was quite realistic. She was feeding it with the toy bottle containing pretend milk – also realistic. As the bottle was tilted it appeared to empty, as though the doll was drinking the milk, and then it refilled once upright. I didn't need to explain to Faye that a real bottle of milk wouldn't automatically refill – she appreciated that this was a (realistic) toy – but I did have to show her how to hold the 'baby'. Faye's movements were sometimes uncoordinated and clumsy, which wasn't conducive to holding a baby. I placed the doll carefully in her arms and explained how gentle we had to be when handling a baby, although of course she couldn't control her lack of coordination; it was part of her condition. She did well, though, and was incredibly gentle when holding and feeding the 'baby'. Sammy, who was now sitting beside her on the sofa, looked on, interested. At one point Faye paused from feeding the baby and pushed its head under Sammy's nose so he could sniff it.

'You wouldn't do that with a real baby,' I said, and Faye laughed.

The front door opened as Paula returned home from college.

'We're in here,' I called from the living room.

'Hi,' she returned.

She came to the living-room door and smiled when she saw Faye with the bottle and the baby doll. 'I used to love playing with that bottle,' she said.

'I'm feeding my baby,' Faye said proudly.

'She's practising,' I said.

I then went out of the room to explain to Paula that the decision had been made that after the birth Faye would be going to a mother-and-baby unit and would be given the chance to keep her baby, so I was teaching her all I could. Paula then told me about a decision she'd had to make at college regarding a choice of subjects for an extended essay. We chatted for a few minutes and when I returned to the living room Faye was still holding and feeding the doll. I said that baby had probably had enough food now and needed winding. I carefully sat the doll upright on my lap and showed Faye how to support its head while gently massaging its back to release trapped wind. I didn't expect Faye to remember all of what I was showing or telling her. I knew I'd have to repeat it often, but it was a start.

Once the baby was winded, I showed Faye how to change the doll's nappy. It was just like the real thing, only it had Velcro tabs to fasten it so it could be reused, rather than the sticky tabs of real nappies. Faye thought this was great fun and put the nappy on and took it off quite a few times.

'I'll show you how to clean a baby's bottom another time,' I said. 'We need cotton wool and warm water, and also some cream.'

She put the nappy on one more time and then cradled the doll in her arms while I went to start making the dinner. Ten minutes later Lucy arrived home and came straight into the kitchen to pour herself a glass of water. I told her about the change of plans for Faye and that she was being given the chance to keep her baby. Like Paula, Lucy didn't comment, and I guessed they both shared my concerns that Faye had an awful lot of learning to do to get anywhere near the level that was required to parent a child.

Lucy went into the living room to say hi to Faye and I heard her ask what the baby was called.

'Snuggles,' Faye said.

'No, I mean, have you thought of a name for your baby?' Lucy asked.

'Snuggles,' she said again.

Lucy, tired from a day at work, lost interest and went up to her room to relax and listen to music until dinner was ready. When Adrian arrived home just before six o'clock, I told him, as I'd told Lucy and Paula, of the new plans for Faye. It is important in fostering that all family members are aware of important changes to a young person's care plan so that no one inadvertently says something inappropriate, and also so that we can all help them achieve the best possible outcome while they are with us. Fostering involves the whole family, not just the main care giver.

'I guess that's good news then,' Adrian said. 'But what will happen at the end of the six months if it doesn't work out?'

'The social services will apply to court to have the child freed for adoption,' I said. 'But I'm trying not to think of that. Faye can learn. It just takes her longer.'

He nodded thoughtfully and then went to shower and change, as he was going out after dinner.

Faye didn't want to be separated from the doll when it was dinnertime and brought it with her to the table, and kept it tucked on her lap. With her bump in the way and her lack of coordination, it wasn't long before gravy splashed on the doll. As I wiped it off I took the opportunity to say that it wasn't a good idea to have a real baby at the table for this very reason – that hot food and drink could be accidentally spilt on it, and a baby's skin is very delicate. I said there was a doll's crib in the loft and I'd fetch it down after dinner, so she'd have somewhere comfortable and safe to leave the baby when she wasn't holding it, just as a mother would with a real baby. I stored some larger toys in the loft and brought them down as and when they were needed by the children we fostered, as there simply wasn't enough room in the house for all the toys I'd collected over the years. There was also a doll's pram in the loft, but that would be far too small for Faye to practise with.

After dinner Adrian went into the loft for me and brought down the doll's crib, which I'd wrapped in a large bin bag to protect it from dust. It was already made up with a complete set of bed linen, and I put it in the living room where Faye was. She loved it and spent the next half an hour playing: putting the doll to bed, picking it up, feeding and changing it and then putting it to bed again, all of which seemed very positive. Children and adults learn through play. She then placed the crib beside her while she watched television, left it there while she had a bath, and then returned to the sofa in her dressing gown to watch more television.

'Faye,' I said gently. 'You do realize that if that was a real baby it would be crying to be fed every two to three hours. You've been able to eat dinner, watch television, have your bath and then watch more television without being disturbed. That wouldn't happen with a real baby. You would have fed and changed it at least twice during the evening. And it might have taken a while to resettle, so you will have missed some of your programme.' She needed to know the reality.

She smiled amicably and I don't think she had the least idea of the point I was making. 'A baby demands a lot of attention and its needs always come first,' I added.

She smiled again and returned to the television. Again, I thought we could have done with one of those life-size electronic baby-simulator dolls that are programmed to cry every few hours and react to external stimuli. They're used in teaching situations and can't be switched off. They record if the baby's needs are being met, how it's handled and how long it's left unattended. But I didn't force the issue. Faye was happy and we'd covered a lot during the first day.

When it was nine o'clock she wanted to take the doll and the crib up with her to bed, which seemed like a good idea, as in reality she would have her baby in her room with her at night. Although, again, that was the only similarity, for this 'baby' wouldn't be waking her every two to three hours to be fed and changed, and then possibly still cry and need soothing and resettling to go back to sleep. Faye liked her sleep and needed it. How would she cope with being woken every few hours? As every parent knows, sleep deprivation takes its toll; no matter how much you love your baby, you can feel utterly wretched without enough sleep.

During the evening I'd wondered a few times how Stan and Wilma had reacted when Becky had told them of the change in Faye's care plan. I was soon to find out. Having said goodnight to Faye, Snuggles and the baby doll, I came downstairs and sat in the living room. The girls were in their rooms, doing their own thing or getting ready for bed, and Adrian was out. It was nearly nine forty-five when the landline rang. 'Hello,' I said.

'Cathy, it's Stan.' His voice was low and subdued. I felt my pulse step up a beat.

'Hello, Stan.'

'I hope I'm not disturbing you. You can probably guess why I'm phoning.'

'About the change in the care plan?'

'Yes. Wilma was going to call you but she's too upset.'

'I'm sorry.'

There was a pause before Stan said, 'I really don't know what to think. Wilma is blaming herself. She says that if Faye had stayed here with us then the idea of keeping the baby would never have occurred to her.'

'Wilma shouldn't blame herself,' I said. Although it was true that Faye had been living in Wilma's shadow, and since coming to me she'd begun to find herself, which wasn't necessarily a bad thing, was it? 'I hope you don't think I persuaded Faye to change her mind.'

'No. Becky said it was Faye's idea, but I think we should have been consulted before any decision was made. We've brought her up and we know her best. We've had very little help from the social services all these years, and now they're trying to drive a wedge between us and take Faye.' Which was how many parents felt when the social services became involved in their family.

'What has Becky said?' I asked. 'You know I wasn't aware of the decision while we were out earlier today.' I didn't want him to think I'd been keeping it a secret. 'Becky telephoned me just before she telephoned you.'

'I know. She said she'd just spoken to you. She was nice enough. But she said that, as Faye was an adult, she had the right to have her wishes taken into account, and they thought it was appropriate for her to be given the chance to look after the baby. I think she said for six months. But then what? Becky knows we can't look after the baby and Faye. It's as much as we can do to look after ourselves.'

'The staff at the mother-and-baby unit will teach Faye parenting skills,' I said. 'As well as assess her.'

'I know, and Becky said you would be helping her too. But what good will that do in the end? Unless there is a miracle, the baby will still have to go for adoption at the end of six months and it will be more upsetting then. Faye might be an adult in age, but she's a child in all other respects. You know that.'

'I understand how difficult it is,' I said. 'I can't promise a miracle, but now the decision has been made to allow Faye to try to keep her baby, I will do all I can to help her. If she is able to parent the baby then perhaps adult social services will be able to find long-term support. I don't know what's available.'

'Nothing, as far as we know. It's usually the family that steps in, and we're Faye's only relatives.'

Had the baby's father been known then the social services would have explored that avenue to see if the father or one of his close relatives could help long term, or even foster or adopt the child. Relatives are always considered by the social services as the next best option if a parent can't look after their child.

'I don't know what else I can say, Stan,' I said. I felt dreadful. He sounded low and very different from the man who'd proudly taken us all out to lunch earlier.

There was a pause before he said, 'Could you try and persuade Faye not to go ahead with this? I know she can be stubborn, but she may listen to you. It would be best in the long run.'

'I'm sorry, I can't do that,' I said. 'It would be unethical for me as a foster carer, and also against my own personal feelings. I have to help Faye and give her every chance. I hope you understand.'

'Wilma said you'd say that, but it won't be you who has to deal with the mess when it goes wrong and she comes back to us.'

'I'm sorry,' I said again. I didn't know what else to say.

He wound up by saying a rather curt goodbye and that they'd see Faye as usual the day after tomorrow. I felt bad, but there was nothing else I could have said or done, and I hoped Stan and Wilma wouldn't put pressure on Faye to change her mind when they saw her, for I thought it could backfire. Faye wanted to try to keep her baby and, difficult though it was for them to accept, her grandparents needed to respect her decision.

CHAPTER FIFTEEN

OPTIMISTIC

The following morning Faye brought the crib with the baby doll in it downstairs and set it on the floor beside her while she ate her breakfast. I had to chivvy her along, as we had an antenatal appointment at 9.45. Despite using the time chart on her bedroom wall, Faye was taking so much longer to do everything now that she was feeding and changing the 'baby'. While this was of course similar to what would happen in real life – it takes forever to get out of the house with a young baby – I didn't think we were going be able to use the doll as an excuse if we were late for the appointment. Faye also went to the toilet, forgetting that she needed to take a urine sample with her to the clinic, so we had to wait until the mug of tea had worked its way through and she could produce a sample.

I didn't see a problem in Faye bringing the baby doll with us until we were in the waiting room at the doctor's surgery when I heard a young boy say to his mother, 'Look, Mum, that woman is playing with a doll and she's grown up.'

Faye didn't appear embarrassed by the comment, but I was for her, and while I let her continue to hold the doll I took away the toy feeding bottle and put it in my bag for safe keeping. When it was our turn to go in she carried the doll in her arms across the waiting room and to the consultation room, as one would a baby. It was the same midwife as before and she smiled as we entered.

'No Snuggles today?' she asked, glancing at the doll.

'He's on my bed at Cathy's,' Faye said as we sat down. I passed the maternity folder and sample pot to the midwife. 'I'm keeping my baby. So I'm learning how to look after it,' Faye said.

The midwife looked at me questioningly.

'Faye's been practising on the doll,' I clarified. 'I'm doing what I can to teach her. Once the baby is born she'll be going to a mother-and-baby unit.' I didn't know how much the midwife knew.

She nodded and brought up Faye's details on the computer screen and then asked her, 'So, how have you been, Faye?'

'I'm all right,' Faye said.

She smiled. 'You don't make much fuss, do you? Some women find the last trimester of pregnancy very uncomfortable.'

'Faye rarely complains,' I said. 'I know she's uncomfortable sometimes because I see her shift position or rub her tummy, but she doesn't say.'

'Well, that bodes well for the delivery then,' the midwife quipped, throwing Faye a smile. 'Let's check your blood pressure first. I'll also have to take a blood sample this week.' She stood and, taking the pressure sleeve from the desk, placed it around Faye's upper arm.

Faye cradled the doll as the midwife took her blood pressure and then a blood sample, weighed and measured her, and checked the urine sample, the results of which were all normal. She took the doll with her to the couch and held it beside her as the midwife applied the gel and then ran the Doppler over her bump. The baby's heartbeat sounded loud and clear.

'My baby,' Faye announced proudly with a huge smile.

'Yes, it is,' the midwife said. 'It's got a good, strong heartbeat.'

'I'm keeping my baby,' Faye told her again.

'I know, you said.' It was impossible to gauge what the midwife thought of this; her tone and manner were completely professional.

Faye returned to sit beside me, the doll on her lap, as the midwife updated the maternity folder and then the computer. As she finished she asked us, 'Have you been going to the antenatal classes?'

Faye looked at me.

'No,' I said. 'It wasn't thought appropriate before. Perhaps we should go now, though?'

'The classes can be useful,' she said. 'You'll have missed some, but it might be worth going to the remaining ones. Faye would have been given a sheet with the dates and times at her first visit to the hospital.'

'I'll find out,' I said. 'Thank you.' I knew I hadn't seen this timetable so I guessed Wilma hadn't passed it on, as Faye wouldn't be going to them.

We said goodbye, and as we left the midwife reminded us to collect another sample pot from reception and to make an appointment for the next antenatal visit in two weeks' time.

Once home I made us a drink and a snack as Faye went upstairs and fetched Snuggles. She laid him in the cot beside the baby doll and then played with them both. And it was playing, as a young child might play, rather than practising parenting. I wasn't sure how much use this was, and I was concerned that Faye might think she could play with a newborn baby like a toy, so I pointed out the differences. Then I opened the laptop and brought up a good website I'd found, which had detailed pictures of many aspects of parenting. I clicked through to the page that showed the correct way to hold a baby and how it should lie in a cot, and showed Faye.

'Look at the picture of the baby,' I said, pointing to the screen. 'You always lie a baby on its back with its feet at the very bottom of the cot so it can't slip down under the covers.'

But Faye wasn't interested. She glanced at the screen and then continued to play with Snuggles and the doll, so I closed the laptop and said we'd have a look at it again later. Faye's attention span could be limited sometimes, like a child's, and it was no good forcing learning upon her if she wasn't in the right frame of mind.

Becky telephoned that afternoon to advise me she'd arranged a review for the following Monday at Wilma and Stan's flat at two o'clock, and I was invited. I updated Becky on the antenatal appointment, including that the midwife had suggested Faye go to the antenatal classes. Becky said she wasn't sure how much Faye would gain from the classes, but I could try one and see how it went. I said I'd telephone the hospital to find out the dates. I told her I was using a doll to teach Faye, and I asked her if she knew where I could borrow an electronic baby-simulator doll from, as I thought it could be very useful. She agreed it would be useful and said she'd look into it. I also said that I thought I should go shopping with Faye soon to start buying what she needed for the baby, and I mentioned some of the items on my list.

'Buy the essentials,' Becky said. 'First-size babygrows, nappies, lotions, bottles, formula and so on, but not the big items. The home has all the equipment Faye will need for the baby and she can borrow one of their prams.'

From which I assumed that Becky wasn't looking further than the initial six months, which may have been practical but was also disheartening.

I telephoned the hospital maternity unit and it took a while to find the right person to speak to about the antenatal classes. Then I was told that Faye should have filled in a form at the start to say she wanted to attend the classes, as numbers were limited, but when I explained the position the person I was speaking to said she would be able to attend the two remaining classes, and also visit the maternity unit, which she was already booked into. I said I would be accompanying Faye and I was her birthing partner. She said that was fine, most mothers had someone with them – their partner, mother or a friend – and you were allowed up to two people in the delivery room with you.

That afternoon I tried again to teach Faye the correct way to hold a baby and lay it in its cot. This time with more success. She'd tired of playing with Snuggles and the doll as toys by then and was now treating the doll like a baby again. I emphasized how important it was to always lay the baby in the cot the way I was showing her: on its back with its feet at the very the bottom of the cot so it couldn't slip under the covers and become overheated. I didn't go into the reasons why this position was recommended – that research had shown it reduced the number of cot deaths, also known as Sudden Infant Death Syndrome (SIDS), as Faye would have found it too confusing and possibly upsetting. She practised with the doll a number of times, putting it to bed in the correct position, getting it up, feeding and winding it, and then settling it in its cot again. She did well, I praised her, and again I felt we were making good progress.

Edith, my support social worker, telephoned that afternoon and I updated her on Faye. She said she'd been in contact with Becky to see how things were going and would visit me the following week. Had I been fostering a child Edith would have normally come to the review, but she didn't feel this was necessary, as it was only a short meeting compared to a child's review. We arranged a date and time for her visit and I asked her, too, if she knew where I could borrow an electronic baby-simulator doll. She said she knew secondary schools used them, but didn't know where I could hire one from and that she'd look into it.

Later that day I telephoned my mother to check it was convenient for us to visit at the weekend, and also to tell her of the change to Faye's care plan – that she was going to try to keep her baby. I knew that Faye would tell Mum as soon as she saw her and I didn't want it to come as a shock. Mum had got to know Faye quite well during our visits, so her reaction was what I thought it would be.

'Really?' she said, surprised. 'She's going to need an awful lot of help, isn't she?'

'Yes, but she is learning. And I know that if she can learn enough to parent, she'll make a wonderful mother. Loving, kind and gentle, just like you.'

Mum laughed, embarrassed. 'I do hope she can manage to do it. That would be a wonderful ending.'

'Yes, it would, and I'm doing all I can to make it happen.'

Mum then mentioned that my brother had been helping her clear out the garage. Dad's car had been sold, but the garage was still full of Dad's work tools. He was a great handyman, could fix anything, and liked decorating and carpentry. If he wasn't in the house or garden, he could be found in the garage, soldering metal, tinkering with the car or gluing and nailing wood. He'd even made a chest of drawers and a cabinet, such were his skills and craftsmanship. While I knew the garage needed to be cleared out – Mum wasn't going to take up carpentry or decorating – the finality of removing the things that were so personal to him hit me hard and I felt a sudden stab of sadness deep inside. It was the end of an era and it was very difficult to accept.

The following day Faye saw her grandparents. It was the first time since they'd been told of the change in the care plan, and Faye made the sensitive decision not to take the doll with her; she left it in the cot and took Snuggles instead.

'I think it will make Gran more upset if she sees me with the baby doll,' Faye said.

'Yes. That's very sensible,' I agreed.

It was perceptive of Faye to realize this, and it was at moments like this that I was more certain Faye had the intelligence to learn what she needed to parent her child.

Stan and Wilma were slightly cold towards me when I went in with Faye. They weren't rude, just distant and not their usual chatty selves. I knew they had a lot to think about and that to some degree they probably blamed me for Faye changing her mind. As Wilma had said, it was highly unlikely that she'd have done so had she stayed at home with her. I appreciated how upsetting it must be for them when they'd brought up Faye for all those years. They wanted what was best for her (and the baby) and believed they knew what that was.

When I collected Faye she was ready with her coat on in the living room and I immediately sensed an atmosphere. She stood and gave both Wilma and Stan a perfunctory kiss on the cheek without its usual warmth, then they all said a muted goodbye. Stan didn't come with us to the door to see us out as he usually did but stayed in the living room.

'Is everything all right?' I asked Faye as we waited for the elevator.

She brought Snuggles up to eye level and said, 'We had to tell them, didn't we?'

'Tell them what?' I asked her, not Snuggles.

'We had to tell them not to keep trying to make me change my mind, didn't we, Snuggles? I know it's difficult looking after a baby, but they don't have to keep telling me. Snuggles and me said if they didn't stop, we wouldn't come and see them next time. We'd see the horses instead.'

'And did that stop them?' I asked as the elevator arrived and we stepped in.

'Yes. But I wouldn't really have gone to see the horses instead. I was just saying that.'

'I know, love.'

But well done Faye, I thought. She was the least assertive person I knew, especially around her grandparents, but when it had come to sticking up for her rights in respect of her baby she'd stood her ground and told them how she felt. This was confidence-building and another small step towards inde-pendence, which would help her when it came to looking after her baby.

* * *

The following day I took Faye shopping for the essential items we needed for her baby. With only six weeks to go before the birth, I didn't want to leave it any later in case it arrived early. I'd persuaded Faye to leave Snuggles and the doll at home, saying she wouldn't be able to carry them with all the things we had to buy. After the boy's comment in the doctor's waiting room, I appreciated how strange it must look to others to see a grown woman carrying a doll and soft toy. People sometimes stared at her anyway, and I didn't want to make it worse by attracting more unwanted attention.

In the shopping centre I was taken aback to see that some Christmas decorations were already up, although I shouldn't have been, as it was the first week in November and stores seem to decorate earlier and earlier. I knew I needed to make a start on my Christmas shopping, as I had a lot of people to buy for: family and friends, foster children I was still in contact with, and this year Faye, her grandparents and the baby, which was due on 14 December, would be added to my list. I would secretly make up a stocking for Faye's baby and surprise Faye with it just before Christmas. However, today I was concentrating on buying essential items, and top of my list were the bottles, sterilizing unit and formula milk – very important, as I wanted plenty of time to teach Faye how to make up the bottles of milk.

We went to the same shop we'd been to before that sold everything for the mother-to-be and her baby and chose these items, plus some first-size nappies and vests, without much deliberation. But when it came to choosing baby clothes, Faye wanted to buy lots of pretty outfits for girls, which, although cute, weren't practical, as we didn't know the sex of her baby. I promised Faye I would come back to the store and buy some dresses as soon as the baby was born, assuming it was a girl, and then persuaded her to buy two packets of first-size unisex babygrows – eight in all. Faye would receive a maternity allowance from the state, but it would take a while to come through, so I was funding these purchases. We also bought a shawl for wrapping her baby in, a bottle brush, baby lotion, cream and cotton wool for cleaning its bottom. Faye wanted to buy a pram, but I explained the mother-and-baby home would have one, as well as a cot. I'd already told her this in the car on the way to the shops, but clearly she'd forgotten.

Once we'd finished shopping we had lunch in one of the cafés on the lower ground floor of the mall and then returned home. Faye was excited about all our purchases and wanted to make up a bottle of milk straight away, so while she unpacked I looked at the instruction sheets. Those for the sterilizer appeared straightforward, but when I looked at the instructions printed on the side of the can of milk formula my heart sank. The entire label on the 900-gram can, apart from a small area at the front bearing the product name, was covered in tiny print. It was so small and compact that I couldn't even read most of it without my glasses. How could they make the instructions so complicated? Faye would never understand this in a million years.

I studied the first section, which was a feeding chart with columns and sub-columns divided into the approximate age and weight of the baby (in kilograms and pounds) and how much formula you would need for single feeds, with level scoops subdivided into millilitres and fluid ounces. Then there was a column headed 'Number of feeds in 24 hours'. Underneath this chart were half a dozen lines of even smaller print saying that this chart was only a guide and a baby may need more or less than stated, which wasn't helpful to someone like Faye, who needed clear and precise guidelines. This section included a recommendation to seek professional help if necessary, from a doctor or midwife. The next box was headed 'Important feeding information' and beneath was a list of dos and don'ts on making up, storing and warming feeds. Moving round the tin, the next twenty or so lines of tiny print were headed 'How to open and prepare your baby's feed', starting with removing the seal. I scanned down the list of instructions and then, turning the tin again, looked at the next box, headed 'Important notice'. It began by stating that breast milk was best for babies and why, and then there was another list of dos and don'ts on when and when not to use formula milk. The next section, with more tightly packed print, was a long list of ingredients. Next to that there was another long list of the milk's nutritional values – energy, fat, carbohydrates, etc. And to the side of that were three sections detailing the different types of formula milk available: 1) From birth; 2) From six months; 3) One–three years. Which took me back to the front of the tin again. A lot of this information wasn't required for making up feeds and I knew I would have to extract what Faye needed and simplify it so she could understand what to do.

Faye had finished unpacking and was now standing beside me, eager to get started, but when she saw the lines and lines of tiny print, charts and measurements on the can she sighed despondently. 'I can't ever read all of that,' she said.

'I know. I'm struggling to work out what we do,' I said. 'But don't worry. We'll leave it for now and then when I have a chance later today I'll write down exactly what you need to do, step by step, so you will understand it. OK?'

She smiled, relieved. 'That's what they do at the day centre,' she said. 'We have instruction sheets for doing things like making a cup of tea.'

It was possible that Faye might breastfeed, but I couldn't rely on that. I didn't want her panicking at the home when her baby was screaming with hunger and she was unable to make up a bottle of milk. Or to make it up incorrectly – a too thin or too concentrated formula can harm a baby, depriving it of nutrients or overloading its kidneys and digestive system.

It was evening, while Faye was watching television, before I had the chance to sit down quietly at the kitchen table with a sheet of A4 paper, a pen and the can of formula milk. I read all the instructions and charts again and then began writing down the steps needed, in bullet points, on how to prepare a bottle of milk. As I worked Adrian passed by on his way to make a drink and, pausing, came over to see what I was doing. I explained I was simplifying the instructions, but I could see from his expression that he was sceptical this was necessary. However, when he looked more closely at the instructions on the tin his expression changed. 'What!' he exclaimed.

'Exactly. Faye couldn't possibly decipher this lot, but once she learns what she has to do she'll be fine. We'll practise it over and over again until she knows it off by heart.'

'Cup of tea, Mum?' he asked, leaving my side.

'Yes, please.'

It took me nearly an hour before I was satisfied that I had the instructions Faye needed. I also wrote a separate sheet for using the sterilizer, although this was much shorter. Now that I'd extracted just the information Faye needed to make up a bottle, I felt sure the task would appear far less daunting to her. She'd gone up for her bath and I now typed up both sets of instructions on the computer, using a reasonably large, bold font. I printed out the pages and then placed each in its own plastic sheet protector. I could do more of these instruction sheets for other things if Faye needed them. When Faye came downstairs I proudly showed her the sheets and said we'd try them out tomorrow, but she was more interested in getting back in front of the television to watch the rest of her programmes.

That night when I tucked Faye and Snuggles into bed she gave me a big hug and thanked me for taking her shopping and buying the things for her baby.

'You're welcome, love,' I said. 'It's important you have everything you need ready in plenty of time. We should pack your hospital bag soon as well, in case you go into labour early.'

'What's labour?' she asked, although I'd explained this many times before.

'It's when you start to have your baby. Do you remember, I told you that it starts slowly with little tummy pains called contractions? Then the tummy pains – the contractions – get bigger and more often. We go into hospital and you then work hard to push your baby out. That's why it's called labour.'

'Oh yes,' she said. 'I remember now.' She gave me another hug and then looked thoughtful. 'I *can* remember things, can't I?'

'Yes, of course you can. You've remembered lots of things all your life.'

'Gran says I can't remember enough to look after a baby, but I'm going to show her she is wrong.'

'That's the spirit. Once your gran sees you looking after your baby and knows you can do it, I'm sure she'll feel much happier.'

'I want Gran and Grandpa to be happy so we can all live together again. Me, Gran, Grandpa and my baby.'

'That sounds good,' I said, but I didn't say any more. I'd no idea if Faye and her baby would ever be able to live with her grandparents.

CHAPTER SIXTEEN

TEACHING FAYE

The following morning, Saturday, once Faye was up and dressed and had finished her breakfast, she was eager to learn how to make up a bottle of milk. It was ten o'clock, Adrian had gone to work and Paula and Lucy were wandering around in their dressing gowns, taking their time getting up, as it was the weekend. Faye came with me to the kitchen where I set the two instruction sheets in their plastic sleeves side by side on the work surface. I carefully explained what each was for.

'You can do that one,' Faye said, pointing to the sheet for sterilizing the bottles. 'I want to put the milk in the bottles.'

'You have to learn to do both,' I said. 'All the bottles must be washed well in warm water and sterilized before you make up the milk.' I'd explained this when we'd gone shopping for the sterilizer, but as with many new things Faye had to hear it a number of times before it was committed to memory. 'If you don't sterilize the bottle, germs could make your baby sick,' I emphasized. 'So what is the first thing you do?' I pointed to number one on the step-by-step instructions for sterilizing the bottles.

'One. Wash all the bottles in warm water,' she read slowly, as a young child might.

'Good. Go on then. There are the bottles and the bottle brush in the sink ready. Just run the hot water and add a squirt of washing-up liquid. I know the bottles aren't dirty, but they will be once you start using them. Always take off the tops of the bottles – the teats – to wash them.'

'I'm good at washing up,' Faye said. 'I do it at home for Gran.'

'Excellent.' I stood to one side and watched as she slowly and rather laboriously began cleaning the first bottle. 'That's right, push the brush right down to the end of the bottle and turn it round and round,' I said. 'Great. Now the next one.' She carefully set the first bottle on the draining board and picked up the next. 'When you've had your baby and you are doing this for real, you'll need to have bottles cleaned and sterilized in plenty of time so you always have a feed ready, but we'll cover that another time.'

It took Faye a good ten minutes to wash and rinse the four bottles and teats and place them on the drainer. She set the bottle brush beside them and then carefully tipped the water from the bowl. She turned to me with a big smile of satisfaction from a job well done. 'Can I put the milk in the bottles now?'

'Not yet,' I said, passing her the towel to wipe her hands. 'We have to do something else first. Something very important. Can you remember what it is? If not, read number two on the list.'

She returned to the work surface and studied the instruction sheet for the sterilizer as I stood beside her. 'What does number two say?' I asked gently. 'Do you know?'

'I can read some of it,' she said. 'Two. Fill the …' She didn't know the next word.

'Measuring jug,' I read, then helped her with the rest of the sentence, 'with two hundred millilitres of water. Here's the jug,' I said, passing it to her. 'Can you see the line on the jug for two hundred mils?'

She studied the side of the jug and then pointed to the correct line.

'Excellent,' I said.

Pleased, she stood there looking at me, the jug in her hand.

'What do you do now?' I asked. She continued looking at me. 'If you've forgotten, look at the instruction sheet again. I've written it to help you.'

She looked down at the sheet and read the line out again. 'Fill the measuring jug with … Oh yes. I put the water in it.'

'That's right. Good. Use the cold water. Fill the jug to the line that shows two hundred mils.' It was possible that Faye had never used a measuring jug before.

She turned on the cold tap and the water came out in a rush. 'It's too much,' she said, panicking slightly and quickly turning off the tap again.

'Don't worry. Just tip a little out until you have about two hundred mils.' She licked her bottom lip as she concentrated.

'That's two hundred,' she said.

'Excellent. Bring the jug over here and we'll look at the next step.'

I helped her read the third stage, pointing to each word as we read: 'Take out the tray in the sterilizer and pour the water into the base.'

I showed her where the tray was and she tipped in the water.

'Good. Next,' I said. 'You're doing well. It will all become easier with practice.'

'Put the tray back in,' she read.

I helped her slide it back into place and then we read the next step together: 'Place the bottles and teats in the top.' I did one to show her and she loaded the others.

'Well done.'

'Put the lid back on,' she read slowly from the sheet.

'And check it's properly closed.' I showed her how the lid went on the sterilizing unit.

She returned to the instruction sheet again and I helped her read the next line: 'Place the sterilizer in the microwave.'

'I know how to use microwaves,' she said, pleased. 'We have one at home.'

'Great. They're all slightly different, but the staff at the mother-and-baby home will show you how to use the one there. But, Faye, you understand that if you breastfeed you may not need to make up bottles. This is just in case you do need to.' She looked confused, so I knew I should leave that explanation for another time and concentrate on the task in hand.

'Open the microwave door and put in the sterilizer,' I prompted. Which she did. 'What do you do now?'

'Switch it on?' she said.

'Yes, but for how many minutes? Look at the instruction sheet.'

I helped her read: 'Set the microwave timer for six minutes.' Then I showed her the timer. There was little point in writing instructions for my microwave, as the one at the home could be different again. I helped her set the dial and she pressed the start button. As the microwave whirred Faye returned to the instruction sheet and I helped her read the next step: 'Do not take the lid off the sterilizer straight away. Let it cool for three minutes.'

'That's important,' I said. 'You must leave the sterilizer to stand for three minutes or the steam could scald you – burn.'

'I know what three minutes is,' Faye said proudly, raising her watch to eye level.

'Yes. But it's three minutes from when the microwave has finished. Not now. It's still going, isn't it?' She nodded but continued to look at her watch.

Deep in thought, I looked at her. Performing a new task like this highlighted the extent of Faye's learning difficulties. Sterilizing bottles using the microwave was a relatively quick and easy task, but I knew that Faye was going to have to repeat the process with me by her side many, many times before she could safely and competently do the task alone and just follow the step-by-step instructions. And of course she'd have to remember to clean and sterilize the bottles in the first place. Would a member of staff at the home remind her that they needed doing? Or would they view that as part of assessing her competency as a parent? I feared the latter, for if she couldn't remember to wash and sterilize bottles at the home then the chances were she wouldn't remember once she'd left.

The microwave pinged, signalling that the cycle had ended.

'It's finished,' Faye announced, lowering her watch.

'Yes, so what do you do now?'

'Make up the bottle of milk,' she said excitedly.

'But not straight away. We have to leave the bottles to cool. For how long?'

There was a moment's hesitation before she said, 'Three minutes.'

'Yes, that's right. Good girl.'

'I'll tell you when three minutes is up,' Faye said, pleased, and, raising her watch again, she began counting off the minutes. 'Time's up!' she called.

I watched her as she carefully removed the sterilizer from the microwave and set it on the work surface, and then I showed her how to remove the lid.

'Now we can make up the milk,' I said. 'What's the first step?'

I pointed to the second sheet and together we read: 'Wash your hands before touching the bottles.'

'That's important,' I said. 'The bottles are clean and you have to make sure your hands are too.'

She returned to the sink and I waited while she washed and dried her hands. Then, following the instructions, we began the process of making up a bottle of milk. Paula and Lucy wandered in and out in their dressing gowns a few times while we were working but did eventually get dressed.

'Isn't that a waste?' Paula asked while later, seeing three bottles of milk lined up. 'We haven't got a baby.'

'I know we haven't got a baby,' I said, throwing her a look. 'But doing a task is the best way to learn and remember it. Do you remember all the time you spent practising tying bows so that you could do up your shoelaces?'

'Yes, and it was only last week!' Lucy joked as she came in. Paula laughed good-humouredly.

'Laces are difficult,' Faye said, completely missing the joke. 'Don't worry, Paula, I can't do them.'

'She can really,' Lucy said. 'I was joking.' But even then Faye didn't understand and there was an uncomfortable silence. 'Show us how you make up a bottle then,' Lucy said, making amends.

Faye smiled proudly as Lucy and Paula came closer to watch. I stood by, ready to help and prompt as necessary, and ten minutes later, with a lot of help, Faye had made up another bottle of milk. We all applauded.

'Well done,' I said.

Although there was still a lot to cover in respect of feeds and bottles – warming the milk, testing it to make sure it was at the right temperature, storing the milk in the fridge and so on, all of which would take Faye time to learn – for now I was pleased with the progress we'd made that morning.

After lunch Lucy and Paula said they were going into town shopping and asked Faye if she would like to go with them, but she smiled shyly and said, 'No, thank you. I have to learn to look after my baby.'

'You can go with them,' I encouraged. 'You've done enough learning for one day and I'll be busy for a couple of hours. The change will do you good.' But she couldn't be persuaded and preferred to stay at home with me.

She occupied herself while I was busy, looking at some books and then doing a simple jigsaw puzzle, but when I told her I was going to bake a cake to take with us to my mother's tomorrow she wanted to help. Faye liked nothing more than to be at home with an adult and involved in domesticity. It was what she was used to and felt comfortable with, which of course augured well for parenting. She certainly wouldn't be yearning to go out partying.

She helped me make the cake and then once it was cool she filled it with jam and butter icing. When everyone came home they all remarked on the delicious smell of home baking and Faye proudly told them, many times, that she'd helped me bake a cake. She often repeated herself; whether this was because she'd forgotten she'd told us or thought we'd forgotten, or because her grandparents repeated things, I didn't know. But it was a habit of Faye's to tell us things more than once, and we always listened as though we were hearing it for the first time and just accepted it as part of her character.

That evening we all ate together and then Adrian, Paula and Lucy went out, which left Faye alone with me again. She didn't seem to tire of my company, as I'm sure many young people would, and was happy to just be around me. Sometimes I felt as though I had a shadow, for she was never far from my side if it was just the two of us. The television programmes Faye watched during the week didn't show at weekends, but she wanted to watch a game show she usually watched with her grandparents. After that she had her bath and then I suggested a few games of dominoes, which I knew she enjoyed. As she stood to put away the domino box she rubbed her tummy. 'I've got those pains you told me about,' she said. 'Am I having a labour?'

'No, I don't think so, not yet. They are more likely to be Braxton Hicks. Do you remember, I explained about Braxton Hicks contractions?'

She gave a small nod but I was pretty sure she didn't remember, so I explained again. 'Braxton Hicks are small contractions that make the wall of your tummy feel hard for a few seconds. They are normal and you will feel them more often towards the end of pregnancy. It's the body's way of getting ready to go into labour and give birth. Has it stopped now?'

'Yes.'

'I'm sure that's what it is. But that reminds me, let's go and pack your hospital bag while we think of it.'

'Why? Am I leaving now?' she asked.

'No, not yet. Your bag is for when you go into hospital to have your baby, which probably won't be for another six weeks. But the notes the hospital gave you say you should have it ready now.'

She came with me upstairs and I placed the weekend bag I'd bought for her on her bed. When she'd first arrived she'd come with a large suitcase and a small shoulder bag, neither of which was suitable for a short hospital stay.

'Is that mine?' she asked, referring to the weekend bag.

'Yes. Do you like it?'

She nodded. 'I've had lots of new things since I've been with you.' She threw her arms around me and gave me a big hug. Bless her.

Using the list of items that had been included in the maternity folder, we packed what she and the baby would need for a couple of days. I didn't know what arrangements would be made after the birth for the rest of Faye's belongings, but I anticipated visiting her often, so I could take whatever else she might need.

'It's like going on holiday,' she said. 'That's what Grandpa will say.'

'Yes.' I smiled. Although my recollection of giving birth was that it was no holiday!

Going to my mother's house where just she greeted us at the door was becoming a little easier now. As usual she was very welcoming and pleased to see us when we went on Sunday.

She thanked us for the cake and Paula placed it in the kitchen. As I'd anticipated, within a couple of minutes of our arrival Faye was telling her: 'I'm going to keep my baby and I'm learning how to look after it.'

'That's lovely,' Mum said. 'You can tell me what you've learnt so far while you help me make everyone a cup of tea.'

I saw Lucy and Paula exchange a pointed look and I wondered if they resented the amount of Mum's time Faye took up when we visited. She rarely left Mum's side, as she did with me at home. But I'd already explained to Lucy and Paula that this was because Faye had spent her whole life with people of Nana's generation and felt more comfortable with them, rather than people her own age. However, a few minutes later, when I caught them whispering while Faye was in the kitchen helping Mum, I asked them if there was a problem.

'Not with us,' Lucy said a little caustically.

'What's that supposed to mean?' I asked.

'Faye keeps telling Nana she's keeping the baby. But it's not definite yet. She's got to prove to the social worker she can do it, and from what I've seen she's got a long way to go yet.'

'Nana knows that,' I said. 'So does Faye.'

'Does she?' Lucy asked. 'When Faye talks to us about it, it seems definite: my baby this and my baby that. She's even thought of a name.'

'Has she?' I asked. 'She hasn't told me.'

'Snuggles!' Lucy said, and both girls laughed.

'Don't be unkind,' I said. 'It doesn't suit you.'

'Sorry,' they said, and looked suitably chastised. They weren't unkind, far from it. They shared their home, love and life unreservedly with all the children and young people we fostered. Humour is often a way of coping, but if they had concerns I needed to explore them.

'I'll speak to Faye later,' I said, 'and make sure she understands what will happen. Thanks for telling me.'

And the rest of the day continued pleasantly.

That evening, once home, I explained to Faye again what would happen after her baby was born: that after a day or so in hospital she would go to the mother-and-baby unit, where she would be taught to look after her baby and also be observed. Then a decision would be made on what was best for her and the baby.

'I know,' Faye said. 'They will be watching me to see if I do it right.'

'Yes. That's about it.'

'And I will do it right,' she said. 'You're teaching me.'

'I'm doing my best, and I know you will do yours.'

CHAPTER SEVENTEEN

AN 'OFF DAY'

To begin with I thought Faye might be worried or preoccupied by the review on Monday afternoon, for that morning she was confused and very forgetful. Her movements were lethargic and slower than usual and she forgot the most basic things, like brushing her hair, cleaning her teeth and which cupboard the cereal was in. She always poured her own cereal for breakfast and the box was in the cupboard where it had always been. She even forgot where Snuggles was, and I found him on her bed where he normally sat when he wasn't with her.

'Are you all right?' I asked her eventually.

She smiled and nodded.

'Is anything wrong?'

'I'm just having an off day. That's what Gran calls it. I'm not ill.'

'OK. And you're not worrying about anything?'

'No.'

I'd noticed before that sometimes, for no obvious reason, Faye had days when she was disorientated and disengaged from what was going on around her. I'd put it down to living in a new house with people she wasn't completely familiar with, but now it seemed it had been happening before she'd come to live with me. Around mid-morning Faye asked if we could make up some more bottles of baby milk and I agreed. Everyone else was out and her review wasn't until two o'clock. I should have realized that if Faye was having an 'off day' she wouldn't be able to concentrate on what, for her, was a complicated task. It soon became clear that not only had Faye forgotten everything we'd covered on Saturday, but she also seemed to be struggling with basic common sense.

I arranged everything she would need, including the instruction sheets, on the work surface and then told her to run the hot water and add a squirt of washing-up liquid to wash the bottles. She did this and then just stood there, hands immersed in the soapy water, looking at the bottles on the drainer.

'Put the first bottle into the water,' I prompted. 'Use the bottle brush to clean it well and then rinse it.'

Faye hesitated again as though she was processing what I'd said before she took the first bottle and began to clean it slowly. I prompted her to rinse it and then move on to the next. It took her fifteen minutes to wash all four bottles. While she was working I busied myself in the kitchen, though still keeping an eye on her. Having washed and rinsed the bottles, she had no idea what to do next, and even with me reading the instructions from the sheet she'd completely forgotten that we had to use the sterilizer and why. I explained again, repeating everything I'd told her before, and finally helped her to sterilize the bottles, as I didn't want her to become disheartened. Now she was ready to do the bit she liked best – making up the feeds. But when she added the first scoop of milk powder to the bottle it caught on the rim and half of it flicked onto the work surface and floor. She was going to scoop it up and use it!

'Faye, you can't do that,' I said, concerned. 'It'll have germs in it. If that happens, clean up what you've spilt, tip the contents of the bottle away and start again.'

'But some of it went in the bottle.'

'Yes, but you don't know how much. The milk needs to be made up to the correct strength. And you never use what you've spilt.'

She looked deep in thought for a moment and then stepped away from the kitchen cabinet. 'I think it's better if I don't do any more today,' she said. 'When I have an off day Gran tells me to take it easy, so I sit with Snuggles.'

'OK, love,' I said. 'No worries. We'll do it again another day.'

All very well, but what would happen if Faye had an 'off day' when she had the baby? It would still need feeding, changing and looking after. I would have to explain this to her when she was more receptive.

Faye wasn't upset or fazed by having an 'off day' and sat happily on the sofa in the living room with Snuggles on her lap, taking it easy for the rest of the morning, as her gran had advised, which essentially meant doing nothing but staring into space. She told Snuggles she was having an off day, and then said it again while we were eating lunch, although having an off day thankfully didn't seem to affect Faye's appetite. She reminded Snuggles again that she was having an off day as he sat on her lap in the car and I drove to her grand-parents' flat for the review. I guessed it was a term Wilma used and it had stuck.

Becky answered the door, saving Stan and Wilma the trouble, and Faye told her straight away she was having an off day.

'Are you, love?' Becky said, apparently unaware of what this meant.

Once in the living room Faye told her grandparents, even before she'd kissed them, that she was having one of her off days.

'Never mind,' Wilma said. 'Sit yourself down and take it easy.' Which Faye did, sitting heavily on the sofa beside her.

Wilma, Stan and I all said a polite hello and I sat on the chair Becky had drawn up for me so that we formed a small circle. Faye tucked Snuggles in between her and Wilma and folded her hands in her lap in a mirror image of her gran. I thought Stan and Wilma both looked tired and drawn, which was hardly surprising, considering how worried they must be by Faye's change of mind. The atmosphere was polite but strained, as it had been the last time I'd met them.

'Well, we all know each other,' Becky began, sitting with a notepad and pen on her lap. 'So there's no need for us to introduce ourselves.' She smiled convivially. 'It'll only be a short, informal meeting. I need to run through what's happening as the short-term plans for Faye have changed. I'll make a few notes as we go along. Faye, if you have any questions or there is anything you don't understand then please stop me.'

'You always say that to me,' Faye said, and I smiled.

'As we are aware,' Becky said, 'Faye has made it known that she would like to try to look after her baby and the social services have found her a place at –' She named the specialist mother-and-baby unit. 'We feel this is appropriate, and Faye can stay there for up to six months. I'm aware of the travelling issues for you,' she said, addressing Wilma and Stan. 'I'm looking into what transport help we can offer so you can visit Faye at the home.'

Wilma gave a stiff nod.

'While Faye is staying at the mother-and-baby home,' Becky said, 'she will be well supported and taught parenting techniques as well as being observed.'

'Cathy is teaching me now,' Faye put in.

'Yes, I know, that's good,' Becky said. 'And the home will build on that learning. During her time at the home Faye will also be monitored, leading to an assessment at the end, which will give us a clearer picture of what the next step should be. I shall also be visiting her.'

As Becky continued to talk I glanced at Wilma and Stan. Both were concentrating on Becky, their expressions neutral. Like me, they already knew how the care plan had changed, but this review was procedural and used to clarify any points and address questions that Faye or her grandparents might have. It was a lot less formal than the reviews I attended for the children I fostered, which were usually held in my house. Children in care have regular reviews, which the child's parent(s), social worker, teacher, foster carer, the foster carer's support social worker and any other adults closely connected with the child all attend. The meeting is chaired and minuted by an independent reviewing officer and usually lasts an hour.

'So, that's the plan at present,' Becky said, rounding off. 'Does anyone have any questions?'

'Only what we've already raised,' Stan said. 'What's going to happen at the end of the six months?'

'We don't know yet,' Becky said. 'We'll have to wait for the outcome of the assessment.'

'No. I mean, what if Faye's allowed to keep –' He couldn't bring himself to say 'the baby', but used the northern term 'bairn' instead.

'We're looking into various options that could offer the support Faye would need – supported lodgings or a semi-independence unit,' Becky said. 'Although I'm afraid they are all out of the immediate area.'

'But I'm right in saying that none of them are long term?' Stan said, so I assumed this issue had been discussed before.

'That's right,' Becky said with a small nod. 'The maximum stay is two years.' I heard Wilma sigh. 'But that's a long time ahead,' Becky continued, 'and it might be felt by then that Faye has the necessary skills to live independently.'

Another small sigh escaped Wilma's lips, but neither she nor Stan commented further.

'Cathy,' Becky said, turning to me. 'I know you see Wilma and Stan regularly when you bring Faye and collect her, but perhaps you'd like to give us an update and say a few words on how Faye is doing with you now.'

'Yes, of course.' Foster carers are usually asked to speak at a child's or young person's review, so this wasn't unexpected. 'Faye's antenatal checks are now every two weeks until she is full term,' I began. 'At these check-ups Faye is weighed and measured by the midwife and her blood pressure and urine are checked. She also listens to the baby's heartbeat. Both Faye and the baby are doing well. There are no medical concerns. I've noticed Faye is becoming more tired, especially in the evening, but that's to be expected at this stage in the pregnancy. Her last blood test showed that her iron levels were normal and they will be checked again at her next appointment. Faye seems to be coping well with all the changes and is generally very happy.'

'She's always happy,' Stan said.

'Because she doesn't see the problems as we do,' Wilma added.

Becky nodded and I continued. 'Faye gets on well with my family, and joins us on days out. She decided she didn't want to continue going to the day centre, and because she can't go to the stables I've been taking her to see some horses in a field, which she enjoys.' Stan and Wilma both nodded. 'Faye has established a good morning routine, which I believe is similar to the one she has here. She also has an evening routine, which includes a bath and watching her favourite television programmes. I've started teaching Faye the basics of parenting: how to hold a baby, lay it in the crib, feed it and so on.'

'That reminds me,' Becky said. 'I'm afraid I haven't had any luck finding one of those electronic baby dolls you asked for. I'm still searching.'

Wilma and Stan looked puzzled and Becky explained what an electronic baby-simulator doll was.

'I'm using an ordinary doll to practise on,' I said to Wilma and Stan. They nodded, although Wilma looked sceptical.

'And Faye's managing to learn the skills you're teaching her?' Becky asked.

Faye was looking at me. 'Yes, slowly, but we've only just started. Faye did well on Saturday when we began to practise making up bottles of milk. We didn't do much this morning, though.'

'Because I'm having an off day,' Faye told her gran again.

'I see,' Becky said, making a note. 'What does having an off day mean exactly?'

'She forgets everything she's supposed to do,' Wilma said, not unkindly. 'It was investigated when she was a child. Epilepsy was suggested but nothing was found.'

'How long does it last?' Becky asked. 'Minutes? Hours?'

'Most of the day,' Wilma said. 'Then she goes to sleep and she's as right as rain in the morning, unless she's sickening for something. Do you feel unwell?' she now asked Faye.

'No. I'm just having an off day,' Faye replied.

Becky finished writing and I continued by saying that I'd booked a place for Faye to attend the last two antenatal classes and that I would be going with her. I gave the dates and also the date when we would be looking round the maternity ward at the hospital. Becky made a note. I said that after discussion with Becky I'd taken Faye shopping for the essential items like nappies, babygrows and vests, and I finished by saying that we'd packed her bag for the hospital. 'In plenty of time, so we're ready.'

Becky looked up from her notepad. 'Thank you, Cathy. That's helpful.' Then, looking mainly at Wilma, she asked, 'Are we still in agreement that Cathy should be Faye's birthing partner?'

There was silence. I looked from Wilma to Stan; clearly they knew something we didn't. It was Wilma who spoke: 'We think Cathy should go with Faye to the hospital when the time comes, but I'd like her to phone me as soon as they arrive. It takes me a long time to get ready, especially if it's at night and I have to get dressed, and I'll need to call a cab. But I feel I should be there for Faye if possible. We've brought her up and I've been her mother.'

'Yes, of course,' I said, pleased. 'I'll phone you as soon as Faye goes into labour.' Becky looked pleased too, for this shift in Wilma and Stan's attitude – their greater acceptance of the baby – was positive and might pave the way for offering the support that could help Faye keep her baby long term.

'That sounds good to me,' Becky said. Then, looking at Faye, she asked, 'What do you think? Would you like your gran and Cathy to be with you when you go to hospital to have your baby?'

'Yes, and Snuggles,' Faye said, smiling.

'Of course Snuggles must go,' Stan laughed kindly, and the atmosphere improved.

Becky then spent a few minutes explaining to Wilma and Stan about the adjustments that would be made to Faye's state benefit, and how to claim a maternity grant for her. Then, with nothing more to discuss and no further questions from us, she wound up the meeting. She thanked me for coming and then wished Faye luck in case she didn't see her again before the birth, and said she would see her afterwards. Stan and Wilma confirmed that they'd see Faye the day after tomorrow and then, saying goodbye, Faye and I left, followed by Becky. We all waited for the elevator together.

'It sounds as though you're doing very well,' Becky said to Faye with a smile.

'Yes, I am,' Faye said. 'Can I keep my baby?' She asked it with a child's naïve innocence, and Becky looked uncomfortable.

'You'll have your baby with you in the mother-and-baby home,' she said. 'Then we will work out what is best for your baby in the long term.' Which is what Becky had explained to Faye before, but it seemed to satisfy her for now.

As we left the building and said goodbye, Becky again wished Faye good luck and then we went to our respective cars.

Once home Faye wanted to look through the contents of her hospital bag, I think because I'd mentioned it at the review. I lifted it down from where I'd stowed it on top of her wardrobe, and placed it on the bed. She sat beside it and began going through, admiring all the new things we'd bought for her baby. I left her to it but looked in on her a couple of times. She was in her element, unpacking and repacking the contents and pretending she was going on holiday. I told her to make sure she returned everything to the bag when she'd finished, but again the incongruity of seeing a heavily pregnant woman playing like a child struck me. She had a lot of growing up to do to become a responsible parent, and in a very short space of time.

Wilma's assurance that after a night's sleep Faye's 'off day' would go and she'd be 'as right as rain' proved correct. The following morning Faye was up at her usual time and fell into her routine, albeit slowly, but then Faye did everything slowly, as though all tasks required her full and equal concentration. She remembered where the cereal for breakfast was kept without a problem, and after breakfast she knew she had to dress, wash and brush her teeth. Once ready she wanted to make up some more bottles and I took everything we needed from the cupboards and set it on the work surface with the instruction sheets. An hour later, and with a lot of help from me, she'd successfully washed and sterilized four bottles, and had made up the formula milk. I praised her.

That afternoon we went to see the horses, as we hadn't been for a while. It was cold – there'd been a frost that morning – so we didn't stay long. But judging from the way the horses and ponies galloped across the field as soon as we approached the fence, they were as pleased to see Faye as she was to see them. She petted and stroked them with her gloved hands and remembered some of the names she'd given them. They whinnied and snorted appreciatively, their warm breath fogging in the cold air. Since the change in the care plan Faye had stopped counting down the number of sleeps to when she could return to the stables. She understood that, as she'd be living out of the area and looking after her baby, going to the stables wouldn't be practical, and neither would going to the day centre.

The following day, after I'd taken Faye to her grandparents, I continued into town to do some Christmas shopping. I knew what Adrian, Lucy and Paula wanted – they'd dropped hints – and I'd decided to buy Faye a camera. She didn't own one and her phone was too basic to have one included. I thought that like all parents she'd want to take lots of photographs of her baby, so it seemed an ideal present. I wanted a camera that was easy to hold and use, but that took good photographs. I went to the large electrical store in the shopping centre where a helpful assistant showed me a range of cameras that matched my criteria and were within budget, and I found exactly what I was looking for. From there I went to the maternity and baby store I'd previously shopped in with Faye. It was bursting with Christmas gift ideas and, taking a basket, I headed for the display marked 'Baby's First Christmas'.

I was like a kid in a candy store as I filled the basket. So many gorgeous gifts, it was difficult to choose. I began by placing a bright-red Santa sack into my basket. It had a large motif on the front showing a jolly, smiling Santa and the words 'My First Christmas'. Then I chose a rattle, an outfit with pictures of reindeer on it, a bib with a snow scene on the front, a photograph album for baby's first year, a velvet-soft cuddly toy, and so on. Eventually I had to drag myself away. As I stood in the queue to pay I pictured the look of delight on Faye's face as she hung the Santa sack on the end of her baby's crib on Christmas Eve, and then the following morning as she opened the presents for her baby. If the baby arrived on time it would be two weeks old on Christmas Day. I also imagined her delight when she opened her own presents and could begin to take photographs of her baby.

Leaving this shop, I went to the department store, where I bought presents for family and friends from my list, some stocking fillers and a Santa sack for Faye. Adrian, Paula and Lucy still had their sacks from when they were little, and despite being young adults now they still liked to find them by their beds on Christmas morning. In recent years I'd found a Santa sack bedside my bed too, containing perfume, bath oil and chocolates. I wonder how Santa knew they were my favourites! I planned to take Faye's and her baby's presents to the mother-and-baby unit a day or so before Christmas.

I left the shopping centre, laden with bags and parcels, with that warm feeling that comes from knowing you are going to make the people you love and care for very happy. Although it was true that thoughts of Christmas this year were tinged with the sad knowledge that it would be the first without my father, I was still looking forward to it. I intended to ask Mum what she wanted to do on the day itself. In the past she and Dad, and my brother and his family, had all come to me for Christmas Day. It was possible that this year she might want to do something different, which might include visiting Dad's grave. I needed to discuss the arrangements with her, but I was putting it off, for once I'd had that conversation I'd have to accept that future Christmases would never be the same again. There would always be someone missing, which made me sad.

CHAPTER EIGHTEEN

EXCITED AND CONCERNED

Although I recorded events objectively in my fostering log, as carers are supposed to, I was now feeling anything but objective. In teaching Faye, the fight for her to keep her baby had become personal as I tried to instil knowledge into her, willing her to learn so she had the best possible chance. In the months Faye had been living with us we'd become very close. She'd spent a lot of time with me – more than most foster children, as they would normally have been in school. All that time, plus her vulnerability, had drawn us closer, and I felt fiercely loyal and protective of her (as I appreciated her grandparents did). Faye was a dear, kind soul who I knew would love her baby unconditionally, if only she could be taught the skills to parent. I knew my children felt the same. Adrian didn't say much, but I often found him explaining something to Faye or praising her for a job well done to build her confidence. Lucy and Paula took every opportunity to encourage and praise Faye too, and because Lucy worked in a nursery she sometimes offered Faye practical childcare advice – usually at the weekend when she wasn't tired from work. Without doubt, we'd all bonded with Faye and were on her side. We were like her support army, ready to do all we could in the battle for her to keep her baby. The possibility that we might fail was too painful to consider.

The rest of the week flew by, and the following week Edith visited. Faye was with us in the living room most of the time and proudly showed Edith how she fed and changed the baby doll. Edith praised her and the way I was teaching Faye. I was pleased. I'd had no formal training in caring for or teaching adults with learning disabilities, so it had been trial and error. Edith made some notes on my fostering, which would be included in the report she wrote for my annual review. She'd forgotten about trying to find an electronic doll and made another note to remind herself. She was with us for nearly three-quarters of an hour, observing Faye and talking to her and me. At the end she read and signed my log notes. I would email her and Becky a monthly report, as all foster carers are now expected to do. The amount of paperwork has steadily increased over the years, and I know some carers find it a burden.

During that week Faye and I also attended the first of the two antenatal classes, held in a function room at the library. It took Faye a while to grasp that this building wasn't anything to do with the hospital where she would be having her baby but was purely being used for the lecture. We signed in and then sat together on the seats arranged in four rows facing a flip chart. There were eight pregnant women with either their partner or mother there, and one woman by herself. All the others appeared to know each other, presumably from the previous classes, which rather singled us out from the start. The lecture was entitled Mother and Baby's Wellbeing and was given by a midwife (though not the one we saw at the doctor's surgery) and a student, whose job it was to distribute the handouts and turn the sheets of the flip chart. The topics included good nutrition for the mother and baby, what to eat and what not to eat, exercise, baby vaccinations, keeping baby at the right temperature, postnatal depression and so on. Faye's literacy skills weren't good enough for her to be able to make sense of much of the handouts, and it soon became obvious that what the midwife was saying was going over her head too. It didn't help that the midwife's voice was rather low and monotonous, and the chairs were hard and uncomfortable. Faye very quickly lost interest and concentration, and then, without the inhibitions that might have kept most adults focused and hiding their boredom, she began yawing and gazing around. Thankfully Snuggles was in the car; otherwise I think she'd have begun playing with him. She examined the walls and ceiling, and then began staring at the others to our left and right and then turning in her seat so she could see those sitting behind. I kept trying to draw her attention back to the front and what was being said, and I told her to sit still.

'I can't,' she said. 'My bum hurts on this chair.'

The woman in front tittered and nodded.

We stayed until the end of the talk – two hours – but only just, and I knew Faye had learnt nothing. She was a tactile learner who needed practical, hands-on experience to acquire and retain knowledge. She also needed one-to-one teaching so she could learn at her own pace. As we came out of the room she yawned. 'Do I have to come here again?'

'Not if you don't want to,' I said.

'I don't. Can I see the horses instead?' Which rather confirmed how little Faye had gained from the talk.

Once we were home and I had a moment free, I sent Becky an email explaining why I thought the class hadn't been useful for Faye and that I was thinking of cancelling the next one, although I would still take her for the visit to the hospital. I'd tell her grandparents the next time I saw them. Becky emailed back the following morning saying I should do what I thought was right, and she understood that Faye would struggle in a classroom situation. I checked again with Faye that she didn't want to attend the other class, which was about labour, the birth and breastfeeding, and she said she didn't. I telephoned the hospital, apologized and cancelled her place but confirmed we'd be joining the group for the visit to the maternity ward.

We also had Faye's next antenatal appointment that week and the urine test showed some traces of protein. The midwife explained that this was not uncommon in later pregnancy and could happen for a number of reasons, including the mother's kidneys working harder to support the baby or because of an infection – in the mother or the baby. Faye had to repeat the urine test, and as there was still a trace of protein present the midwife said that as a precautionary measure she would send the sample to the lab for testing. She would see us again in a week, and weekly from then on until the birth. Faye didn't feel unwell and the midwife reassured us that there was nothing to worry about. That evening I recorded this in my log, as I was supposed to.

On the days when Faye saw her grandparents I continued going into town to Christmas shop. By 1 December I had bought most of the presents, Christmas cards, wrapping paper and bows, and finally had that conversation with my mother. Typical Mum, I shouldn't have worried so much. She was positive and looking forward to Christmas.

'Of course I'd like to come to you on Christmas Day,' she said. 'Just as usual. I'll be going to the cemetery in the afternoon on Christmas Eve. Shall I make a trifle as an alternative to Christmas pudding? I did that last year and it worked well. And some cupcakes? You all like those.'

'Yes, please, that would be great.'

Having spoken to Mum, I telephoned my brother and 'officially' invited him for Christmas Day. He, too, was pleased that we were all getting together and said he'd visit the cemetery with Mum on Christmas Eve. I'd go again the next time I went to see Mum.

The first weekend in December we decorated the house, apart from the Christmas tree, which we'd buy fresh nearer the time. Everyone helped, and Faye said she usually helped her grandparents decorate the flat and she'd do it next time she saw them. With less than two weeks to go before she was due to give birth, she was very large now and I warned her against going up stepladders to hang decorations, but she said they didn't have those sorts of decorations; they had ones that stood on the floor and the sideboard, and a holly wreath on their front door.

The weather had turned cold and this, coupled with Faye being large, meant that she didn't want to go out much, so we spent more time at home. I used every spare minute to continue teaching her about babies and parenting. I felt a sense of urgency now, as the time was running out, although I never forced her to learn and I always stopped if she was tired or had lost interest. I have to admit, though, that there were moments when I had to hide my frustration when she forgot something very basic that we'd already covered many times. As well as revising what we'd already learnt – holding a baby,

226

making up bottles, feeding, changing, bathing, etc. – I also talked to Faye about the more abstract aspects of parenting; for example, how to know what a baby wants when it cries, establishing a routine, the importance of giving a baby stimulation, bonding and interacting with the baby. I knew the parenting assessment would include all of this, and it was as important as feeding and changing a baby. I used our practical aids where possible: the doll (an electronic one hadn't appeared), bottles, nappies, the toy crib, babygrows for dressing and so on. I went online for the videos. There were informative educational clips of everything, including the actual birth, breastfeeding and generally caring for a baby. I hoped the visual input would help Faye understand more and reinforce what I was telling her. Although of course all this was academic. The real test would come when she had to put it into practice.

The visit to the labour ward went well. It was with the same group of mums-to-be and partners who'd been at the antenatal class. The midwife made a point of welcoming Faye and said she was pleased to see her again, which was nice. Because this tour was practical and visual – we could see for ourselves what the midwife was telling us – Faye remained engaged and interested throughout, although I knew I'd have to explain some aspects of what we'd been told later, such as an epidural, monitoring the baby's heart and a forceps delivery. Some of the women grimaced in the delivery suite when this was mentioned, but for Faye ignorance was bliss. With little real understanding of what lay in store, Faye wasn't worried about the birth and, smiling, remarked out loud that she was looking forward to seeing her baby.

'So am I,' one of the other women said. 'I just wish it wasn't me giving birth.'

The other women agreed.

The tour ended with a visit to one of the four bedded wards where the mothers had had their babies and were now resting before they were discharged home. Seeing the tiny newborns in their cribs or cradled in their parent's arms banished unpleasant thoughts of the delivery room. Oohings and aahings could be heard coming from our group and everyone had a smile on their face by the time we left. This was the last of the antenatal group meetings and the midwife wished everyone good luck as she said goodbye.

With Christmas and Faye's due date fast approaching, the excitement and sense of anticipation grew. We were all looking forward to Christmas and Faye giving birth to her baby. Each time I telephoned Mum, the first thing she asked was how Faye was, and my close friends and my good neighbour Sue always asked after Faye when they saw me.

Did I have doubts about Faye's competency to parent her baby? I'd be lying if I said no. I often woke in the early hours worrying about something she hadn't grasped or that needed emphasizing or I'd forgotten to tell her, and I'd make a mental note to go over it in the morning. Faye's success had become my success, and I felt her possible failure and the loss of her baby would be my responsibility.

If anyone asked Faye whether she'd thought of a name for her baby, she still said Snuggles, which was starting to irritate me. What had once been cute now appeared ludicrous, with her due date looming and Faye about to become a mother. It seemed to typify and emphasize Faye's learning disabilities and make her look silly, with the implication that if she was silly in this then she could be silly in other, more important matters connected with parenting. The subject of choosing a name must have come up at Faye's next visit to see her grand-parents. Since her review her grandparents had been talking a little more about the baby, rather than ignoring what was happening, although I don't think they discussed long-terms plans. When I collected Faye at the end of her visit she said, 'Gran helped me choose a name for my baby. If it's a girl it'll be Mary after my mum, and if it's a boy, Edward, which is Grandpa's middle name.'

'Excellent,' I said, pleased. 'Good choices.'

Adrian, Lucy and Paula were pleased, too, when she told them.

'Much better than Snuggles,' Adrian said.

The lab results for Faye's urine test were clear – there was no sign of infection – and the sample we took to the following antenatal check-up was clear too. Her pregnancy continued to go well; in fact, it had been an easy pregnancy. Faye hadn't suffered from morning sickness and there'd been no compli-cations. At the check-up on 14 December, Faye's due date, she had an internal examination. The midwife had told her she would be doing this when we'd seen her the previous week. It was to make sure the baby was in the correction position, with its head engaged, ready for the birth. I'd talked to Faye about this and what would happen at the examination, but even so it was very uncomfortable for her and she grimaced, moaned and bit her bottom lip. The midwife confirmed that the baby was positioned correctly and she also said that sometimes this internal examination could cause labour to start.

She was right. That evening, as Faye came downstairs in her dressing gown after having her bath, she said her tummy was hurting her. The pain only lasted a short while – about twenty seconds – but it was intense. Half an hour later, while she was watching television, she grimaced and said her tummy was hurting again. It lasted about twenty to thirty seconds and stopped. I began to keep an eye on the clock and forty minutes went by before she experienced another contraction, again lasting about twenty seconds. It was now nine o'clock and her television programmes had finished. Faye asked if we should go to the hospital now. I explained that if this was the start of labour, this stage could go on for a couple of days and that she should go to bed as usual. I went up with her and waited on the landing while she brushed her teeth, went to the toilet and then climbed into bed. As I was saying goodnight to her (and Snuggles) she experienced another contraction, which was about half an hour after the last one. I told Faye to try to get some sleep and that I'd leave her bedroom door and mine open so I'd hear her if she called out for me in the night.

Lucy and Paula had spent most of the evening after dinner in their rooms. Adrian had gone out. As I said goodnight to the girls I told them that I thought Faye could be in the first stage of labour but I doubted anything would happen during the night. They were both excited and concerned for her and went round to see her, but she was already asleep, with Snuggles on the pillow beside her.

Faye didn't call out in the night, but I checked on her at two o'clock, and when I heard her get up at four o'clock to use the toilet I went to see her. She was still half asleep and I asked her if she'd had any more pains. She shook her head and said a groggy 'No', so I wondered if the contractions had been a false start. However, as soon as she woke in the morning she said her tummy had started hurting again and that it hurt a lot. I timed the contractions. They were coming every half an hour and seemed to be more intense. She had breakfast in her dressing gown without a contraction, and Adrian, Lucy and Paula said goodbye and good luck as they left the house.

As Faye finished her breakfast she had another contraction, about forty minutes after the last one. I went with her upstairs and waited while she washed and dressed so I could reassure her if another one took hold. Sammy came with us. He hadn't left her side since she'd got up this morning, as if sensing something important was going on and she needed his attention. He went with her into the bathroom and she left the door slightly open. She had another contraction as she washed and then again as she dressed. Downstairs I telephoned Faye's grandparents – she was supposed to be seeing them today. Stan answered and said Wilma was still getting up. I told him I thought Faye could be in the first stage of labour, as she was having contractions every half an hour, so I wouldn't be bringing her to visit today. He said he'd tell Wilma and she'd phone once she was dressed.

Faye and I were sitting side by side on the sofa when another contraction gripped her; this time it was twenty minutes after the last one. I gently rubbed her lower back and reassured her. She clearly wasn't in any frame of mind to do much today, so when she asked if she could watch television I passed her the remote. I sat with her for a while as another contraction came, and then I completed a few jobs around the house, popping into the living room every so often or when I heard her groan or call out. My calm exterior belied my mounting excitement and apprehension. The contractions were now coming every twenty minutes and appeared to be more intense. It's very difficult to gauge another person's level of pain because all our thresholds are different, but when Faye was in the throes of a contraction she went rigid and couldn't speak until it had passed. I tried to help her relax and reassured her that this was normal for the first stage of labour, but she wasn't impressed.

'Why's my baby hurting me?' she moaned. 'That's not nice.'

'It's not the baby's fault,' I said. 'It's nature's way of pushing it out.'

'I don't want it out if it hurts.'

At midday, with the contractions still coming every twenty minutes, I telephoned triage at the hospital, using the number in Faye's maternity folder. They confirmed what I already knew: that we should wait until the contractions were coming every five minutes or Faye's waters broke, and then phone again and go in. I explained this to Faye, reassured her and rubbed her back. Wilma telephoned and apologized for not phoning sooner but she'd misplaced my number. I told her the contractions were now every twenty minutes and what the hospital had said, and that I'd phone her if anything happened, and definitely before we left to go to the hospital. She thanked me and asked to speak to Faye. She didn't sound anxious or excited, just matter-of-fact. I supposed she'd had to deal with many crises in her life and now took things in her stride. I silenced the television and passed the phone to Faye.

232

'My baby's hurting me,' she told her gran straight away. I couldn't hear what Wilma said, but Faye nodded and then said, 'I'll try to be brave. I love you too.'

The afternoon wore on, with the contractions still coming every twenty minutes and Faye watching television in between. I was surprised by just how many repeats of the soaps could be found if you channel-hopped, and Faye knew where to find them. I sat beside her on and off for most of the afternoon, reassuring her and trying to help her relax and breathe when a contraction took hold. Wilma telephoned at five o'clock and I told her nothing much had changed. She spoke to Faye again and must have said that babies sometimes took a long time to come, for Faye said, 'I wish my baby would hurry up, and stop hurting me.'

We were all in for dinner that evening and all furtively watched Faye as we ate. She had two contractions during the meal but still managed to clear her plate. As soon as she'd finished eating, though, she rushed to the kitchen sink and was sick, bringing up all her dinner. I reassured her there was nothing wrong and that this could happen at the start of labour, and then I poured her a glass of cold water. I felt sorry for her. I knew what it felt like to be in labour and at the mercy of your body. Adrian, Lucy and Paula, who'd seen Faye being sick and could be a bit squeamish, took refuge upstairs. Faye settled on the sofa again with Snuggles on her lap and Sammy at her feet and watched the evening soaps. By 7.30 the contractions were coming every fifteen minutes and my anticipation and apprehension grew. She had her bath as usual, although I waited on the landing to make sure she was all right. I gave her fresh clothes to put on, rather than her dressing gown. 'In case we have to go to the hospital this evening,' I said.

I sat with her again in the living room as the contractions went from every fifteen minutes to every ten minutes and seemed to grow in strength and intensity. I held her hand, massaged her back, reminded her to breathe and reassured her that this was all normal. Faye groaned and tensed when a contraction took hold but didn't say much, other than how she wanted it to stop. Adrian, Paula and Lucy came down a few times during the evening, but they were subdued and worried when they saw Faye in pain and knew there was nothing they could do to help. They were all in bed by 10.30. I brought Faye's hospital bag down from upstairs and placed it with the maternity folder in the hall ready, and then returned to the living room. We sat together on the sofa with the television on, Snuggles on her lap and Sammy at her feet. The Christmas garlands stirred in the warm air rising from the radiators. The clock on the mantelpiece ticked by and at midnight I was satisfied that the contractions were coming every five minutes. Using the telephone in the living room, I dialled the hospital and told the triage nurse the frequency of the contractions. She said I should bring Faye in. I telephoned Faye's grandparents and to my surprise Wilma answered straight away.

'I didn't go to bed,' she said. 'I've been waiting up for any news.' I told her the contractions were now coming every five minutes and we were leaving for the hospital shortly. 'I'll phone for a taxi,' she said. 'Can I have a quick word with Faye first?' I waited until Faye's contraction had passed and handed the phone to her.

'The baby's hurting me,' Faye said. Wilma said something and then Faye replied, 'Don't be late. Love you too.' She returned the handset to me.

'I'll be there as soon as I can,' Wilma said to me. 'Look after her until I get there.'

'I will.'

Faye wanted to use the toilet before we left for the hospital and I went with her upstairs. She had to pause at the top of the stairs as another contraction took hold. Paula and Lucy must have heard us, for they appeared from their rooms in their nightwear, and I explained that we were going to the hospital. Then Adrian came out of his room, still dressed, and asked if I'd like him to drive us to the hospital.

'That's kind of you, love,' I said. 'But you need your sleep. You're on an early shift tomorrow. We'll be OK.'

They came with us downstairs to see us off and I reminded them to set their alarms, as I wouldn't be there in the morning to wake them. Adrian put Faye's bag and the folder in the car and wished her luck. The girls kissed and hugged her, but she was soon in the grip of another contraction, which made her gasp out loud. I slid my arm around her waist and waited for it to pass, then I helped her out of the house.

'I'll phone as soon as there's any news,' I said to my family. 'The next time you see Faye she'll be a mummy.' And a little cheer rose from them and into the night.

CHAPTER NINETEEN

BABY EDWARD

Faye sat rigid in the passenger seat, gripping Snuggles as another contraction took hold. 'Breathe,' I commanded, glancing at her as I drove. 'Remember what I taught you about deep breathing.'

'I can't!' she cried. 'It's hurting too much.' Which of course is what many women in labour feel. Easy practising relaxation techniques in a class or at home, but rather different when labour sets in and the pain really starts.

As the contraction ended Faye let out a big sigh and relaxed back into the seat. 'It's gone,' she said. 'No more.'

'Faye, there will be more. You must try to relax and keep breathing as we've been practising. If you are tense, the pain will be worse.'

'OK, I'll try,' she said amicably.

But as soon as the next contraction came she stiffened, clutched the edge of her seat, her knuckles white, and groaned loudly.

'Take deep breaths!' I said as I drove. 'Stay in control.' I was worried. This was just the start of labour. The pain would build steadily until the baby was born.

I glanced at the clock on the dashboard. The contractions were still coming every five minutes. She had two more before

I drove into the hospital car park. I parked in the bay closest to the maternity unit. Although it was after midnight and Faye was in labour, I still had to feed the meter and display a parking ticket in the windscreen. A large sign said that those failing to do so would be wheel-clamped, and a note in Faye's maternity folder had warned the same. Faye had another contraction as I paid and then placed the ticket on the inside of the windscreen. 'Breathe in. And out. In. And out,' I said, slowing my breathing to remind her how it was done. I could see she was panicking, which would make the pain worse. I talked to her calmly for a moment and then helped her out of the car.

I carried her overnight bag and maternity folder and she linked her arm in mine as we crossed the car park. I could feel how tense she was as she braced herself for the next contraction. 'Relax and breathe slowly,' I said again.

The night was cold but clear. Stars twinkled brightly in the heavens far away, befitting a night only two weeks before Christmas. I helped Faye up the three steps to the entrance of the maternity wing, where I pressed the security buzzer. A nurse's voice came through the intercom and I gave Faye's name and said that I'd telephoned. 'Push the door and it will open,' she said, releasing the security lock.

We stepped in. It was a different world to outside. Bright, warm and decorated for Christmas. A large artificial Christmas tree festooned with silver tinsel and multicoloured baubles stood to our left. I'm sure Faye would have appreciated it had she not been gripped by another contraction. A nurse appeared pushing a wheelchair.

'Hello, Faye,' she said, smiling cheerfully. 'I'm Eunice, a student nurse. Would you like a ride up to the ward?'

Faye nodded and collapsed gratefully into the wheelchair, and Eunice pushed it the short distance to the elevator. 'I'm Cathy,' I said. 'Faye's carer and birthing partner. Her grandmother is on her way.'

She smiled kindly. 'We'll soon have Faye settled and comfortable. It's a busy night. You're the third mum to go into labour this evening. Pre-Christmas rush.' Eunice was very pleasant, a mature student nurse who was trying to put Faye at ease. 'I see you've brought your lucky mascot with you,' she said, referring to Snuggles, but Faye didn't answer.

The maternity ward was on the second floor and as the elevator stopped and the doors opened Faye had another contraction. She went rigid and, clutching the arms of the wheelchair, cried out in pain.

'Remember your breathing techniques,' Eunice said, as I had been saying all day.

'I can't,' Faye gasped.

'Yes, you can,' Eunice said firmly but kindly. 'Deep breaths, and you'll be able to have some gas and air soon. That will help you with the pain.'

Eunice wheeled Faye to the nurse's station, where another nurse took over. I thanked Eunice and she said she'd see us later. I passed Faye's maternity folder to the nurse and she began completing the paperwork for her admission, which she said would just take a few minutes. Faye groaned in pain, shifted in her chair and clutched Snuggles. I talked to her calmly, reassuring her, in between answering the nurse's questions. Not far away a baby cried.

'Listen, Faye,' I said, trying to distract her. 'I can hear a baby.'

She wasn't interested. She was completely absorbed in her pain and discomfort. Once the paperwork was complete the nurse helped Faye from the wheelchair and we were shown into an examination room – sterile white and similar to the one we'd been shown on our tour. The nurse handed Faye a small cup and asked her to give a urine sample. We had to return to the corridor for the Ladies. I waited outside the door, and presently I heard Faye moan loudly as another contraction took hold. It was a while before she emerged with the sample. I handed it to the nurse to be tested and we returned to the examination room. Another contraction took hold and Faye leant on the examination couch while I rubbed her back and told her to breathe. The nurse reappeared with a hospital gown but said Faye could use her own if she preferred. Faye wanted to use the hospital gown, so when the contraction stopped I helped her into it. She lay on the couch while the nurse took her blood pressure, pulse and temperature and noted them on a form. She asked Faye if she'd had anything to eat recently and Faye shook her head. I explained she'd had dinner at six but had vomited, and since then she'd just had water, which the nurse also wrote in the notes. She then said she needed to take a sample of blood. Faye hadn't made much fuss when the midwife at the doctor's surgery had taken blood samples, but now this seemed to be one pain too many. It took a lot of persuading and distracting before the nurse was able to take the sample.

The nurse left and a midwife arrived. 'Hello, Faye, I'm Gemma,' she said cheerily, 'one of the midwives who will be looking after you tonight.'

I introduced myself and then Gemma explained to Faye that she was going to examine her to make sure the baby was

OK. I held Faye's hand and talked to her calmly, but she moaned loudly as the midwife felt her stomach and then screamed when she examined her internally.

'I'm sorry, pet,' Gemma said. 'I know it's uncomfortable.' Then, 'Well done. You're five centimetres dilated. Baby is on its way.'

While this meant little to Faye, I knew it was good progress. Although Faye's baby might not be born for many hours yet, she was now in the active stage of labour.

'Are you having a boy or a girl?' Gemma asked Faye.

'Don't know,' Faye said.

'Have you thought of any names?'

Faye shook her head.

'Mary if it's a girl and Edward if it's a boy,' I said.

'Those are nice names. Let's get you into the birthing room.'

I helped Faye from the couch and we followed the midwife through to a birthing room, which was exactly the same as the one we'd seen during our visit. I hoped its familiarity was reassuring for Faye. She climbed onto the bed and tucked Snuggles on the pillow beside her.

'Lucky mascot?' Gemma asked, just as the student nurse had done. So I thought it probably wasn't so unusual to bring a treasured object into hospital for comfort and security.

Gemma showed us how to use the gas and air but warned Faye not to use it constantly, as it could cause nausea. I explained this to Faye and that it would help her with the pain. Gemma asked Faye if she was having an epidural. When I'd discussed this with Faye she'd said she didn't want a needle in her back, but I now asked her again, explaining that it would help with the pain. She still didn't want it. When the next contraction came I guided the mouthpiece of the gas and air to her mouth. She took a breath and then, removing it, cried, 'I've wet myself!'

'I expect your waters have broken,' Gemma said calmly. 'It's nothing to worry about. It's part of labour. I'll check.'

'No!' Faye cried as Gemma went to lift the sheet covering her. 'Don't touch me.'

Gemma paused and looked at Faye, unsure of how to proceed.

'I'm sorry,' I said.

Then we all turned as the door to the room began to open slowly. It was a moment before the front steel legs of a walking frame came into view and Wilma awkwardly shuffled in. I immediately went over to hold the door open for her. 'Good to see you,' I said.

'There's a lot of noise in here,' she said, making her way towards the bed. 'I could hear you from the corridor, Faye.'

'Gran!' Faye cried, pushing herself upright. 'You're here!' Tears sprang to her eyes.

'Of course I'm here, you silly sausage. I said I'd come.'

'This is Faye's grandmother,' I said to Gemma as I drew up a chair for Wilma.

'Nice to meet you. I'm one of the midwives looking after your granddaughter.'

I helped Wilma sit down. She was very stiff and her ankles and feet were swollen. She was wearing sandals despite it being winter, and I guessed these were the most comfortable footwear for her. I moved the walking frame out of the way to one side so that Wilma could sit closer to the bed and she hugged Faye. I returned to my chair on the other side of the bed.

'Are you being good?' Wilma asked Faye as she collapsed onto the pillow again. 'I see you've brought Snuggles.'

'It hurts,' Faye said, grimacing, and then cried out as another contraction took hold.

'Remember the gas and air,' I said, directing Faye's hand to the mouthpiece.

'Breathe normally,' Gemma said.

Whether it was the gas and air or her gran's presence I wasn't sure, but Faye began to relax and became more cooperative, now doing as Gemma asked. Without any fuss, she allowed Gemma to check if her waters had broken. They had, and Gemma said she'd get a fresh sheet for the bed. She left the room and returned almost immediately with a sheet and Eunice, the student nurse we'd seen on our arrival, who smiled and asked Faye how she was doing. The nurse and the midwife quickly and efficiently changed the sheet without Faye having to move much. Once Faye was comfortable Gemma said she'd be back later and they both left. I knew from the literature Faye had been given by the hospital and from my own experience of being in labour that the midwives and nurses wouldn't be in the room the whole time, not until the next stage of labour when Faye had to push and the baby would be delivered. That's why it's so important for the woman to have someone with her.

Now it was just a matter of time and nature taking its course. In between contractions Wilma and I talked, and I was soon seeing another side to her. In the past she'd often appeared cool, a little severe and sometimes hard, but now that tough shell gave way to a softer, gentler person full of compassion, sympathy and concern. She was still firm with Faye as the contractions gripped her and she cried out, but that approach seemed to help her. I now realized that perhaps my approach with Faye since she'd gone into labour had been too soft. Wilma spoke to her quite forcefully, as though addressing a wilful child. 'Breathe the gas and air,' or, 'Lie still.' Faye did as she was told, although of course she was just used to doing what her gran told her, as she'd brought her up. Whatever the reason, much of Faye's screaming and crying out stopped and she controlled the pain much better with the gas and air. I asked Wilma if she wanted me to leave. Giving birth is such an intimate and life-affirming experience, I wondered if she'd prefer it if there was just the two of them.

'Good gracious, no,' she said. 'She needs us both. I'm not much help other than talking to her.'

'Stay,' Faye said.

Between contractions Wilma and I talked across the bed. Wilma was holding Faye's free hand and I was holding her other with the gas and air, ready to guide it to her mouth when necessary. Occasionally Faye joined in with our conversation, but most of the time she lay with her eyes closed, sedated by the gas and air. Wilma told me she'd been with her daughter, Mary, at Faye's birth, and then confided more about Mary and the happiness of her childhood before she began drinking heavily as a teenager. Her face clouded as she recounted how she had fought but failed to try to keep Mary sober. She'd died of multiple organ failure as a result of alcoholism, she said. By then Wilma was already looking after Faye and continued to do so, giving up work to invest everything in her granddaughter.

'I still torment myself sometimes that perhaps I could have done something different that would have saved her life,' Wilma admitted sadly. 'Maybe I should have been stricter with her, or perhaps I was too strict.' She shrugged. 'I don't know, but as a mother you blame yourself, don't you?' I nodded.

Wilma also mentioned the unknown father of Faye's child, wondering again who it could be and the circumstances in which Faye had become pregnant. 'We'll get to the bottom of it one day,' she said. We glanced at Faye, but she had her eyes closed and gave no indication she'd even heard.

As we talked Wilma asked me about my life and how I came to be by myself. I explained my husband had left me for someone at work many years before, and the devastation I'd felt when I'd found out he'd been cheating on me. I think the intimacy of the delivery room invited confidences that we probably wouldn't have shared at another time. As Faye's labour progressed I talked about the births of my own children, and my eyes filled when I thought of their father, so proud and emotional as he'd cradled them in his arms at their births. Now he only saw Adrian and Paula for a few hours every four to six weeks.

When Faye grew hot I rinsed a flannel under the cold-water tap and wiped her forehead. 'I've seen this on the television,' she suddenly said, smiling bravely.

The early hours of the morning rolled on and at five o'clock the doctor came with the midwife to examine Faye again and said she was fully dilated. The room quickly filled as the medical staff we'd seen on and off during the night – midwife, doctor and two nurses – were all in the room together, giving instructions and encouragement as Faye entered the final stage of labour. Wilma and I repeated the instructions to Faye and added encouragement and praise of our own, as she now had to push with the contractions and then relax and pant in between them. We mopped her brow and helped her with the gas and air.

Half an hour passed with Faye pushing when told to and trying to relax in between contractions, and she was exhausted. She said she'd had enough and wanted to go home. Gemma was so kind and reassuring and said that it wouldn't be long now before her baby was born. Faye held Snuggles very tightly and with the next big push she cried out.

'Good girl,' Gemma said. 'Your baby's head is crowning. Nearly there. I can see a mop of brown hair.'

'What's happening?' Faye gasped.

'Your baby is being born,' Wilma said.

A few more concentrated pushes and the baby's head appeared, followed by the sound of suction as one of the nurses cleared its airways – suctioning out the mucous from its mouth and nose. A few more strong pushes, with all of us encouraging Faye, and one shoulder appeared and then the other. A final big push and her baby was born.

'It's a boy!' Gemma said as the baby cried. She held him up. 'Look. You have a son, Faye.'

My eyes filled. I kissed Faye's cheek. Wilma did the same. 'Well done, love,' I said. 'Look at your beautiful baby.' This was probably one of the most emotional moments I'd ever experienced in fostering. Wilma was reaching for a tissue to wipe her eyes. Tears of happiness and relief that mother and baby were safe and well.

Faye appeared unable to believe that her ordeal was finally over and, looking bemused, she braced herself for the next contraction.

'Faye, look at your baby,' I said. 'He's beautiful.'

She raised her head slightly so she could see. Gemma had cut and clamped the cord and was now wrapping him in a blanket. As an experienced midwife she must have delivered hundreds of babies, but she made this birth feel as special and unique as the first. Having wrapped him in the blanket, she put a little white hat on him and placed the precious bundle in Faye's arms. Wilma and I looked on in awe and admiration. I asked Faye and Wilma if they'd like me to take some photographs; I was the only one with a camera, and they did. I took about a dozen before the nurse said she needed to take Edward to be weighed, measured and generally checked over. She carefully lifted him from Faye's arms and carried him to the scales on the other side of the room. Faye was still looking bemused so I explained what was happening.

'Seven pounds three ounces,' the nurse announced after a moment. 'He's a good weight.' She checked him over and listened to his heart and said all was well and he was very healthy.

Then she wiped him clean and wrapped him in a fresh blanket and returned him to Faye.

'Baby Edward,' Wilma said, gazing at her great-grandson. 'Baby Edward.' And her eyes filled again.

'Don't cry, Gran,' Faye said. 'You have to be happy.'

'I am,' Wilma said. 'Really, I am.' And I knew that, for now at least, all the worries of the past and the challenges that lay ahead had disappeared in the love she felt for that baby.

Presently Gemma suggested to Faye that she dress Edward in the clothes we'd brought with us, and I opened her overnight bag and took out one of the little vests, a babygrow and a nappy. I'd brought a hat with us but we didn't need it, as the hospital had provided one.

'They're like dolls' clothes,' Wilma said, smiling. 'I'd forgotten just how small newborn clothes are.'

'Can you do it for me?' Faye said to her gran. 'I'm too tired and sore.'

'Yes, of course,' Wilma said, only too pleased to help. 'Cathy can help me.'

I went round to Wilma's side of the bed and set the baby clothes and nappy within her reach. I then carefully lifted little Edward from Faye's arms and laid him on the bed; so small, fragile and precious. Faye propped herself up and watched as Wilma and I gingerly manoeuvred Edward's little arms and legs into the vest, then put on his tiny nappy, taking a side each, and finally the babygrow. It was a joint effort, but Wilma's arthritic fingers couldn't manage the press-studs on the babygrow, so I fastened them. He barely stirred.

'What a smart little fellow,' one of the nurses said.

'Just like his great-grandpa,' Wilma said, referring to Stan.

Now Edward was dressed I took more photographs: Faye with Edward in her arms. Faye with Edward and Snuggles. Faye with Edward and Gran. Gran with Edward in her arms, and then she took one of me with Faye and Edward. A hospital orderly arrived with breakfast for Faye and a welcome cup of tea for Wilma and me. Following Faye's instructions, I placed Edward in the hospital crib by the bed while we ate and drank. Wilma wanted to tell Stan the good news, so I lent her my phone, and then I telephoned home.

Despite the early hour – it was 6.30 a.m. – Paula, Lucy and Adrian were awake and delighted when I told them, and asked me to pass on their congratulations to Faye. One of the nurses who'd helped with the delivery returned to see if Faye would like to start breastfeeding and said she'd help her put the baby to the breast and latch on. I'd previously explained to Faye that breast milk was best for her baby and that a nurse would show her what to do. But Faye said she was very tired, understandably, and just wanted to sleep. The nurse, like all the maternity staff, was lovely and said she'd come back later after Faye had rested. The doctor returned to examine Faye and I took the opportunity to pop out to the bathroom.

Faye then fell into a deep sleep with Edward asleep in the hospital crib beside her. Wilma and I continued sitting on either side of the bed, sometimes talking quietly but mainly gazing at Edward. The nurse who'd offered to help Faye start breastfeeding called back twice during the morning, but, seeing both mother and baby sound asleep, said she wouldn't disturb them and that a nurse from the next shift would help Faye later. I thanked her, and before she left she took Faye's blood pressure, pulse and temperature and noted them on her chart. Faye didn't wake, and Wilma said she'd always been a heavy sleeper, which I'd noticed too. Wilma said that once Faye woke she'd tell her she was going home for the afternoon, and then she and Stan would come back this evening. I said I needed to go home for a few hours too, so I'd give her a lift and also drop her back to the hospital this evening if she wanted. She was grateful and thanked me.

When Faye's lunch arrived a little after midday she woke, and once she was settled with her food within reach on the bed table Wilma asked her if she minded if we went home for a few hours, and then we'd come back in the evening. She said she didn't mind and that she was hungry, so, saying goodbye and congratulating her again, we left her happily tucking into pie and mash, which did smell appetizing.

Wilma was quiet as we walked to the car. I think she was emotionally and physically drained. I know I was. I helped her into the passenger seat and stowed her walking frame in the boot. She remained quiet as I drove, but then neither of us had had any sleep, and she was a lot older than me. But as I drew up outside the flats she turned to me and asked, 'Do you really believe Faye could look after the baby with help?'

'Yes, I do,' I said.

Wilma nodded thoughtfully. 'I think Stan and I need to talk. If we had a bungalow or ground-floor flat that had room for us all, then perhaps ...' Her sentence was left unfinished, although I knew what she was thinking: that now she'd seen the baby, everything had changed, and a future that had once seemed impossible needed to be explored to help Faye keep her baby.

CHAPTER TWENTY

SECOND THOUGHTS

It seemed like a lifetime since I'd left the house with Faye in the first stage of labour, and as I let myself in I was still elated, although exhausted. I knew I needed a few hours of sleep to see me through the rest of the day. I made a hot drink and then, sitting on the sofa, telephoned Mum to tell her the good news. She was delighted of course and said to give Faye her congratulations and she'd send a card and hoped she'd have a chance to see the baby, although I wasn't sure when that would be. I then telephoned Becky, but she already knew – the hospital had phoned her.

'Faye did very well,' Becky said. 'We were half expecting her to need a caesarean.' Which I hadn't known. 'I've arranged for her to spend two nights in hospital so the nurses can help her establish feeding. Then we'll transfer her to the mother-and-baby unit. I'll call in to see her this afternoon.'

Lastly I telephoned Edith, but it went through to her voice-mail so I left a message, then I lay on the sofa and closed my eyes. It was nearly four o'clock when I woke as Paula let herself in the front door. We had a chat and I made a quick dinner for us to have later. Usually, a first-time mother stays in hospital one night after giving birth if it's a normal delivery, but Becky had arranged an extra night to help Faye, which seemed sensible. I didn't read any more into it than that, but it meant that my children could visit tomorrow evening, which I thought was appropriate, as Stan hadn't seen his great-grandson yet and he was going tonight. I ate my dinner early, said a quick hello to Lucy and Adrian as they came in and then goodbye to all three of them as I left to collect Wilma and Stan. It was dark and cold outside and it took a few moments for the heater to warm up the car.

I parked under a street lamp outside the flats and then phoned Wilma and Stan to say I'd arrived as we'd arranged. They were ready with their coats on, but even so, with their mobility problems it took them ten minutes to come down. I helped them into the car, stowing Wilma's walking frame in the boot and Stan's stick beside him. I thought they both looked tired and a little strained, although Wilma said she'd managed to doze in the chair that afternoon. Stan admitted he hadn't slept the night before, worrying about Faye in labour. I didn't know what discussion they'd had, if any, in respect of offering Faye long-term support so that she could try to keep Edward, and it wasn't for me to ask. Any commitment they felt able to make would need to be practical and sustainable: a decision of the head and not just the heart, for it was a huge undertaking. Stan had a supermarket carrier bag tucked on his lap, which he said contained snacks for Faye: grapes, crisps, a box of chocolates and bottles of fizzy energy drinks. 'To build up her strength,' he said.

When we arrived at the hospital Faye had been moved from the delivery suite to the maternity ward, as was normal practice. A nurse showed us to her bed. The curtains were partially closed, as were some of the others on the ward. Wilma went in first, followed by Stan and then me. Faye was awake, propped up on her pillow with Snuggles, and Edward was in the crib beside her bed, fast asleep. She was so pleased to see her grandparents, especially her grandpa, and, sitting up in bed, she spread her arms wide for a big hug. Wilma and I hugged her too, and then I spent some moments arranging chairs for Stan and Wilma on either side of the bed. There was just enough room. I saw Stan stealing glances at Edward, whose crib was on his side of the bed. Once Wilma and Stan were settled I said I'd leave them to have some time with Faye and Edward and then I'd come back a bit later.

'There's no need for that,' Wilma said, but I thought it was right, so I left Faye tucking into one of the packets of crisps Stan had brought and went to find a coffee.

When I returned half an hour or so later Faye was offering around the box of chocolates. I thanked her as I chose one and then perched on the edge of the bed. Edward was still sound asleep. Swaddled in a hospital blanket with his tiny white hat over his forehead, only his little face was visible. He was already losing that scrunched-up look, but as with many newborns I couldn't see a family likeness.

'Have you had a hold yet?' I asked Stan.

'No. He's been asleep.'

'How's the feeding going?' I asked Faye. I was hoping that Edward would be due for a feed soon so we could all have a hold.

Faye shrugged. 'The nurse will tell you.'

'One of the nurses fed him,' Wilma said, clearly having had a conversation about this already with Faye. 'Faye hasn't been out of bed yet.'

'Oh. Why not?' I asked. Faye had delivered twelve hours previously. A new mother would usually be up and tending to her baby by now after a normal delivery.

'I got up to go to the toilet,' Faye said, choosing another chocolate. 'It hurt, so I'm staying in bed.'

'You're bound to be sore for a while,' I said. 'That's normal. Have the nurses given you some tablets for the pain?'

She nodded as she ate.

'I wonder if the doctor should examine her,' I said to Wilma. 'To make sure everything is all right.'

'She has,' Wilma said. 'A nurse told us they'd called the doctor and everything is as it should be.'

'Here, you can have a coffee cream,' Faye said, pushing the box of chocolates towards me. 'None of us likes coffee creams.'

Stan and Wilma gave a small laugh.

'I do,' I said, and helped myself to one of the coffee cream chocolates. 'Thank you. Did Becky come and see you this afternoon?' I asked Faye. 'She said she was going to.'

'Yes,' Faye said, and then spent some moments choosing another chocolate from the box.

We continued chatting, mainly about the hospital routine, as Faye enjoyed the chocolates her grandpa had brought for her. She had never been an inpatient in hospital before and was fascinated by all the comings and goings, especially the trolley that arrived with the meals. Her only complaint was that there wasn't a television, so she was missing her favourite programmes. I consoled her by reminding her that she would only be in hospital for two nights and I was sure there would be a television at the mother-and-baby unit. Edward stirred, wrinkled his nose and sighed but didn't wake. Wilma, Stan and I were watching him, fascinated, but Faye was more interested in showing Snuggles the box of chocolates. I appreciated it must be very strange for her to suddenly be a mother and that it would take time for her to fully understand what that meant. It would probably take her longer than the average mother to adjust and bond with her baby, but the specialist mother-and-baby unit would help her.

At eight o'clock Wilma said that she and Stan were very tired and told Faye they would go home soon. She said they'd visit her again the following afternoon. Turning to me, she said, 'We'll book a cab. Our neighbour wants to come as well. Perhaps you could visit Faye in the evening. We couldn't manage the journey twice in one day.'

'Yes, of course,' I said. 'I'd be pleased to.'

'I'm very thirsty,' Faye said. 'Aren't I, Snuggles?'

'Hardly surprising with the number of chocolates you've eaten,' Stan said affectionately. Unscrewing the top of one of the fizzy drinks he'd brought, he passed it to her.

I refilled her glass from the jug of water on her beside cabinet and put that within her reach too. Then we all began to say goodbye. I glanced hopefully at Edward in the crib and thought he must be due for a feed soon, but he stayed firmly asleep. I seemed to remember being advised by a maternity nurse to wake Adrian and Paula to feed them when they were newborns, but I didn't want to interfere. The nurses would be advising Faye. I said goodbye first and then waited at the end of the bed while Stan and Wilma kissed Faye and then manoeuvred themselves out of the cubicle. We walked slowly to the elevator to take us to the ground floor.

The night was inky black and a frost had settled while we'd been inside. Salt and gravel had been scattered on the pathways and in the car park, and our feet crunched over the hard surface. Once inside the car I switched on the heater to defrost the windscreen before pulling away. Stan and Wilma were both quiet; exhausted and possibly deep in thought. Wilma stifled a few yawns during the journey and then apologized, while Stan actually dozed off for a while. As I pulled up outside their block of flats I asked them if they'd like me to give them and their neighbour a lift to the hospital the following afternoon, rather than use a cab, but Stan thanked me and said they'd be all right and I'd done enough already. I saw them safely to the entrance and then returned to my car and drove home. I wondered what arrangements would be made to move Faye from the hospital to the mother-and-baby home the day after tomorrow. I needed to know before too long, as I had to pack Faye's belongings and get them to her, presumably at the unit, wherever that was. I didn't have an address yet. I thought that if Becky hadn't telephoned me by the following afternoon then I'd phone her to find out.

Once home I told Paula, Lucy and Adrian that Faye was well and suggested that they came with me to visit the following evening. Adrian said that unfortunately he couldn't as he was working until eight, but the girls were free to come. I had an early night and, having had no sleep the night before, I slept like a log and was woken by the alarm. When I opened the curtains it was onto another cold, crisp day. Everything was covered with a deep hoar frost and the pavements, roads and rooftops glistened. With my dressing gown on, I headed downstairs to make a coffee and feed Sammy before I woke the children.

It was strange not having Faye at home. Her routine had become part of my routine, so there were now gaps and I had too much time to do what I usually did: make my coffee, shower and dress, and then have breakfast. I thought of Faye in hospital, probably tucking into her breakfast between feeding and changing Edward. I hoped they had the cereal she liked. Adrian, Lucy and Paula found Faye's absence strange too, and said they wondered how she was getting on. Sammy clearly missed Faye and wandered from room to room looking for her. Eventually he went upstairs and curled into a ball on her bed – something he'd never done before. I'm sure animals are a lot more intelligent than we give them credit for and can sense things in a way we can't comprehend. Sadly, there was no way I could explain to him that Faye was safe and well and in hospital, having had a wonderful baby boy.

Once the children had left and I'd cleared up the breakfast things, I decided to do Faye's packing. Although I didn't know the arrangements for moving her to the mother-and-baby home, I did know for certain she would be moving the next day, so it made sense to be ready. I began by bringing her laundry up to date, and then I took down her large suitcase from on top of the wardrobe and started packing it with her clothes. It's always sad when a child or younger person we've been fostering leaves us, but this wasn't as sad as many children we'd had to say goodbye to, as Faye had a beautiful baby, which is a joyous occasion. And she was leaving us so she could learn to parent her baby and hopefully keep him. It was therefore a positive outcome, and although we'd miss her I was anticipating seeing her regularly at the mother-and-baby unit, and hopefully she'd keep in touch after she'd left.

Faye had far more clothes now than when she'd arrived, and it wasn't long before the suitcase was full. I closed it, put it to one side and broke for lunch. In the afternoon I continued packing, using the holdalls I kept as spares for the children I fostered. With all her clothes packed, I put her personal items into her shoulder bag and then checked the room for any stray items. Leaving all the cases there ready for the following day, I came out and closed the door. It was now 3.30 p.m. and I decided that while I had the time I should start wrapping Christmas presents. It would be 16 December tomorrow, as our advent calendars showed, and I didn't know when I'd have another opportunity. I always bought a few extra presents just in case a child arrived close to Christmas, or even on Christmas Eve, so I put those to one side. I began by wrapping Edward's presents and carefully placing them in his 'My First Christmas' sack. I was in my element. I was working in my bedroom so that when I had to break off I could leave all the paraphernalia of wrapping – the paper, sticky tape, scissors, ribbon, bows and gift cards – on the floor without it being in anyone's way. An hour later, when I'd finished wrapping Edward's presents and had begun on Faye's, the landline rang. I reached over and picked up the handset from my bedside cabinet. I was pleased to hear Becky's voice.

'I was about to phone you,' I said chirpily. 'I've packed Faye's bags ready.'

There was silence – uncharacteristic for Becky, who was always upbeat and communicative. 'I'm afraid there's a problem, Cathy,' she said sombrely.

'With what?'

'Wilma telephoned me. When they arrived at the hospital this afternoon the staff nurse took them aside to speak to them. Faye hasn't been feeding or changing her baby. In fact, she hasn't done anything since he was born. The nursing assistants have been doing it all. The staff nurse asked Wilma if she could talk to Faye. She thought it might help, but it didn't. Stan and their good friend and neighbour were there too, and they all tried talking to her. But Faye refused to engage and buried her head under the sheets.'

'But why?' I asked, horrified.

'I'm not completely sure. Wilma says it's because Faye's having second thoughts about looking after Edward.'

'No, I'm sure it's not that. It can't be. Faye's probably over-whelmed by all the changes. It's a huge upheaval, having a baby, physically and emotionally. She's in an unfamiliar place with a very different routine and surrounded by people she doesn't know.'

'I appreciate that, Cathy. But when I visited her yesterday it crossed my mind that she should be interacting more with her baby. I put it down to her being tired from the birth and the shock of all the changes. I've now spoken to the staff nurse. I can't send Faye to the mother-and-baby unit unless she's looking after her baby. They'll help her, but they won't do it all for her, and at present she won't have anything to do with Edward.'

My mouth was dry and my heart began thumping loudly in my chest. 'Let me talk to her,' I said. 'I'm sure Faye just needs some encouragement and time to adjust.'

'Yes, please. And explain she can't stay in hospital indefi-nitely. She's well enough to leave and the doctor is ready to discharge her.' Becky paused. 'But, Cathy, if Faye isn't going to look after her baby I'll have to speak to children's services to arrange an emergency foster placement for him. I know this isn't what we were hoping for, but I have to be practical.

And if the baby comes into care, Faye will have to return to live with her grandparents.'

'Where are her grandparents now?' I asked.

'Home.'

'I'll go to the hospital and talk to Faye straight away. I'm sure I can make her see sense.'

'Phone me when you've spoken to her, please. My office number will go through to my mobile if it's out of hours.'

As I replaced the handset I felt sick with fear. What had gone wrong? Faye, what are you thinking of? Of course you want to keep your baby. That's what we've been working towards all these months. And you can do it. I know you can. You're just lacking the confidence at present. You need to see how precious he is. What you are going to lose? I stood and stepped over the wrapping paper and presents, the joy of Christmas now a long way off. I hurried downstairs and, taking my mobile from my handbag, quickly typed a text message to Adrian, Lucy and Paula: *Have 2 go 2 the hospital 2 c Faye. She's feeling low. I'll explain later. Please make dinner. Love Mum xx.* I pressed send, quickly checked that the back door was locked and then, stuffing my feet into my shoes, grabbed my coat and bag and flew out the front door.

I had no idea what I was going to say to Faye. Whatever it took to get her out of bed and caring for her baby. Perhaps I should have encouraged her yesterday, I thought as I drove, instead of letting her lie in bed and eat chocolates, but it hadn't really occurred to me that anything was wrong, and I don't think it had to Stan and Wilma either. Faye knew how to look after her baby if she thought about it. Once she started putting into practice everything I'd taught her, she'd be fine. I had every confidence in her. Of course Edward wouldn't be going into foster care; he was staying with his mother. As I'd told Becky, Faye was simply overwhelmed by all the changes. We should have spotted the signs earlier, maybe even foreseen it. Poor little Edward, lying there in his cot without his mother's care. Thank goodness the nurses were looking after him. I glanced at the speedometer and realized I was driving over the speed limit. I touched the brake and, taking a deep breath, tried to calm myself.

It was dark by 5 p.m. in December and the hospital car park was lit by a few lamps over the payment meters. I fed in the coins, placed the ticket on the windscreen and then hurried to the maternity entrance. Inside, the fluorescent lights were dazzlingly bright and the tinsel sparkled on the Christmas tree. I didn't wait for the elevator but ran up the couple of flights of stairs to the maternity ward. I paused briefly outside the swing doors to disinfect by hands with gel from the pump dispenser on the wall and then pressed the security buzzer to enter the ward. The curtains were still partially closed around Faye's bed and, easing one aside, I went in. Faye was in bed, on her side, cuddled up to Snuggles and facing away from the young nurse who sat in a chair by her bed feeding Edward. The nurse looked up and smiled.

'I'm Cathy. I was Faye's carer.'

'Hello,' she said sweetly. 'Would you like to give him the rest of his bottle? We're very busy on the ward tonight.'

'Yes, or perhaps Faye would,' I said pointedly, looking at her.

Faye responded by pulling the cover further up over her face.

Slipping off my coat, I went to where the nurse was and sat in the chair she vacated. She carefully laid Edward in my arms.

'It's a long while since I've fed a newborn,' I said apprehensively.

'I'm sure you'll be fine. Use the call button if you need help.' She waited until he'd latched onto the teat. 'There,' she said, smiling. 'He's feeding well.' I was relieved.

'I'm leaving Cathy to feed your baby,' the nurse said to Faye. 'I'll see you later.' But Faye didn't so much as look at her. I guessed the nurse knew there was a problem.

'Thanks for your help,' I said as she disappeared through the gap in the curtains.

I looked at Edward in my arms. His eyes were closed tight as all his effort and concentration went into feeding. So small, fragile and vulnerable, so perfect and beautiful. I glanced up at Faye, who was still on her side, facing away from me.

'It's a big step, having a baby,' I said gently as Edward suckled. 'I guess you must be feeling pretty scared and worried right now. I can remember how I felt when I had Adrian. I didn't know anything about babies then. I was sure I'd do something wrong that would hurt him, or even drop him.' I wondered if this was a worry of Faye's. She was aware she was clumsy and uncoordinated, so perhaps she wasn't touching him for fear of harming or dropping him.

'You won't hurt him,' I said. 'You'll sit down to feed him, and when you carry him you'll hold him close to your chest. Just as we practised at home with the doll. Then, when you go out, he'll be in a pram, so no harm will come to him. You'll do fine, I know you will.' I glanced up, but there was no response, then down at Edward as he continued suckling.

'Faye, no one is expecting you to know everything all at once,' I continued gently. 'The nurses are helping you now, and then once you move to the mother-and-baby home the

261

staff there will help you. You can phone Becky, your grand-parents and me any time if you have a problem, and we'll all visit regularly. I can come and see you every day if necessary, and I'm on the end of the phone if you have a question.' I paused and glanced at her again. 'Is there anything in particu-lar worrying you? If so, tell me and I'm sure I can help you with it now.' I waited, but there was no response. I returned my gaze to Edward, who was now draining the last of his bottle.

'Faye, love, I know you can look after your baby. I'm posi-tive you can. He needs you and you need him. Why don't you turn over and look at him? He's gorgeous. In a moment he'll need winding and maybe his nappy will need changing. It's a long while since I changed a nappy. You and I used to practise on the doll at home, do you remember? We did it so many times. Let's see if we can do it together. We'll help each other.' Still nothing. Edward took the last of the milk and I gently eased the teat from his lips and placed the bottle on the table.

'Time to wind him,' I said, hoping Faye's interest would now be sparked enough that she'd at least turn over to look at him. I didn't understand her resistance. I eased little Edward into a sitting position and then, supporting his head with one hand, I began to gently rub his back with the other, just as Faye had practised on the doll at home.

'Look, Faye, it's simple, love. I'm sure you'll remember. You support his chin and massage his back.' But she remained facing away.

I concentrated on Edward and a few moments later I was rewarded with a burp. 'Well done, little fellow,' I said, as pleased with myself for bringing up his wind as I was with him. 'Did you hear that, Faye? He burped.'

I looked again towards the bed and now saw the smallest movement, but it wasn't Faye getting up or even turning over. She was crying. 'What is it, love? What's the matter? Why are you upset? Please tell me.'

CHAPTER TWENTY-ONE

AN IMPOSSIBLE DECISION

Edward could really have done with some more winding, but my priority now lay with Faye. I carefully wrapped him in his blanket and placed him on his back in the crib, then I repositioned his little hat. I went round the end of the bed and sat in the chair on the other side so I was facing Faye. The sheet covered her mouth and her eyes were closed, but tears silently escaped and ran down her cheeks.

'Faye, what's the matter, love?' I took a tissue from the box and gently wiped away her tears. 'Why are you upset? Edward is fine. He's had his bottle and is asleep in the crib. We can change his nappy later. There's nothing for you to worry about.'

'Yes, there is,' Faye said, without opening her eyes.

'What? What's wrong? He's a lovely baby. You've done well.' Another tear escaped and ran down her cheek. I wiped it away. My heart ached for her. 'Faye, love, can you try to tell me what's wrong? I'm sure I can help.'

'You can't,' she said. 'There's nothing you can do.'

'So tell me what it is. What is it that's upsetting you?'

Her brow creased, then she opened her eyes and looked at me, her expression one of deep sorrow and regret. 'Cathy, I can't learn all I have to. Really, I can't.'

'You can,' I said, relieved I'd found the reason. 'Not all at once, but slowly, one step at a time. And when you start looking after him you'll find it gets easier. You'll remember what to do. You know more than you think, Faye, and the nurses here and the staff at the home will help you.'

She gave a slight shake of her head and then heaved herself from under the covers and propped herself onto the pillow. Her face was red and tear-stained.

'That's better, I can see you now,' I said positively. I passed her a tissue and then took one of her hands in mine as she stared down at the bed. 'Come on, love. Tell me exactly what it is that's worrying you,' I encouraged. 'Then we can sort it out.'

'There's too much for me to learn,' she said despairingly. 'Lots and lots of things I can't remember.'

'Like what?'

She thought for a moment. 'Cleaning the stump. I heard the nurses talking about it and I don't know what to do.'

Faye was referring to the clamped umbilical-cord stump on the baby, which would need cleaning for the first week or so until it dropped off.

'I'll show you,' I said, with an encouraging smile. 'It's easy once you know how. Is there anything else?'

'Yes.' She turned to look at me properly, fear and pain in her eyes. 'Cathy, I'm different from you. You can learn things and keep them in your head, but I can't.'

'Yes, you can, Faye. You have learnt lots of things.'

'But I forget them,' she said more forcefully. 'Some days I forget everything. You know. You've seen me like that. You can't forget things when you have a baby.'

'But that's only when you have an off day. On all the other days you remember things.'

'But not enough.' She paused before continuing. 'You're a nice person, Cathy, a really nice person. You've done your best to help me. I thought I could learn when we were using the doll, but now I've seen my baby I know it's not enough. I'm very worried, Cathy. I love my baby, but I can't look after him.'

I paused as I looked at her. 'Did you tell your gran this?'

'Yes.'

'What did she say?'

'She understands. She's known me all my life and understands.'

'In a way I don't?' I asked quietly.

Faye nodded. 'I know I'm going to be sad when I have to say goodbye to Edward, but I want him to be adopted. I want him to have a proper mummy and daddy who will love him as much as I do. Ones who can drive and take him out in the car to see lots of wonderful places, like you do. I want his mummy and daddy to be clever and teach him things so he does really well at school. I can't ever do that. I want him to be smart like Adrian, Paula and Lucy. Please try to understand like my gran does, Cathy. It's for the best.'

I felt my eyes mist as a lump rose in my throat, and for a moment I couldn't speak. The sounds of a busy ward continued in the background on the other side of the curtains as I sat quietly holding Faye's hand.

'Can you understand?' Faye asked after a while.

'Yes, but Faye, listen to me. Don't you think you should at least try to look after Edward? Give yourself the chance. You could go to the mother-and-baby home and see how you get on looking after him. You might surprise yourself. Isn't it too early to make that decision?'

She paused and took a breath, her brow furrowing. 'Cathy, it's going to hurt me badly now when I have to say goodbye to him. It would hurt me even more if I looked after him and then had to say goodbye. It would hurt him too. He doesn't know me now, but he would in a few months. He'd love me as I love him. I don't want to hurt him. He's too precious. I know I can't look after him. I'm certain. Gran knows too.'

I nodded slowly and wiped the moisture from the corner of my eye. Faye had spoken with wisdom and insight and I knew she'd given this a lot of thought. Of course she was right about bonding with Edward if she tried to look after him for six months. In that time she and Edward would grow close, and to say goodbye then would be even more traumatic and distressing than it would be now. Faye had considered this and the complexities of looking after him and knew what she was capable of, as did her gran. I realized then I had to put aside my own feelings of failure and listen to what she was telling me. This was her decision and, heartbreaking though it was, I needed to accept it.

'Your grandparents agree?' I asked.

She nodded. 'Grandpa said it had to be my decision. They said if I wanted to try and look after Edward they would help me, which was kind of them. But they're old, Cathy, and they need help, so they couldn't really help me. Even with their help, I know I couldn't manage. I'd be very worried all the time, like I am now. Like I have been since he was born. Grandpa says it's the responsibility. I told them I wanted Edward adopted, and I was sorry I changed my mind and upset them.'

I lightly rubbed her hand in mine and glanced at Edward, sleeping peacefully in the crib, and blissfully unaware of the dramatic and far-reaching change that was about to take place in his future. I could barely look at him for the sorrow I felt.

'Faye, you understand that if you are certain you're not going to look after Edward, he will stay with a foster carer for a while before he is adopted. And you will go home to live with your grandparents.'

'I know. That's what I want, Cathy,' she said quietly. 'It's best for us all, and especially for Edward. He's the most important person in this. Not me, Gran, Grandpa or you. He deserves the best and I want him to be happy.' Said with such selflessness and understanding … I was very moved. I gave her hand a reassuring squeeze.

'I understand and I respect your decision, Faye,' I said. 'You're a very brave, kind girl.'

'Am I, Cathy?' she asked, childlike and vulnerable. 'That's nice, thank you.' I could have wept.

The nurse who'd been feeding Edward when I'd arrived returned briefly to check on him. I guessed the nurses checked on him regularly, as Faye wasn't looking after him.

'He finished his bottle,' I said, straightening in my chair. 'But I didn't change his nappy.'

'OK, thanks. We'll do it later.' Then to Faye: 'Are you all right, pet?'

'Yes, thank you,' Faye said. 'I've had to make a very difficult decision, haven't I, Cathy?' I nodded. 'That's what Grandpa called it – a very difficult decision.'

The nurse threw her a small, professional smile. 'I'll look in later then,' she said. She glanced into the crib and then, picking up the empty feeding bottle, left the cubicle.

I sat back in my chair and tried to relax. I felt emotionally drained, as I was sure Faye did, having struggled with this decision for two days and nights. I shuddered to think of the pain this must have caused her as she lay alone in her hospital bed, considering the alternatives and finally accepting she couldn't ever parent her son. We were both quiet for some time, and then I heard her take a breath.

'Cathy?' she asked, turning her head slightly towards me.

'Yes, love?'

'Can I ask you to do something for me?'

'Yes, of course. I'll help if I can.'

'Will you phone Becky and tell her what I've told you, and that when the foster carer comes to take my baby I want you here with me. Gran and Grandpa will be too upset. Can you be with me?'

My eyes filled again. 'Yes, if it's possible. I don't know what arrangements Becky will make, but when I leave here I'll phone her and find out.'

'Thank you. That's kind of you.' Her eyes closed and her head relaxed back in a mixture of exhaustion and relief.

I stayed for a while longer, but when it became clear Faye was asleep I moved quietly away from the bed, checked on Edward and then left. I stopped by the nurses' station on the way out to tell them I was leaving and that Faye and Edward were asleep, then I slipped on my coat and left the ward.

Outside, the cold air hit me as I hurried, head down, across the car park, fighting back my tears. Faye had originally come to live with me with the intention of placing her baby for adoption, so in a way we had come full circle. Not that this was any consolation. All my hopes and aspirations for her and Edward had been dashed. While we'd been working towards her keeping her baby, I'd put aside any doubts I might have had about her ability to parent, and had concentrated on teaching her and preparing her for the birth and parenthood. I'd covered what I thought Faye needed to know time and time again, repeating things as often as was required. I'd done my best, but clearly that hadn't been good enough. Could I have done more? I honestly didn't know. We never did get that electronic doll, but I doubted that would have made much difference to the outcome. Practising on any doll, however sophisticated, was a long way from the reality of caring for a baby, and Faye had found the responsibility just too much to cope with. She knew what she was capable of, as did her grandparents, and I had to respect that.

It was nearly six o'clock now. With the key in the ignition but the engine off, I took my phone from my bag and telephoned Becky. She answered straight away.

'It's Cathy. I've just seen Faye.'

'Yes?'

I took a deep breath. 'She told me she wants Edward to be adopted. She says she's sure she can't look after him, and it's better if he goes now rather than her trying to look after him and then having to give him up.'

'That's what Wilma said. Do you think her grandparents put her under any pressure to come to that decision?'

'No. Faye said they told her they'd back whatever decision she made. They said they were willing to help if she decided to try to keep him.'

'All right. Thank you. I'm leaving the office soon and I'll go from here to see Faye. Then I'll need to make arrangements for the baby to come into care. I'm thinking on my feet, but as it's getting late it might be better if he stayed at the hospital tonight and then I'll move him tomorrow. I'll have to check with the hospital if that's all right. Faye can go home this evening. Is she up and about yet?'

'No. Becky, she asked if I could be there when you take the baby. I told her I would if I could but I'd need to check with you.'

'I see. Could you manage tonight if necessary?'

'Yes.'

'I'll go to the hospital now and then I'll phone you later.'

'Thank you.'

I returned my phone to my bag and then drove home, deep in thought and haunted by the image of Faye giving up her baby. Yes, I'd be there if that was what she wanted, but I wasn't sure how much use I'd be. Every time I thought of Faye and little Edward my eyes filled. It was heart-rending and I didn't know how I'd cope.

The girls heard the front door open and as soon as I stepped into the hall they appeared from the living room. Adrian was working until eight again.

'I thought you were taking us to see Faye and her baby tonight?' Paula said, a little disgruntled.

'There's been a change of plan,' I said as I hung my coat on the hall stand.

'So aren't we going then?' Lucy persisted.

'No. Let's go and sit down and I'll explain.' I could smell dinner cooking – Lucy and Paula must have made it – but I wasn't hungry.

In the living room the girls sat together on the sofa and I took one of the easy chairs. They looked at me and waited.

'I guess it's not good news then,' Lucy said.

I shook my head and drew a breath. 'Faye has decided she can't look after Edward and he should be adopted.' They stared at me, serious and concerned.

'Oh,' Paula said after a moment, while Lucy remained silent.

'I've spoken to her social worker and Edward will go into care either this evening or tomorrow. Faye will go home. It's obviously not what any of us was hoping for, but it's her decision.'

'That's very sad,' Paula said at last.

'But it's not completely unexpected, is it?' Lucy said. 'I mean, Faye was going to struggle to look after her baby and it's better if it happens now than in a few years' time.'

Lucy had been badly neglected before coming into care so had a very personal view of a mother trying, but failing, to parent her child.

'And adoption is good for the child,' Lucy added. 'Look at me.'

I managed a weak smile. 'But even so, it's very sad when a mother has to give up her child, for whatever reason.'

'Aren't we going to see Edward at all then?' Paula asked forlornly.

'I don't think so.'

'We bought a present for him from us all,' Paula said. 'It's a big teddy bear.'

'And a congratulations card for Faye,' Lucy said. 'But that's not really appropriate now, is it?'

'No,' I agreed quietly. 'It isn't. But I'm sure I can get the present to Edward somehow, when I know the arrangements. I've bought Christmas presents too.' I looked away and swallowed hard as we all fell silent.

Sammy sauntered in, looked at us and, deciding this wasn't much fun, went out again. A Christmas garland stirred gently, its gaiety now perversely at odds with our sadness.

'So. There we have it,' I said at last. 'We did our best. We've faced upsetting situations in fostering before and I don't suppose this will be the last.' But my bottom lip trembled, undermining the brave stoicism of my words. The girls saw and came over and encircled me in their arms. I put mine around them and we hugged. A group hug. We've group hugged since the children were little and it's helped us all at some time or other when one of us has been upset. The warmth and reassurance of having the arms of loved ones around you is comforting and heartening. Sometimes we have a group hug when we're not upset, just because we want to.

After a while we drew apart and Paula said more brightly, 'We've made dinner, Mum. You'll be surprised by our culinary efforts. Shall we dish it up now?'

I hadn't the heart to say no, that I wasn't hungry, when they'd gone to so much trouble. 'Yes, please, but just a little for me.'

They insisted I waited in the living room until they were ready. The food certainly smelt good. Sometimes when I asked them or Adrian to make dinner because I was rushing around and hadn't the time, they took the easy way out and defrosted convenience food from the freezer, but that hadn't happened tonight. When they called me in I was very impressed. A steaming pasta, ham and vegetable bake topped with a delicious cheese sauce and browned to perfection stood on a pad in the centre of the table, and beside it garlic bread and a bowl of salad.

'Wow,' I said. 'You'll have to cook more often.'

'No, thanks. It took us ages,' Lucy said.

'It must have done.'

We served ourselves and it was delicious, although the conversation as we ate was more subdued than usual. Once we'd finished I said I'd clear away, as they'd made dinner, and there were audible sounds of relief. When Adrian came home I told him straight away of Faye's decision, even before he'd showered.

'I'm sorry to hear that,' he said. 'I guess she knows best, and the baby will be loved and well looked after with the adoptive parents.'

'Yes.'

That was all he said, although I knew he'd be thinking much more. Adrian's never been one to wear his heart on his sleeve, but Faye giving up her baby would have affected him as much as it had the rest of us.

After he'd eaten he complimented the girls on their cooking. He sometimes teased them if they cooked, feigning stomach pains, as they did to him. But tonight he was all praise and said, as I had, that it was delicious, and then added that surprisingly he still felt quite well, which won him a light-hearted smack on the arm from the girls.

It was now 8.45 and I was still waiting for Becky to telephone with the arrangements for Edward going into care. I wondered if I should call Mum and tell her what was happening, but decided to wait until the following day when the deed was done and hopefully I would feel stronger, more positive and less likely to burst into tears.

At nine o'clock I was sitting in the living room, the phone within reach, and writing up my log notes for the day – my visit to the hospital and Faye's decision. It wasn't easy and my eyes kept welling, making it difficult to see what I was writing. The phone rang and I reached out and picked up the handset. It was Becky on her mobile, just about to leave the hospital. She'd been there for two and a half hours, talking to Faye and making arrangements.

'Edward can stay here tonight,' she said, 'and then tomorrow he'll go into foster care. I'm aiming to have him collected at eleven o'clock in the morning, but I'm waiting for confirmation on the time from the carer's social worker. Faye asked me if she could stay in hospital tonight so she can spend one last night with Edward, and I've agreed this with the staff nurse. Faye won't be looking after him, the nurses will, but she just wants to be close to him. I've moved his crib right up beside her bed so she can see him during the night.' Becky's voice fell away and it was a moment before she could continue. 'Once I've had confirmation from children's services about the time tomorrow, I'll phone you, Cathy. Probably in the morning now, as it's getting late. I shall be at the hospital tomorrow when the carer arrives, but Stan and Wilma won't. I've spoken to them and they'll be waiting at home for Faye. I'll take her there once the baby's gone. I've told her she needn't be there, she doesn't have to hand the baby to the carer, but she wants to.' She stopped abruptly as emotion again got the better of her. 'It's been a long day.'

'Yes.' I took a deep breath and then, focusing on the practical, said, 'Faye's belongings are here. I'll have to get them to her at some point.'

'Perhaps you could take them to her once she's home? If not, I will.'

'I can take them,' I said.

'Thank you. Give her a day or so. She's bound to be upset, and she'll still have some clothes at home she can wear. I'll phone you in the morning as soon as I hear.'

We said goodnight and I stayed where I was for a few minutes, composing myself, then I went upstairs to tell Adrian, Paula and Lucy what was happening. They were in their bedrooms, reading, texting or listening to music, and I went in and out of each of their rooms and told them that I wasn't going to the hospital tonight, as Edward would be going into care tomorrow. I didn't tell them what Becky had said about Faye asking if she could spend one more night with her baby, as I knew my composure would crack and they'd find it very upsetting. I also told them I was having an early night and reminded them to make sure that Sammy was in for the night. Now they were older I sometimes went to bed before them and read or listened to the radio, but not tonight. I just wanted the comfort of my bed.

I'd forgotten that I'd been wrapping Christmas presents when I'd taken the telephone call to go to the hospital, and as I entered my bedroom and switched on the light the first thing I saw was Edward's sack – 'My First Christmas'. Beside that lay the camera I'd bought for Faye, which I'd been about to wrap – her present from us so she could take lots of photographs of Edward on Christmas morning. That was it. The tears I'd been fighting back all evening now fell. I closed my bedroom door so no one could hear, sat on the floor with my back against the door and, with the presents in view, wept.

I cried for little Edward who wouldn't be spending this Christmas, or any other, with his mother. I cried for Faye, the kindest, most gentle person I knew, who, despite her learning difficulties, had tried her best to learn to parent and then, facing an impossible decision, had made the ultimate sacrifice. I cried for my darling dad, whom I missed dreadfully as we faced our first Christmas without him. Then I cried for all the pain and suffering in the world – for those whose lives had been blighted by war, famine or years of abuse, sadness or loss. Then I just cried.

It's said that a good cry helps, but as I finally wiped my eyes and began packing away the presents, ribbon and paper I didn't feel much better. In a little over twelve hours I'd be with Faye as she said goodbye to her baby, and it was agony.

CHAPTER TWENTY-TWO

SAYING GOODBYE

I needed to be strong for Faye. She'd asked me to be with her for support, and I couldn't let her down. As I showered and dressed the following morning I clung to that thought and tried to contain my emotion. But the image of Faye saying goodbye to Edward and then handing him to the carer tortured me. I hadn't slept well, although as I'd tossed and turned I'd also been dreading the night being over, as it would take us closer to that fateful moment. Did I secretly hope that Faye would change her mind at the last minute? Yes, but I doubted she would. I knew she hadn't taken the decision lightly; she'd been wrestling with it since Edward's birth, which was why she hadn't wanted anything to do with him. And perhaps part of me felt it was the right decision, and that it was inevitable.

I couldn't face breakfast but drank a large mug of coffee. Paula, Lucy and Adrian didn't mention what was about to happen until I saw them off at the door one at a time.

'Good luck,' Lucy said, with a very serious expression as she kissed my cheek.

'I'll be thinking of you,' Paula said, hugging me hard.

'Phone me at work if you need me,' Adrian said, and patted the top of my head. With him being that much taller than me, it was usually comical, and I managed a small smile.

Once the house was empty, save for Sammy and me, I put the contents of the laundry basket into the washing machine and then tidied up the kitchen. At nine o'clock the landline rang and my heart stepped up a beat.

'Hello, Cathy.' It was Becky telephoning from her office. 'I'll be at the hospital by ten thirty,' she said evenly. 'The foster carer will be arriving at eleven, so I suggest you arrive at ten forty-five. I haven't met the carer, but she sounds very nice. She has two older children of her own and special-izes in fostering babies and toddlers. She's just moved a toddler to adoptive parents and is looking forward to caring for a baby again.'

'Good,' I said, with as much enthusiasm as I could muster. 'What's her name?'

'Patsy.'

'Patsy McDonald?'

'Yes. Do you know her?'

'A little, from our fostering support group meetings and training. I've spoken to her. She is very nice, a lovely person.' I felt very slightly better.

'Excellent. You'll be able to reassure Faye. I'm going to telephone Stan and Wilma now and confirm what time I'll be bringing Faye home. I'll see you at ten forty-five then.'

'Yes.'

I now had an hour to fill before I needed to leave for the hospital. I knew I couldn't settle to much, so I took a duster and began wiping various surfaces. They weren't really dusty, but I thought being on the move and doing something physical might distract me. I also put away the doll, doll's bottle, crib and clothes Faye and I had been practising with. I didn't want any reminders when I came home. I'd already put Edward's Santa sack and Faye's presents out of sight in what had been her bedroom.

It was almost a relief when it was time for me to leave for the hospital; waiting for the inevitable had become agonizing. I went through my usual routine of locking and checking the back door, and then I put on my coat and shoes and left the house. I was dressed smartly but soberly in a plain navy skirt, blue jumper, ankle boots and a grey coat. The weather was clear and dry. I reversed the car from the driveway and then concentrated on the road ahead. I could feel my stomach churning, and as I neared the hospital my mouth went dry and I shivered, but I managed to keep the tears from my eyes. I parked the car in view of the maternity block and then suddenly panic gripped me. I was sure I was going to let Faye down. I switched off the engine and sat for a minute to compose myself, then I got out, fed the meter, placed the ticket on the windscreen and crossed the car park to the maternity entrance.

The Christmas tree was lit up, but any joy it represented evaded me. A young couple, both smiling broadly, came out of the elevator, the man carrying their newborn baby in a carrier car seat. They searched for eye contact, wanting the world to share their happiness, and I smiled back. Leaving hospital for the first time with your newborn is a glorious moment, one that Faye wouldn't now experience. It was exactly ten forty-five as I entered the ward and I stopped dead as anxiety gripped me. The curtains around Faye's bed were open and she and her baby were gone.

'Where's Faye?' I asked the auxiliary nurse who was making up the bed. Had I misunderstood the instructions and come too late?

'We're in here, Cathy!' Becky's voice came from behind me. I turned, relieved. Becky was standing in front of a door marked 'Visitors' Room'. 'I've been looking out for you. We'll be more private in here.'

'How is Faye?' I asked as I went over.

'She's being very brave. She'll be pleased to see you.'

With my heart thumping loudly I went in and Becky closed the door behind us. My gaze went to Faye, who was sitting in the corner of the room with Edward asleep in her arms. She was dressed in the fresh clothes I'd packed for her, and with her hair brushed she looked a bit brighter.

'Hello, love,' I said. I went over and sat beside her.

'Thank you for coming,' she said, glancing up.

'You're welcome.' I touched her arm reassuringly.

Becky sat in the chair on the other side of Faye and the three of us gazed at little Edward, his features relaxed in sleep. He was wearing one of the babygrows and the shawl Faye and I had bought together, with the little white hat. It was impossible to know what to say for the best. In all my years of fostering I'd never been in this position before. *He's gorgeous* or *You've got a lovely baby* didn't seem appropriate and were surely likely to upset Faye.

But then Faye said, 'I think he looks a little like me, don't you?'

'Yes. He's very handsome,' I said, and Becky agreed.

'I was looking at him a lot last night,' Faye said. 'I think he's going to be handsome and very clever, don't you?'

'Definitely,' I said. Becky nodded. I thought she was struggling to contain her emotion as much as I was.

'He will be clever and able to learn things, won't he?' Faye asked, turning to Becky. We both knew what she meant.

'Yes,' Becky said. 'You don't have to worry about that. He's perfect in every way.' Although Faye had been told that her condition – Foetal Alcohol Syndrome – couldn't be inherited, I think she needed the reassurance.

'That's good,' Faye said quietly, with the smallest of smiles, and my heart clenched.

We continued to gaze at Edward for some moments as he slept and then Faye said to me, 'I'm going home to my gran and grandpa's when I've said goodbye to Edward.'

'Yes, I know, love. They'll look after you. I'll phone you in a couple of days to arrange to bring your belongings to you.'

'Thank you. But don't bring the baby things. I don't want those,' she said. 'They'll make me sad.'

'No, just your things,' I confirmed.

There was another small silence and then Faye said, 'It will be Christmas soon. I'll be with Gran and Grandpa. Will you be with your mummy?'

'Yes,' I said.

'Will you say goodbye to her from me?' Faye said. 'She's a nice lady. She was very nice to me. I'm sure your daddy was nice, too, but I didn't know him.' Said with the innocent tactlessness of a child, but the mention of my father at this emotional time brought the tears to my eyes. I quickly turned away so Faye couldn't see and, taking a tissue from my pocket, I wiped my eyes. Becky saw and understood.

'It's all right, Cathy,' she said kindly.

'Say goodbye to Paula, Lucy and Adrian,' Faye added. 'They were kind to me too. I like them.'

'I will,' I said, facing her again. 'We all liked having you to stay, Faye. Hopefully we'll see you again.' But I didn't know when or how.

I looked at her as she continued to gaze down at Edward sleeping peacefully in her arms. It was the perfect image of a mother and her child, if you didn't know what was about to happen. At least at his age, I consoled myself, Edward wouldn't be aware of the separation that was about to take place. Older babies, toddlers and children scream and cry, and cling to their parents when they are taken into care, but Edward would just go from one pair of loving arms into another. It was a small consolation.

'I gave him his bottle this morning,' Faye announced proudly after a moment. 'I didn't make up the milk, the nurse did, but I gave it to him by myself.'

'Well done,' I said. Becky nodded in agreement.

'The nurse watched me for a while and then left me to do it by myself. Then she came back and helped me wind him. I did well, didn't I?'

'Yes,' Becky and I said. As far as I knew, that was the only time Faye had fed Edward.

'I'm going to give Snuggles to Edward,' Faye now said to me. 'Can you get him from my bag?'

I glanced over to Faye's overnight bag ready by the door. Snuggles sat on top of it. I'd seen the bag when I'd first walked in and had assumed Snuggles was going home with her.

'Are you sure, Faye?' I asked. 'You've had Snuggles a very long time.'

'Since I was a baby,' she said. 'Mummy gave him to me. I want Edward to have him so he has something from me. When I think of Edward he will have Snuggles looking after him, just as he looked after me.'

I saw Becky wipe the corner of her eye.

'Well, if you're sure,' I said, standing.

'I am.'

I took Snuggles from the top of the case and tucked him on Faye's lap between her and Edward. A knock sounded on the door and my stomach tightened.

'That'll be the foster carer,' Becky said. She stood and went over and opened the door. 'Come in.'

Patsy stepped in carrying an empty carrier car seat and a large baby bag on her shoulder. 'Hello,' she said, with a reassuring smile.

I smiled back. 'This is Faye and little Edward,' I said, introducing them. 'Faye, this is Patsy. She's the foster carer. I know her.'

Faye watched her as she set the car seat and bag on the floor. 'Is she your friend?' she asked me.

'Yes. She's also a great foster carer,' I said.

Patsy came over and sat beside Faye in the seat Becky had vacated. 'He's a beautiful baby,' she said, 'and very content.'

Faye gave her a little smile. 'He's going to be intelligent and learn lots of things, isn't he?'

'Yes, we'll make sure of it,' Patsy said. I could see Faye was warming to her. 'I will look after him very well, but please tell me if there is anything special you want me to do for him.'

'I want him to have Snuggles,' Faye said, pointing to the soft toy. 'He must have him every night, like I did. And when he goes shopping with you,' she added as an afterthought.

'Good. I'll do that then. Is there anything else you'd like me to do?' Usually when a baby or child goes into care the parent tells the carer something about the child's routine to help the baby or child settle in, but Faye hadn't been looking after Edward so hadn't established a routine.

She thought for a moment. 'I want you to feed him, change him, bath him, play with him and read to him so he learns lots of things.'

'I will do all of those things and more, I promise you, Faye,' Patsy said, her manner just right. 'I'll take very good care of him. The best ever. Is there anything else?'

Faye shook her head.

'When was he last fed?' Patsy asked practically.

Faye didn't know. 'About an hour ago,' Becky said.

'So he'll be all right until I get him home,' Patsy said. 'Although I've got a couple of bottles with me just in case. He's on formula milk?'

'Yes,' Becky confirmed.

'Does Faye have a photograph of her with her baby?' Patsy asked. 'I've brought my camera with me.' Clearly Patsy had more experience of babies going into care than Becky or I did.

'I'm not sure,' Becky said. 'I haven't taken any.'

'I have,' I said. 'On the day he was born.'

'Faye, would you like a photograph of you and Edward now?' Becky asked.

Faye shook her head. 'No, thank you. This is a sad day and it will make me more sad when I look at it.'

'I understand,' Becky said. 'Cathy has some photographs. You might like those.'

'You'll have to ask my gran,' Faye said. 'I don't know.'

'Don't worry,' Becky said. 'I'll ask her another time.'

'Is there anything else?' Patsy asked, glancing at us all. 'I'll be sending regular reports on Edward's progress through my support social worker.'

'I don't think there's anything else, thank you,' Becky said.

The room fell silent and the enormity of what now had to be done weighed heavily upon us. No one spoke or moved for some time as we all gazed at Edward, still asleep in Faye's arms. Then, without looking up at Patsy, Faye said quietly, 'I know I've got to give you my baby now.'

Patsy immediately teared up. 'Sorry,' she said, embarrassed, and sniffed. 'When you're ready, Faye, we'll put Edward in the car seat and I'll take him home. I promise you I'll look after him very well and give him the best care ever.'

Faye didn't move but continued to gaze down at Edward.

'When you're ready, Faye,' Becky said gently after a minute or so.

Faye began to stand. We stood too. Carefully cradling Edward against her chest as I'd taught her, and with Patsy by her side, Faye took the couple of steps to the car seat and together they placed Edward into it. He barely stirred.

'There's a good little chap,' Patsy said reassuringly. She fastened the safety harness as Faye watched, and then tucked the shawl over him. 'He'll be nice and warm in there,' she said.

As Patsy straightened, Faye knelt forward and kissed Edward's cheek. 'Bye,' she said quietly, almost in a whisper. 'I'll always remember you, really I will.' She tucked Snuggles in the carrier beside him. 'I love you so much.'

A tear slipped from my eye and I wiped it away. I saw Patsy and Becky do the same.

'If ever you're lonely or afraid,' Faye told Edward, 'Snuggles will keep you safe. He was my mummy's and he always looked after me. He'll look after you too. When you see him, think of me, please.'

It was heartbreaking but it was as though Edward had heard and understood, for his eyes briefly opened.

'Bye, my little baby,' Faye said. 'I'm so sorry I couldn't look after you. You'll have a proper mummy and daddy. I love you.'

I wiped my eyes again, as Patsy was doing too. Faye remained on her knees in front of the carrier, taking all she could from that last look at Edward. Then Patsy said quietly to Becky, 'I'll go now then?'

Becky nodded. I snapped to. I was supposed to be supporting Faye, so I went over and helped her to her feet. I slipped my arm around her waist as Patsy looped the bag over her shoulder and then picked up the carrier car seat.

'Bye, Edward,' Faye said. 'I'll always love you. Sorry I couldn't be your mummy.' Resting her head on my shoulder, she wept openly. My tears fell too.

Patsy knew she shouldn't prolong the agony and took the few steps to the door. Becky held the door open for her and, without turning, Patsy continued through, giving us our last view of Edward fast asleep in the carrier with Snuggles beside him. Faye was sobbing quietly now and I led her to a chair and eased her into it. I sat on one side of her and Becky sat on the other, and we offered what comfort we could. There was little we could say or do beyond holding her hands and waiting for the raw pain of parting to begin to ease. I've experienced many sad moments in my life, as have most people, but this was one of the worst, up there with my father dying and his funeral. Yet if it was bad for me, it was far, far worse for Faye. It was probably the worst day of her life and would remain so forever, for how does a mother get over losing her child? I honestly don't know.

After some time Faye's tears began to subside, for now she couldn't cry any more.

'Are you ready to go home?' Becky asked her gently.

Gazing down at her hands in her lap, Faye nodded. It was strange not seeing Snuggles there and I hoped Faye didn't ever regret parting with him. Becky and I helped Faye to her feet and then helped her into her coat. I picked up her overnight bag and we silently left the room. The staff nurse from the ward came over. I'd seen her before – a largish woman, very caring of her patients, with a strong Irish accent.

'Take care and good luck, love,' she said to Faye, giving her a hug. 'My sister in Ireland had to give up her baby thirty years ago. He came looking for her last year. A big strapping lad. A merchant banker. So don't give up hope, love.'

I didn't know if Faye found her words comforting or not. She seemed numb with grief right now.

'Thank you for looking after Faye so well,' Becky said.

'You're welcome, take care.' And with an encouraging smile she returned to her ward.

Faye walked between us to the elevator, quiet and expressionless. Becky and I didn't speak either, for what could we say? Smalltalk was inappropriate and any words of comfort seemed shallow and impotent set against what Faye was going through. Once outside I carried Faye's bag to Becky's car and put it on the back seat. Becky helped Faye into the passenger seat and fastened her seat belt. Faye didn't look at me but kept her gaze down.

'Bye, love,' I said. I leant in and kissed her cheek. 'I'll be thinking about you.' But she didn't respond. I straightened and Becky closed her door.

'Try not to worry,' Becky said. 'I'm sure she'll start to feel a bit better once she's home with her gran and grandpa.'

'I hope so.'

We said goodbye and I didn't wait around. Faye wasn't looking out of her window, so I went straight to my car. Once inside I took my phone from my bag and pressed my mother's number. I needed to hear her voice.

'I love you,' I said as soon as she answered.

'Well, that's nice. I love you too, dear. What's the matter?'

I told her the whole sad story, from Faye's decision to give up her baby to him being collected by the carer just now.

Mum was quiet until I'd finished and then she said, 'You know, Cathy, Faye might have learning difficulties, but she's got an awful lot of good sense. She recognized her limitations, before any of you did, and made a very sensible decision. She's saved herself and Edward a lot of heartache in the future. Obviously I'm sorry that it couldn't have been different, but that girl deserves a medal. She had the perception and courage to make the most difficult decision any mother could ever make. God bless her.'

CHAPTER TWENTY-THREE

A REVELATION

I didn't go straight home. I decided I needed some fresh air to clear my head, so I drove to the downs, about twenty minutes outside of town. From the top of the downs the view is spectacular. Undulating green hills peppered with scarps and clusters of trees as far as the eye can see. The view continues to the skyline in the distance, and on a clear day it's as though you can see forever. Stony gravel paths lead from the car park over the downs, some for seasoned walkers, others for novices. I set off on one that I knew was about an hour of walking on even terrain. The wind always blows keenly over the downs even in summer, and today it was sharp. 'A brisk walk on the downs will blow those cobwebs away,' my father used to say when my brother and I were children and had been niggling each other and needed some exercise and a change of scenery.

Brisk it certainly was, and after fifteen minutes my cheeks were glowing and my ears stung with the cold. But the beauty and vastness of the landscape touched me now as it always did, and being up there and away from the world below gave me a fresh perspective. The solitude was welcome, too, for there weren't many walking the downs in the middle of winter on a weekday. By the time I'd completed the circuit I felt better able to appreciate all that was good in life and what we had to be grateful for. I returned home and kept myself busy, and when Paula, Lucy and Adrian came in I told them that Faye had been very brave and Edward had slept peacefully throughout. Even so, we were all quieter than usual that evening and tended to keep our own company. It would take time for us to adjust and come to terms with Faye leaving, especially as the outcome wasn't what we'd hoped for.

The following morning Becky telephoned to see how I was, which was kind of her. She said she'd seen Faye safely home the day before. Wilma and Stan had been waiting at the flat and had been very pleased to see her, as she was to see them. Becky had stayed for about an hour to make sure they were coping and had everything they needed. She said that Wilma had brought up the subject of the photographs I'd taken and had asked if it was possible for them to have copies, feeling it was important they had some pictures of Edward to remember him by. She said that if Faye didn't want to look at them now, she'd put them away until she did. For she was certain she would do one day, just as she liked to look at the photographs of her mother. I told Becky I'd get a set printed and take them when I took Faye's belongings. In that connection Becky asked if I could phone Wilma and Stan later to arrange a mutually convenient time to do this, as Faye was asking about her belongings.

That afternoon I went into town and had the photographs printed. The shop offered a special fast-track one-hour service, and while they were being processed I put the time to good use by doing the last of my Christmas shopping. Christmas was less than a week away now. I waited until I was in the privacy of my car before I opened the packet containing the photographs, and of course my eyes immediately filled. Pictures of darling little Edward, only a few minutes old, swaddled in a blanket in Faye's arms. Then some of him dressed in one of the babygrows we'd bought together, with Snuggles and Faye, a couple with Wilma, then all of them together, and finally one of me with Faye and Edward, a copy of which I would keep. As I looked at the photographs I studied Faye's expression for any indication of what she might have been thinking at that time, but there was nothing beyond relief and happiness that her precious baby had been delivered safely. Nothing to say she was changing her mind about being able to look after him.

That evening I telephoned Wilma and Stan. Stan answered, polite as ever, although not chatty, which was understandable. They'd all been through a lot in the last few days. I began by asking how they all were and he said, 'Pleased to have Faye home with us.' I explained why I was phoning and we arranged for me to bring Faye's belongings the following morning at eleven o'clock. He thanked me and we said goodbye. I now had the incentive I needed to go into what had been Faye's bedroom and finish wrapping her Christmas presents, which I would take with me. I was sure Faye would find good use for the camera, even though it wasn't the one I'd envisaged. I neatly wrapped the camera in its box and then the stocking fillers, and placed them all in the Santa sack I'd bought for her. I fetched a large black bin liner from the kitchen and placed Faye's sack in it, as well as the presents I'd bought for Wilma and Stan. I'd ask Stan or

Wilma to put the bag away until Christmas morning, when they'd all have a nice surprise. Before I went to bed I stripped Faye's bed and remade it with fresh linen. Tomorrow I'd vacuum and clean the room. Now Faye had left I could be asked to foster another child or young person at short notice, although I hoped that wouldn't happen just before Christmas.

The following day Adrian helped me load the car with Faye's belongings and I set off to the flat. I'll admit I had reservations about seeing Faye, Wilma and Stan again so soon after the trauma of two days ago. The emotion was still raw for me, as I'm sure it was for them, but Faye wanted her belongings. I parked the car outside the flats and then telephoned their landline to say I'd arrived and was about to make my first trip up in the lift. I imagined having to make a number of trips up and down with all the bags.

'If you hold on a minute,' Stan said, 'I'll send Lewis down to help. He's our neighbour's nephew. He's with them now.'

'OK, fine,' I said. 'That would be a big help.'

I waited by the car and a few minutes later a slightly built lad in his teens appeared. Shy and awkward as teenagers can be, I was grateful for his help and we managed to move everything up in two trips. Stan, leaning on his walking stick, had their front door propped open and took the case and bags as we brought them up. I carried the bin liner containing the presents.

'Thank you very much,' I said to Lewis before he returned next door.

'That's OK,' he said self-consciously. 'It's the least I can do.'

I went into the flat with Stan and explained what the bin liner contained. He was genuinely surprised and grateful.

'Your secret is safe with me,' he said. 'We'll hide it in here.' He pushed open the door to his and Wilma's bedroom and I followed him in. 'Can you put it in the cupboard, lass. Wilma and Faye never go in there.'

I opened the door and lifted in the bulging bin liner. It just fitted.

'Thanks, love,' he said. 'You're a kind lass. That will make our Christmas.' And I knew he meant it.

In the living room Faye was sitting on the sofa beside her gran in a mirror image of her, just as she had been when I'd first met her. She looked up and managed a weak smile as Wilma said a friendly, 'Hello, Cathy.' Faye was again dressed in clothes similar to her gran's and that could have been hers. The television was on, showing repeats of soaps, and Stan picked up the remote and lowered the sound.

'Can we make you a drink?' he asked.

'No, thank you. I'm fine. I had a coffee before I left.'

'Sit yourself down,' Wilma said hospitably.

I drew up one of the dining chairs. Stan sat in his armchair to my right and Faye and Wilma were on the sofa in front of me. There was an awkward silence. 'I won't stay long, but I wanted to see how you were,' I said to Faye.

'I'm all right,' she said, with a small shrug of acceptance.

'You've got a new cuddly then?' I said, referring to the soft toy wedged between her and Wilma. It was of a similar size and shape to Snuggles.

'That's Cuddles,' Faye said, without picking him up. 'He's the baby of Snuggles, and he's staying with me.'

I smiled as Wilma threw me a knowing look. 'It's another one of her mum's toys,' Wilma said. 'We kept all her favourites.'

'That's nice,' I said.

'He's not the same as Snuggles,' Faye said, a little disheartened.

'He will be soon,' Wilma said positively. 'He just needs some TLC. We'll work on it.'

I smiled again and then reached into my bag for the packet of photographs and passed it to Wilma.

'Thank you. How much do we owe you?'

'Nothing. It's my pleasure.'

'That's kind of you.' She tucked the packet down beside her on the sofa.

'I'm not looking at them,' Faye said.

'No, you don't have to, but your grandpa and I will,' Wilma replied. I thought how appropriately Wilma handled Faye; kind but firm. I had no doubt that she would deal sympathetically with Faye as she came to terms with losing Edward, but she wouldn't indulge her. I could imagine the three of them in years to come sitting in this living room, looking at the photographs and possibly speculating about what Edward looked like now and what he was doing. Usually the natural parent(s) of a child that is to be adopted is updated with photographs and short reports on the infant's progress until the actual adoption, and then after the adoption there are sometimes updates, but that would be for Becky and the adoption team to discuss and arrange.

'So, what are you doing for Christmas?' Wilma asked after a moment, making conversation.

'My mother and my brother and his family are coming to us for Christmas Day.'

'That'll be nice.'

'Yes. And you?'

'We're going next door as usual,' Wilma said. 'They invite us every year and make a real fuss of us. We have a lovely time. They're like family.'

'And as they're only next door I can have a couple of scotches and still find my way home,' Stan added, with a laugh. Wilma and I laughed too.

There was another silence and then I said, 'Well, I won't keep you. I'll be off then. I think I've packed everything, but if I find something of Faye's that I've missed I'll give you a ring and then bring it to you.'

'Thanks, love,' Wilma said.

'You haven't packed the baby clothes, have you?' Faye asked, picking up Cuddles.

'No, love. Just all your belongings.'

'You and I have got some unpacking to do,' Wilma said, nudging Faye.

I stood and returned my chair to the table. 'Goodbye then,' I said to Faye. I went over and gave her a hug. 'I'll be thinking of you.'

To my surprise Wilma then hugged me too. 'Thanks for all you've done,' she said quietly. 'We're very grateful. We couldn't have managed without you.'

'It was a pleasure to be of help,' I said as I straightened. I was about to add that I just wished the outcome could have been different, but I stopped myself.

Wilma must have read my expression. 'It's for the best,' she said stoically, looking me straight in the eyes. 'We would have supported Faye whatever, but I think this is right. It's what's meant to be.'

I nodded. We said goodbye and then Stan pulled himself from his chair and leant on his walking stick. 'I'll see you out, love,' he said. 'We can't have a young lady seeing herself out, it's bad manners.'

I said a final goodbye to Wilma and Faye and left them as I found them, side by side on the sofa, watching television. There was something comforting in the familiarity of this scene. Faye was where she wanted to be and belonged, and I had every confidence that with her grandparents' help she would move on with her life, safe in the knowledge that she'd made the right decision and that little Edward was happy with his adoptive family.

Stan came with me to the elevator. 'If I don't see you again, thanks,' he said. He took my hand and gave it an affectionate squeeze.

I hesitated before I spoke, as there was something still bothering me. 'Stan, you do know that I didn't persuade Faye to try to keep her baby. It was her decision.'

'I know,' he said. 'She can be very obstinate sometimes. Wilma and I feel that she probably had to travel that path to be satisfied that having Edward adopted was the right decision.'

I was grateful for the reassurance. The elevator arrived and I stepped in.

'All the best then,' Stan said, with a wave of his walking stick. 'Merry Christmas to you and your family. Have a good one.'

'And you,' I said, and the doors closed.

The lift descended uninterrupted to the ground floor where I got out. I took a couple of steps and then Lewis, their neighbour's nephew whom I'd just met, appeared in front of me in the lobby. He wasn't wearing a coat and had his arms folded across his chest, as if trying to protect himself from the cold. 'You need a jacket on down here,' I said. 'It's freezing.'

I looked at him. He was my height and his nose and cheeks were blue from the cold.

'I've been waiting for you,' he said.

'Why?'

'I need to talk to you,' he said edgily. 'You're a foster carer, aren't you?'

'Yes.'

'So you know about social workers and the law.' His teeth chattered as he spoke.

'A little,' I said, puzzled. I wasn't sure how much of his shivering was due to the cold and how much was nervousness, for he seemed very agitated. 'What's the matter? Are you in trouble with the police?'

'I think I might be.'

'I see. How?' I waited as he shivered and shifted from one foot to the other.

Then he swallowed hard. 'Don't be angry with me, but I think I might be the father of Faye's baby.'

My jaw dropped. I stared at him, and my first thought was that he wasn't old enough.

'What makes you say that?' I asked, trying to hide my shock.

He looked down, embarrassed. 'You know, Faye and me did it.'

'Sorry. It was a daft question. I'm not thinking straight. Have you told anyone apart from me?'

He shook his head. 'I was worried I'd be in trouble, but Faye said I had to tell now.' He looked and sounded like a naughty schoolboy.

'She's right. How old are you, Lewis? If you don't mind me asking.'

298

'Nearly nineteen.' He looked more like twelve. 'I didn't hurt her,' he blurted. 'She wanted me to. She saw it on the television and wanted to do it. I'd never done it before either. I didn't think you could get pregnant just doing it once.' I wondered how many other young people had been similarly caught out, but it wasn't for me to lecture him.

'Lewis, you're going to have to tell your aunt and uncle. Do you live with your parents?' He nodded. 'You will need to tell them too.'

He shifted uncomfortably. 'Can you tell them for me?'

'It will be better coming from you. I will tell Faye's social worker. She needs to know so she can talk to Faye and her grandparents.'

'Will the police want to see me?' he asked anxiously.

'I don't know, but if they do, you just tell them the truth, as you've told me, and I'm sure it will be fine.'

He brightened a little. 'I'll tell my aunt and uncle first. They're easier to talk to than my parents.'

'I should do it now. Don't put it off any longer.' Then curiosity got the better of me. 'Where did this happen, Lewis? Faye never goes out.'

'In her flat. Stan and Wilma were with my aunt and uncle in our flat, so I went round to keep her company. We often do that. Either I go there or she comes to us. The adults play cards in one flat and we watch films in the other.'

'I see,' I said thoughtfully. 'All right, I understand. Just explain what happened. They are bound to be upset to begin with. It will be a shock.'

'I know. I'll tell them now.' He turned and headed up the stairs, taking them two at a time. I looked after him for a moment and then continued out of the building.

I've experienced many a dramatic and surprising turn of events as a foster carer – some disturbing and others happy – but Lewis's revelation was certainly in the top ten for surprise value. To use an expression, I was gobsmacked. I knew that his aunt and uncle, and Stan and Wilma, were close – good friends and neighbours. They were going to be very surprised and shocked. I didn't think the police would need to be involved if Lewis was telling the truth. He and Faye were both over the age of consent, and although Faye was classified as a vulnerable adult, he hadn't forced or coerced her into having sex – she had been willing. However, as the child's father, Lewis had rights and he might want to play a part in Edward's life, even bringing him up, although he appeared little more than a child himself. Certainly the social services would want to talk to him to ascertain his wishes and to plan Edward's future. Now the baby's father was known, it wasn't just Faye's decision.

I was still bemused and mulling over all of this when I arrived home. As soon as I was in I telephoned Becky and updated her.

'Oh my!' she said, as surprised as I was. 'And Wilma's been blaming the day centre and the stables! They'll be relieved to know they're off the hook. But Lewis's aunt and uncle are going to be furious. I've never met Lewis, but I have met his aunt and uncle. They're a good, kind couple who do a lot for Stan and Wilma. They'll be mortified when they find out their nephew is responsible. I think I'll phone Stan and Wilma and prepare them, and I'll need to see Faye. Thank you, Cathy.'

Having said goodbye to Becky, I telephoned Edith and updated her. Not being directly involved in my fostering of

Faye, Edith wasn't so aware of the ramifications of this development or as surprised. She asked me to send in my final report on Faye, which would go on the social services' file, as was normal practice, and then confirmed with me that I was free to foster again if necessary. I said I had some Christmas presents for Edward and that I would like to give them to Patsy, but I didn't know her contact details. Edith said she'd find out. An hour later she called back with Patsy's telephone number and address, having checked with her first (for confidentiality reasons) that it was all right to give them to me. Edith wished me a good Christmas in case she didn't speak to me again beforehand, and I wished her the same. Having said goodbye, I cut the call and then phoned Patsy.

CHAPTER TWENTY-FOUR

A LOVING LEGACY

'I see Santa Claus has come early this year,' Patsy joked the following afternoon as I stood on her doorstep holding Edward's Santa sack. 'Come on in, Cathy. Good to see you. Let me take your coat.'

I put the Santa sack and the bag of baby clothes in the hall, took off my coat and handed it to Pasty, who hung it on their hall stand, and then followed her into the living room. Like many carers who specialize in fostering babies and toddlers, the room looked like a mini nursery, with large boxes overflowing with colourful toys, a play mat, baby walker, high chair, rocker, entertainment centres for various ages, a toy cooker and shop, and so on. I went straight to the Moses basket standing by the sofa.

'Isn't he gorgeous?' Pasty said, already smitten, as we gazed in.

'Absolutely.' Dear little Edward, how pleased I was to see him. He lay on his back in blissful sleep, with his arms flung out either side of him.

'How is his mum coping?' Pasty asked kindly, glancing at me. 'The poor girl.'

'I saw her yesterday and she seems to be doing all right,' I said. 'She's living with her grandparents again and they're looking after her.'

Patsy nodded. 'And how are you?'

'I'm fine.'

She threw me an old-fashioned look, aware that a foster carer is never 'fine' when a child or young person they've been fostering has just left, but that it would take time to adjust.

She offered me a drink and while she went into the kitchen to make tea I continued to gaze at Edward. So peaceful and content cocooned in the crib, away from the outside world and all that was happening there. He had his whole life ahead of him. I sincerely hoped it was a good one. How I wished I could take that journey with him.

Patsy returned carrying a tray of drinks and, setting it on an occasional table, passed me one of the cups. I tore myself away from the Moses basket and sat beside her on the sofa. As we sipped our tea we talked, firstly about the routine she was establishing for Edward, then about our plans for Christmas. She mentioned that she was also fostering a two-year-old girl who at present was seeing her mother at the contact centre. She'd have to collect her later. I told Patsy the bag in the hall contained not only baby clothes, but also nappies, creams, wipes and other small baby items that Faye and I had bought and which I hoped she could make use of.

'Thank you, Cathy. You can never have too many.'

'And the Santa sack contains Edward's presents from my family and me,' I said. 'Also a soft toy that my children bought specially for him.'

'That's kind of them. I'll make sure he has them. We've got him some presents too. Not that he's going to know much about them now, but he will in the future.'

It was then I realized I couldn't see Snuggles anywhere. I set my cup in its saucer and looked around. 'I did give you a soft toy at the hospital – Snuggles – didn't I?' I asked, worried.

'Yes, but I've put him safely away for when Edward is older,' Patsy said. 'I didn't want him getting damaged. I'll explain the significance of Snuggles to Edward's adoptive parents when he eventually leaves me.'

'Thank you. Snuggles didn't just belong to Faye but to her mother as well.'

'Don't worry, I'll tell them.'

It was obvious that Patsy didn't yet know that Edward's father had come forward, which might change the plans for Edward being adopted, and it wasn't my place to tell her. She would be informed by Edward's social worker and then be involved in planning and moving Edward to his permanent home, wherever that might be. Although it wouldn't happen for some months yet. Presently Edward woke for a feed and I stood by the Moses basket and soothed him while Patsy warmed his milk. When she returned she asked me if I'd like to feed him.

'Yes, please,' I said.

But as I sat on the sofa with him cradled in my arms, suckling contentedly, I felt a rush of sadness that it wasn't Faye feeding him, especially after all those weeks of practising. I'd had such high hopes. I wondered what she was doing now and if she was coping. Sitting here with her child just didn't seem right. It's a thought I have often when I'm fostering: feeling that the child should be with their parents instead of me and hoping they were coping without them.

When he'd taken half the milk I paused to wind him and then continued with the rest of the bottle. He barely opened his eyes, bless him. Patsy changed his nappy and then settled him in the Moses basket again. I stayed for another twenty minutes and then Patsy had to leave to collect her other child from contact. She saw me to the door, and as I left we both wished each other a merry Christmas and a happy New Year. That evening I was able to reassure my children that I'd seen Edward and he was being very well looked after, and that he would be given our presents at Christmas.

Christmas was now only five days away. Paula had broken up from college for the holidays, but Adrian and Lucy had to work right up to Christmas Eve. On the day before Christmas Eve I received the telephone call I'd been dreading from Edith, informing me that the social services might be bringing a child into care. Edith said that a young couple with a small child had been arrested by the police after a house raid, and if they couldn't find a family member to look after the infant then they'd need a foster placement. She said she'd call back as soon as she had more details. I quickly checked the spare bedroom and also my cache of emergency Christmas presents. Thankfully, later that afternoon Edith telephoned again and said that an aunt had been found to look after the child until the parents were released from custody, so she wouldn't have to come into care. But even so, what a dreadful upset, and I wondered what sort of Christmas that family would have. I was never told what the couple had done to be arrested and, like most referrals that failed to arrive, I didn't hear any more.

* * *

My family and I had a good Christmas. It was obviously different without Dad, but we enjoyed ourselves, as he would have wanted us to. He loved Christmas like a child and never grew out of playing games and winning prizes from the Christmas tree. We spoke of him a few times during the day as our thoughts went to him, and I think it is true to say that we felt his love and joy shining through, even though he wasn't with us. On Boxing Day the children and I visited the cemetery, taking some of our Christmas flowers with us to put on Dad's grave. It was a very cold day, the clouds were low and the air was perfectly still. Snow had been forecast in some parts of the country and while we were there, to our delight, a few snowflakes fell – the first of the winter.

'Grandpa loved the snow,' Adrian said. 'The toboggan he made for us when we were little is still in the shed.'

'I hope it snows a lot,' the girls said, gazing wishfully at the sky. 'Then we can use it.'

On the way home I drove through more little flurries of snow, although none appeared to settle, but then the following morning when we woke the outside was shrouded in a magical blanket of pure white snow. Suddenly, we were all up and dressed, like children again, excited and eager to be out in the snow. Sammy didn't know what to make of it and he took one look and shot back in through the cat flap. After breakfast Adrian fetched the toboggan from the shed and, wrapped up warm, we set off to our nearby park, renowned for its hill that makes a perfect toboggan run. There were already many others there and we saw friends, neighbours and families from the area. There was a festive atmosphere, with lots of shouting, screaming and laughing, as adults and children of all ages hurtled down the slope on their toboggans – or anything they had: trays, sheets of plastic and cardboard, even a metal dustbin lid, which looked comical but was surprisingly fast. As we flew down, laughing, taking turns on the toboggan that Dad had made all those years ago, I hoped he could see how much fun we were all having.

It's so very sad to lose a beloved parent or grandparent, but my father's legacy, his love of life, his devotion to his family, his kindness, understanding and patience, not just with my children but with all those we fostered, will stay with us forever. I believe it is a testament to the way I was raised that my family is the happy one it is today, and for that I am truly grateful.

EPILOGUE

A new child arrived on 2 January, so I was very busy, but not so busy that I didn't think of Faye and wonder how she was doing. Once a child or younger person leaves a foster carer the social services no longer keep the carer informed of the child's progress, which is a great pity. Any news comes from hearing it by chance or from the child keeping in touch, as it's considered unprofessional for a carer to initiate contact after the child has left. It is thought that it could hinder them bonding with their permanent family and therefore moving on with their lives, although that's not my view. I believe you can never have too many people in your life who love you.

I was delighted, therefore, when halfway through January I received a photograph from Patsy of Edward's first Christmas. The covering note said that Edward was doing well and she thought I might like the enclosed photograph. She'd sent some to Becky for Faye and concluded by wishing me a belated happy New Year and hoped we were all well. I immediately texted a thank you to her. I showed the photograph to Paula, Lucy and Adrian before putting it carefully in the family album.

Then one morning towards the end of January, as I picked up the mail from the front doormat I saw what I thought looked like Faye's handwriting on one of the envelopes. I quickly tore it open and a letter and three photographs fell out. Two of the photographs were of horses in their stables, and the other was of Faye proudly sitting on a horse and smiling broadly. I read the letter.

Dear Cathy, Paula, Lucy, Adrian and Sammy,
Thank you for my lovely Christmas presents. Gran and Grandpa say thank you for theirs. Gran is helping me write this letter with the spellings. Grandpa showed me how to use the camera and I have taken lots of photographs. Some of Gran and Grandpa, some of the day centre and lots of the horses at the stables. I am sending you pictures of my favourite horses. I hope you are all well. Thank you for looking after me.
Love Faye (Stan and Wilma)

I was very moved, and after I'd shown the photographs to my family I added the one of Faye sitting on a horse to the album. I have many family photograph albums, built up over the years, and always include pictures of the children I've fostered, for they are always part of my extended family.

Later that year I bumped into Becky as I came out of a meeting at the council offices, and she was good enough to give me an update. She said Faye was well and happy and had settled into her old routine. Stan and Wilma were well too. They had finally been offered a ground-floor flat not far away from where they lived now, and would move at the end of the month. I eagerly awaited news of Edward, and was finally rewarded. Becky said that he'd been placed for adoption with the childless couple who had originally been matched for him before Faye had changed her mind. Lewis and his family, together with the social services, had decided that realistically they couldn't bring up his child, so it would be kinder for Edward to be adopted as soon as possible. Like Faye's decision this too was selfless and put the child's best interests first. I asked if Lewis was ever interviewed by the police about his relationship with Faye, and Becky said he wasn't. I was pleased; he seemed like a good lad. She said that when she had talked to Faye about what had happened, her account had matched Lewis's, so no crime had been committed. Becky added that when Stan had been told of the circumstances in which Edward had been conceived, and not being a fan of the soaps on television, he'd said, 'I knew no good would come of watching those daft programmes, and I've been proved right!' Becky didn't say if Lewis continued to see Faye, but she did say that Stan and Wilma had remained friends with their neighbours and would do so after the move.

Foster carers always hope that the child or young person they are looking after will be able to have a happy ending to their story, but sometimes, as with Faye, that just isn't possible. Yet, when I look at the photographs of little Edward and the one of Faye smiling broadly at the stables, I think that maybe their story did have a happy ending after all. Faye is now living contentedly with her grandparents again, without the anxiety of a responsibility she would never have been able to cope with. Edward is growing up loved and cherished by a couple who never thought they'd be able to have children and who, thanks to Faye and Lewis's brave decision, are now able to experience the wonderful gift of parenthood. So, yes, I think it is possible to say that Faye and Edward's story does have a happy ending, and I wonder if, in years to come, Edward will search out his birth parents, as some adopted children do, and meet them.

For the latest update on Faye and Edward and the other children in my fostering memoirs, please visit www.cathyglass.co.uk.

If you are interested in fostering adults and would like to know more, contact your local authority or independent fostering agency for schemes in your area.

SUGGESTED TOPICS FOR READING-GROUP DISCUSSION

This book gives an insight into fostering adults. What do you think the similarities and differences are between fostering children and fostering an adult with learning difficulties?

What are the challenges in fostering adults with either a learning or physical disability?

Would you describe Faye's grandparents as overprotective? If so, what would you have done differently if you'd raised Faye?

This book highlights the lack of provision for adults with learning difficulties. Discuss.

Whether to bring the child of a disabled parent into care – and if so, when – must be a difficult decision for any social worker. What criteria would you use in a case such as Faye and Edward's? How much would the grandparents' support influence your decision?

Why might Lewis, the father of Faye's child, be questioned by the police?

Faye has to make a very difficult decision with regard to her child. Is it the right one?

Prior to the birth, what indications were there that Faye might not have managed to parent Edward? Give examples from the text.

It is now generally considered best for an adopted child to grow up aware of their birth family. Discuss the likely positive and negative effects of this.

Cathy Glass

———

One remarkable woman, more
than **150** foster children cared for.

Cathy Glass has been a foster carer for over
twenty-five years, during which time she has
looked after more than 150 children, as well
as raising three children of her own. She was
awarded a degree in education and psychology
as a mature student, and writes under a
pseudonym. To find out more about Cathy
and her story visit www.cathyglass.co.uk.

The Silent Cry

A mother battling depression. A family in denial

Cathy is desperate to help before something terrible happens.

Girl Alone

An angry, traumatized young girl on a path to self-destruction

Can Cathy discover the truth behind Joss's dangerous behaviour before it's too late?

Saving Danny

Danny's parents can no longer cope with his challenging behaviour

Calling on all her expertise, Cathy discovers a frightened little boy who just wants to be loved.

The Child
Bride

**A girl blamed and
abused for dishonouring
her community**

Cathy discovers the
devastating truth.

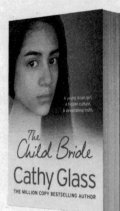

Daddy's Little
Princess

**A sweet-natured girl with
a complicated past**

Cathy picks up the
pieces after events take
a dramatic turn.

Will you
love me?

**A broken child desperate
for a loving home**

The true story of Cathy's
adopted daughter Lucy.

Please Don't Take My Baby

Seventeen-year-old Jade is pregnant, homeless and alone

Cathy has room in her heart for two.

Another Forgotten Child

Eight-year-old Aimee was on the child-protection register at birth

Cathy is determined to give her the happy home she deserves.

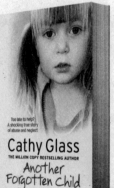

A Baby's Cry

A newborn, only hours old, taken into care

Cathy protects tiny Harrison from the potentially fatal secrets that surround his existence.

The Night the Angels Came

A little boy on the brink of bereavement

Cathy and her family make sure Michael is never alone.

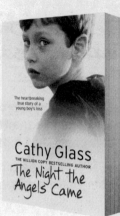

Mummy Told me not to tell

A troubled boy sworn to secrecy

After his dark past has been revealed, Cathy helps Reece to rebuild his life.

I Miss Mummy

Four-year-old Alice doesn't understand why she's in care

Cathy fights for her to have the happy home she deserves.

The saddest girl in the world

A haunted child who refuses to speak

Do Donna's scars run too deep for Cathy to help?

Cut

Dawn is desperate to be loved

Abused and abandoned, this vulnerable child pushes Cathy and her family to their limits.

Hidden

The boy with no past

Can Cathy help Tayo to feel like he belongs again?

Damaged

A forgotten child

Cathy is Jodie's last hope. For the first time, this abused young girl has found someone she can trust.

Inspired by Cathy's own experiences...

Run, Mummy, Run

The gripping story of a woman caught in a horrific cycle of abuse, and the desperate measures she must take to escape.

My Dad's a Policeman

The dramatic short story about a young boy's desperate bid to keep his family together.

The Girl in the Mirror

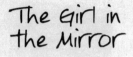

Trying to piece together her past, Mandy uncovers a dreadful family secret that has been blanked from her memory for years.

Sharing her expertise...

About Writing and How to Publish

A clear and concise, practical guide on writing and the best ways to get published.

Happy Mealtimes for Kids

A guide to healthy eating with simple recipes that children love.

Happy Adults

A practical guide to achieving lasting happiness, contentment and success. The essential manual for getting the best out of life.

Happy Kids

A clear and concise guide to raising confident, well-behaved and happy children.

Be amazed
Be moved
Be inspired

———

Discover more about Cathy Glass
visit www.cathyglass.co.uk